Web Services Patterns: Java Edition

PAUL B. MONDAY

Web Services Patterns: Java Edition
Copyright (©)2003 by Paul B. Monday

ISBN (pbk): 1-59059-084-8

Printed and bound in the United States of America 12345678910

Technical Reviewer: Kunal Mittal

Editorial Directors: Dan Appleman, Gary Cornell, Simon Hayes, Martin Streicher, Karen Watterson, John Zukowski

Assistant Publisher: Grace Wong

Project Managers: Sofia Marchant and Beth Christmas

Copy Editor: Kim Wimpsett

Compositor and Proofreader: Kinetic Publishing Services

Indexer: Valerie Robbins

Artist: Kinetic Publishing Services

Cover Designer: Kurt Krames

Production Manager: Kari Brooks

Manufacturing Manager: Tom Debolski

Distributed to the book trade in the United States by Springer-Verlag New York, Inc., 175 Fifth Avenue, New York, NY, 10010 and outside the United States by Springer-Verlag GmbH & Co. KG, Tiergartenstr. 17, 69112 Heidelberg, Germany.

In the United States: phone 1-800-SPRINGER, email orders@springer-ny.com, or visit http://www.springer-ny.com. Outside the United States: fax +49 6221 345229, email orders@springer.de, or visit http://www.springer.de.

For information on translations, please contact Apress directly at 2560 Ninth Street, Suite 219, Berkeley, CA 94710. Phone 510-549-5930, fax 510-549-5939, email info@apress.com, or visit http://www.apress.com.

The source code for this book is available to readers at http://www.apress.com in the Downloads section.

Contents at a Glance

Contents

Chapter 7 Exploring the Business Object Collection Pattern 115

Chapter 8 Exploring the Business Process (Composition) Pattern 131

Chapter 9 Exploring the Asynchronous Business Process Pattern 153

Chapter 10 Exploring the Event Monitor Pattern......*169*

Chapter 11 Implementing the Observer Pattern.........*187*

Chapter 12 Implementing the Publish/Subscribe Pattern...*205*

Chapter 13 Exploring the Physical Tiers Pattern...*225*

About the Author

PAUL B. MONDAY is a software architect who works for Sun Microsystems' network storage division. He has been testing, implementing, designing, and architecting software for many years. During graduate school at Washington State University, he created the System V File system implementation for the early Linux operating system (prior to the 1.0 kernel). After graduate school, Paul began working at IBM. His work included finding mechanisms for reusing software efficiently, with most of his efforts centered on the IBM SanFrancisco project. After IBM, Paul worked for Imation Corporation as an architect and project leader for a series of projects involving device management and network appliances. While there, Paul led an effort to build a network appliance based entirely on open-source software. Since Imation Corporation, Paul has worked on a variety of architecture projects related to enterprise software. Paul is also the coauthor of two books, *SanFrancisco Component Framework: An Introduction* (Addison-Wesley, 1999) and *The Jiro Technology Programmer's Guide and Federated Management Architecture* (Addison-Wesley, 2001).

About the Technical Reviewer

KUNAL MITTAL, an independent J2EE and Web Service consultant, has more than six years of software development experience and has been working with J2EE technologies since early 1999. He specializes in Web Services using the BEA platform and has coauthored and edited several books on J2EE and Web Services.

Acknowledgments

OVER THE COURSE of writing this book, I have undergone many changes in my life. In the middle of the book, I was hired by Sun Microsystems' network storage division. My former manager, Dave Jespersen, was extremely understanding of my prior commitments, including this book. I am excited to be working for Sun and wish Dave J. the best in his future endeavors.

Jennifer Aloi, editor of the IBM developerWorks Java technology zone, helped me hone many of my writing skills and allowed me much creative freedom on the site to try out my ideas. Jennifer also introduced me to John Zukowski from Apress. John spent quite a bit of time noodling over book ideas with me and continues to be helpful as this book goes to press. Thanks, Jenni and John.

During the course of writing, Sofia Marchant nurtured the beginning phases of the book, and then Beth Christmas came in and helped me wrap up the book. The end of the schedule was grueling, but Beth provided the feedback I needed at the right time. Anyone who has ever written a book knows that the author is only the name on the cover; people such as Kunal Mittal (the technical reviewer), John Zukowski (the editorial director), Kim Wimpsett (the copy editor), and Kari Brooks (the production manager) are the ones who helped turn my ramblings into something that is actually readable, informative, and, I hope, useful. The entire Apress team is phenomenal.

I would also like to thank the Eskimo Ski Shop in Littleton, Colorado, and the Loveland Ski Area in Colorado for helping me cultivate my snowboarding skills. The skills came in handy at the end of a long week trying to work through Kunal's and Kim's comments. There is nothing better than some fresh Colorado powder down your back to bring you back to reality.

Finally, my family and dogs (Sapphire and Emma) have been, mostly, patient with me throughout the journey. Thanks for helping me take on the burden of writing a book for the third time. I love you all even though it is sometimes difficult to show from behind a computer screen.

Introduction

THE HETEROGENEOUS NATURE of software and computing platforms leads to a chaotic and fragile web of code in order to make applications appear seamless to the user while sharing data beneath the surface. Further, the salary that programmers demand to rein in the chaos can tax any company and technology department. Even after an application integration job is complete, the resulting system is often unintelligible and difficult to maintain.

Web Services create a common architecture and implementation for exposing the application functionality that helps programmers integrate systems and create seamless business processes that span departments, companies, and computing platforms. Web Services are attractive because programmers do not need in-depth knowledge of every computing platform that will participate in a business process. Instead, programmers need to understand Web Services and their own programming environment.

As you probably have seen with the object-oriented programming paradigm, the Java 2 Standard Edition (J2SE) computing platform, and even the Java 2 Enterprise Edition (J2EE) computing platform, offering a language, an architecture, and a platform to solve problems is not enough. A platform requires an additional layer of organization, known as a *pattern*, to help realize its full potential. Patterns help you see how to address specific problems with the tools that are available from a computing platform. Web Services are no different from any other computing platform in that the documentation of solutions can help you use the platform better and more quickly. This book provides generic patterns and implementations to illustrate how to use the Web Service platform.

What You Will Learn from Reading This Book

It is important to realize where Web Services fit into a complete solution for a business problem. For example, Web Services are not responsible for the behavior of a service; instead, they focus on how to access the behavior of a service. This distinction is critical when studying the category of solutions that Web Services enable. Despite a clear separation between the responsibilities of Web Services and those of a computing platform such as J2SE, there is often much overlap in the patterns that programmers leverage when concentrating on the different platforms.

You will also use new patterns when you embrace the Web Service platform to its fullest potential. The separation of communication from behavior—as well as the separation of service definition and location from the implementation of a service's behavior—enables a new generation of dynamic system behaviors.

By the time you have completed this book, you should have a clear understanding of the following:

- Business drivers that lead to solutions built with the Web Service platform

- Several common patterns and how to implement them using the Web Service platform

- Several new patterns to help you leverage Web Services

In addition to a catalog of patterns that you can leverage after completing the book, it is my intention that you have gained hands-on experience with the patterns through a case study that binds the patterns together. My approach to doing hands-on work is to present a simple case study enabled with open-source software, such as Apache Tomcat, Apache Axis, and MySQL. Appendix A contains a list of software required to run the examples. The samples themselves are open source and are available at SourceForge (http://sourceforge.net/projects/websvcdsnptn). I hope you will have a good understanding of the open-source community that is backing up Web Services by the time you finish the book.

Developing the Case Study

My experience with patterns is that the behavior and implementation of patterns is a mystery even after considerable thought and paper diagramming. Of course, if you are a student, your experience is probably to go ahead and implement the pattern as part of an exercise for class. My intent in this book is to give you the generic perspective that is useful in a pattern yet also hand you an implementation of the pattern that runs within the context of a larger application.

To fulfill this intent, I spend a chapter defining a fictitious company, the business drivers that lead to an update in the company's application, and the requirements that lead to an application that leverages Web Services. It would be exceptional if I could show you how to implement a complete Enterprise Resource Planning (ERP) system and we could sit and dissect it for weeks, but I have decided to use a smaller, more contained application centered on opening a coffee company to the broader world. My grandfather's coffee company, the P.T. Monday Coffee Company (based in Milwaukee, Wisconsin, throughout the early 1900s), serves as the foundation for the case study. What makes this situation unique is showing how a niche player in the coffee industry can take advantage of Web Services to become a player in a larger integrated value chain.

Once I have laid out the groundwork for the company, I spend the remainder of the book showing various patterns and how those patterns fulfill the application architecture, design, and implementation.

At the time of publication, I did not have a complete application; rather, I focused on the pattern samples for Web Services. Over time, my intention is to fill out the application in the SourceForge open-source project. Details about how to download and run the application are available in Appendix A.

Who Should Read This Book

Application architects, designers, and programmers who are interested in refining their knowledge of Web Services should read this book, as well as programmers who are interested in getting hands-on experience with Apache Axis. Ideally, a reader of this book has some sophistication in the Unified Modeling Language (UML), the Java 2 platform, software patterns, and Web Services. Anyone with fewer than three to four years of experience in programming systems, designing systems, or architecting systems should take the time and care to understand the constructs introduced in the book and read the references in the "Additional Reading" sections.

Several chapters discuss the patterns that the Web Service platform embodies. These chapters do not intend to introduce a specific Web Service platform implementation, but they should be enough to give you a good understanding of the underlying motivations and organization of most platforms. When I discuss a specific Web Service platform, I use the Apache Axis platform that plugs into the Apache Tomcat engine.

Finally, my target audience should have practical experience with software patterns. Although this is not a mandatory prerequisite, it is helpful to understand the level of abstraction at which I approach each pattern.

How the Book Is Organized

Pattern books take a variety of directions to portray patterns to the reader. Some books use rigid templates, and others lean more toward readable prose. Purists usually like the prior, and book readers, like me, like the latter. To be honest, I think pattern books should serve both types of readers. I have taken the approach to organize the book as a readable, prose-based, stand-alone piece of work.

A brief introduction to the topic of Web Service Patterns leads off the book. Next, I present the high-level requirements, business drivers, and architecture of the case study. After the case study, the chapters discuss various software patterns and how each one fulfills the system structures embodied in the high-level architecture. I introduce a single pattern per chapter (with the exception of two chapters that introduce variants and a necessary dependent pattern) along with how the pattern fulfills the needs of the case study. In addition to how the pattern specifically addresses the case study, each pattern documents the more general problem and solution that the pattern addresses. Figure 1 illustrates the relationships between the patterns.

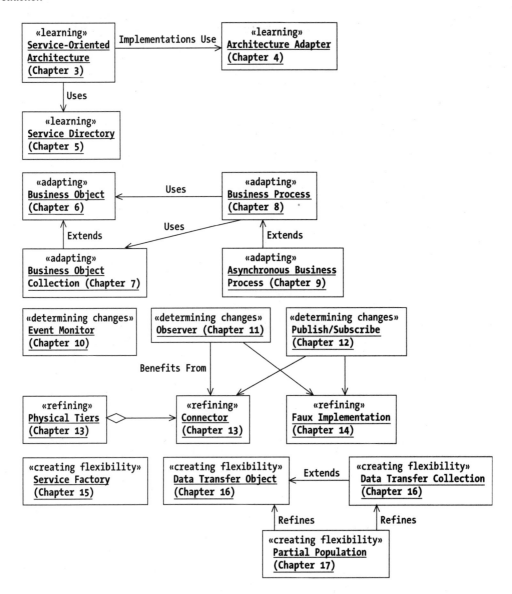

Figure 1. Pattern relationships

The patterns come in five categories:

Learning: It is important to understand the Web Service environment, where it originated from, and the mechanisms that help it fulfill its purposes of implementation and location transparency. The "learning" patterns fulfill this need.

Adapting: These patterns help refine your knowledge of a Web Service environment. These patterns change your way of thinking from object orientation to a flatter, more component-like approach for building representations of data and processes. The "adapting" patterns are used throughout the remainder of the book as base patterns.

Determining changes: Throughout my career I have been interested in messages and events. Although Web Services have asynchronous calls and although the service implementations could be based on a message-oriented architecture, I still find the traditional event patterns (the Observer and Publish/Subscribe patterns) interesting in the environment. They add a mechanism that programmer's expect from today's services.

Refining: These patterns are necessary enhancements to disprove that Web Services are monolithic in nature. Web Services are simply an access mechanism to behavior implemented in a language. These patterns help you understand the Web Service environment better and help you mold the environment to your own needs.

Creating flexibility: Finally, you can create more flexible Web Services that better suit your needs with a few additional patterns. The patterns in this category could easily be shuffled throughout different points in the book, but I chose to put them at the end because they are simply internal mechanisms and contracts to Web Services that help create a more optimized and flexible environment. In essence, they are extensions of the other patterns, not base patterns.

NOTE *Some of the later patterns in the book could easily be rearranged. For example, the Service Factory pattern could follow the Business Process pattern. The Physical Tiers pattern could follow the Service-Oriented Architecture pattern. I chose to structure the book in a way that would help you best learn the Web Service environment. In this spirit, I waited as long as I could before I ratcheted up the complexity with patterns such as the Physical Tiers pattern and Service Factory pattern.*

Finally, I present a variety of architectural, design, and implementation patterns (idioms) in the book. Several times, you will have to switch hats from architecture to design, but I hope to create a logical flow as to how you would go about understanding a complete application.

Next Steps After Reading

You will gain some valuable insights and techniques by reading and studying the examples in this book. On the other hand, you will become an expert in Web Services only if you spend considerable time working with them.

After reading this book, I encourage you to read as many of the Web Service–related specifications as you can. Each specification has its own motivation and patterns. In addition, if you find the implementation code I provide useful and well documented, I encourage you to extend the code with your own experiments and pattern implementations. Further, I would love to see any extensions to the code I provide. One of the reasons for not including the implementation with the book is that I will be able to keep the code base live and updated with new versions of the technology infrastructure on which the code is based.

> **NOTE** *SourceForge contains the active open-source project for adding additional Web Service patterns and enterprise application patterns to the P.T. Monday Coffee Company application* (http://sourceforge.net/projects/websvcdsnptn/). *If you do not want to participate in the SourceForge project, you can contact me at* pmonday@apress.com.

CHAPTER 1

Introducing Web Service Patterns

THE 1990S BROUGHT REVOLUTION to an entrenched computer industry in the form of the Internet. Networks broke out of the walls of companies and spanned nations and the globe instead of floors of a building. The 1990s brought the world e-commerce, e-business, and hundreds of companies that started with the letter *e* and ended in *.com*. Within the first years of the 21st century, however, disaster struck the bulk of the e-companies that put technology, glitz, and marketing strategies ahead of business plans and sound business practices.

As the 21st century continues marching on, people are picking up the pieces of the Internet revolution and deciding exactly what the 1990s have left us, other than smaller mutual funds and depleted retirement savings. With respect to computing and business, the Internet revolution taught us the following:

> The world is much smaller than expected. The ability to conduct business with a company located on the other side of the world is sometimes as easy as, or easier than, conducting business with the company next door.

> Technology's pace is just slightly under light speed. With Moore's Law applied to processor speed, network capacity, and the exponential increase in storage densities, new technology generations are hitting store shelves every nine to twelve months. This pace of technology allows you to write increasingly complex programs that were simply not possible even two to three years ago. A downside to the speed of technology generations is the number of types of hardware and software that are all running and available on the Internet at the same time. Today, everything from Timex Sinclair ZX80s to the latest Sun clusters are powering business and content on the Internet.

> **NOTE** *Moore's Law predicts that the number of transistors per integrated circuit will continue to grow exponentially. This translates into a more common interpretation of Moore's Law that states that the number of transistors will double every few years and thus the speed of the CPU will double every few years.*

An ever-increasing number of device types are being built and networked. In addition to getting information from traditional computers (desktops, notebooks, midrange, and mainframe), consumers and business people request information from their Personal Digital Assistants (PDAs), cellular phones, and watches. In no time, you will find your clothing, your sunglasses, and even your shoes networked together to give you a pervasive and ubiquitous computing experience.

Technology can overcome the widely disparate computing platforms used on the Internet and, even, within the walls of a company.

What the Internet revolution really left us with are the hopes and dreams of a networked world but also a relative chaos in terms of the networked world's implementation. Within businesses, a variety of generations of computers, devices, and software hang together with Enterprise Application Integration (EAI) software that was installed after the fact to get all of the technology and software working together to achieve a business need.

Unfortunately, EAI software is not an ideal situation. Integration most often occurs through the application's databases while the meat of the application logic remains a stovepipe.

The first part of the 21st century is defining itself to be a period in which the following will occur:

- People acknowledge that there will always be competing platforms that must work together to provide for a business.

- Businesses and the companies and customers that participate in making a business operate and become successful span the outside world as well as what is controlled within their own walls.

- People finally figure out how to build software that plugs into an ecosystem rather than software that believes it defines the ecosystem.

Web Services provide an important building block for integrating disparate computing platforms and, indirectly, provide a mechanism to integrate their global value chains. You can build Web Services after the system was originally deployed, making them similar in many ways to today's EAI software, but you can also build them along with new software as the open Application Programming Interface (API) to the application. This chapter introduces Web Services and the patterns that help you build them.

Web Services: Bringing Order to the Internet

Step back in time and think about the order of the Internet *evolution*. In the early Internet days, text-based content was king. Over time, Hypertext Transfer Protocol (HTTP) and Hypertext Markup Language (HTML) evolved to be rich enough to represent acceptable multimedia content. Further, the protocols and markup languages were easy enough that anyone could build and deploy a Web page. By this time, network bandwidth was still catching up to the content offered on the Internet.

Eventually, a critical mass hit the Internet:

- Companies such as Amazon.com started to generate revenue.

- Husbands ordered flowers for their wives on the Internet as a part of the culture rather than as a novelty.

- Virtually all news organizations started to have a Web presence.

Out of all of the business that started to occur on the Internet, one Web page signaled the start of true online business: the FedEx package-tracking page. Although it seemed like a novelty at the time, today it is easy to forget exactly how revolutionary this HTML form was in terms of its impact to business.

The basis for the page was simple; using a tracking number given to you by FedEx, you can track your package as it moves across the country. Suddenly, FedEx was not just a company that moved a package from a supplier to a customer; it was a part of a value chain. This value chain starts with product manufacturing and ends with the consumption of the product by the consumer. The package tracker exposes the customer and the manufacturer to the shipping process and its progress in the value chain. Now, everyone in the value chain knows when a package was shipped and received and can get up-to-date estimates for delivery.

Enabling the Integrated Value Chain

The FedEx package tracking application shows the progress of one business process, shipping, in a chain of many different processes that have to occur in the larger business process known as *order to fulfillment*. The order-to-fulfillment business process starts when a customer places an order with a company and ends when the customer receives the order. Although the separate package tracking application is nice, your customer must deal with two applications for keeping track of a single business process: the package tracking application and your own order processing application.

The ideal situation for a customer is that they can view the entire order-to-fulfillment process from a single location—your Web site. Immediately after placing an order, customers can see the order being located, packaged, and shipped and receive an estimate for the arrival time to their doorstep. It is important to bring the shipping company and its information seamlessly into your own business process. To do this, you need to have your applications tightly coupled with the shipping company's applications. After the product is shipped, you actually want to reflect the shipping company's status rather than your own.

Either the shipping company or the manufacturing company is in a computing platform predicament. How does the shipping company expose their application in a way that all of their customers can easily access it? Should they use the Java platform? With this tactic, a company gains portability as well as a mindshare of more than 50 percent of the computing industry today. Unfortunately, some of the biggest companies do not yet use the Java platform. Further, disruptive technologies are always on the horizon, such as C#, that could make the decision to expose an application with the Java platform unwise.

The choice of the platform to expose your API in should be language neutral and remotely accessible to natural constructs available in any language. Language neutrality will make it equally simple—and equally difficult—for any language to access your API. Remote accessibility makes the service addressable from any language although it resides somewhere on the network. Web Services provide solutions to both of these issues. The World Wide Web Consortium (W3C) defines a *Web Service* to be the following:

> *. . . a software system identified by a URI, whose public interfaces and bindings are defined and described using XML. Its definition can be discovered by other software systems. These systems may then interact with the Web service in a manner prescribed by its definition, using XML-based messages conveyed by Internet protocols.*

If there are two things you should know after the 1990s, they are that everything connects to the Internet, and everything supports Extensible Markup Language (XML). With Web Services, you have solved the dilemma on how to allow access to the package-tracking application from a variety of platforms; you do it with XML-based Web Services that rely on the Internet.

Tying Together Disparate Architectures

FedEx choosing a neutral language and communication mechanism such as Web Services illustrates another important use of Web Services: tying together disparate architectures. Thinking about a shipping company, you cannot predict what computing platforms from which a company will request to access your API.

Consider the situation many companies are in today with multiple software suites serving the employee requirements. Often, these companies purchased their software from different software vendors. Eventually, a company realizes that its customer data resides in both systems, with each system having different data. To reconcile the data and keep it coordinated over time, a company can write batch programs and different proprietary synchronization programs.

To write these synchronization programs, a programmer must be knowledgeable about both systems at some level. Most often, programmers write simple programs that query the database from one system, convert the data to the format of the other system, and insert the data into the second database table. Unfortunately, a change to either application renders the data transfer program useless. Further, system administrators must take the program offline to run the synchronization program; this avoids problems with pushing data into locked tables or getting a partial update from the source system.

Web Services, again, come to the rescue. By surfacing an API in a language-neutral and platform-neutral format, programmers can access data from one system and quickly move it to the other through the Web Service. There are several strengths to this approach:

- Programmers can write the data-transfer programs in any language or platform with which they are comfortable.

- The source and target systems can control the requests and updates of data in such a way that they do not interfere with a running system.

Consider the scenario of a third architecture inserted into a company's integration needs. In this case, a programmer's job without Web Services would become even more difficult as they learn and leverage the various software data formats. With Web Services, they simply learn another API and extend their existing program.

Because your own company's applications are often a microcosm of the Internet's diversity in applications and platforms, Web Services can help with both internal integration projects and external integration projects.

Patterns: Bringing Order to Software

If the Internet with its hundreds of heterogeneous software programs and computing platforms makes your head spin, then a quick survey of object-oriented programs will likely put you over the edge. Consider the number of ways that a simple problem, such as notifying interested parties of a change to an object's state, are solved with a platform such as Java 2 Standard Edition. Some developers may use an intermediate file to track changes, with interested parties reading the file to find out when and how an object changed. Other developers may construct a point-to-point notification system, or even a set of one-to-many Publish/Subscribe patterns. Some developers may have one type of naming convention for the adding and removing of listeners; other developers may not have any naming convention for the same operations.

Without a common way to solve the problem of notifying interested parties of a change to an object's state, everyone has a license to invent their own mechanism. This reinvention does not come free either; a robust notification mechanism can take days or weeks to perfect.

Patterns, simply, are a mechanism to document and educate others on problems that often occur when building software. You can limit patterns to your own software group, expand them to include your customers, or publish them to help the general software community.

Understanding Pattern Usage in the Computer Industry

Patterns exploded on the software scene after the 1995 publication of *Design Patterns: Elements of Reusable Object-Oriented Software*, the groundbreaking book from the "Gang of Four" (Erich Gamma, Richard Helm, Ralph Johnson, and John Vlissides).

> **NOTE**   *Developers refer to this book as the GoF book; we will do the same throughout the text.*

At this stage in software history, patterns are so pervasive that it is difficult to find software professionals without some knowledge of patterns, the most common being the 23 patterns discussed in the GoF book. Since the publication of the GoF book, patterns have emerged in dozens of texts and hundreds and thousands of Internet sites. The patterns range from the trivial idioms that apply to a particular language to the complex structure of a business application. Not only do patterns range from the trivial to the complex, but patterns also apply to situational human scenarios in the process of software development in addition to the more traditional mechanical patterns.

Software patterns that apply to your own software group include the rules and solutions for building applications unique to your company. These rules provide consistency in all of the efforts your software group embarks on, provided your architects, designers, and developers read the patterns. This model fits a traditional closed development lab that produces packaged software, but what if other software groups extend your software? In this case, it is useful to expose your patterns to those who will have to understand the software you build. By publishing to the extended community, you are able to aid your customers in understanding your design and implementation, while also ensuring that they maintain consistency in the designs for extensions and customizations.

The final step of publishing software patterns is what this book accomplishes. A book about software patterns helps you learn about patterns, software that uses patterns, and ways you could leverage the patterns in your own software.

Applying Software Patterns

Patterns apply to any portion of the software cycle. As shown in Figure 1-1, a typical software process goes through many stages (all of which are iterative in nature). Processes usually involve gathering requirements, creating the architecture, designing the software, and implementing it. The length of the individual steps, how the microtasks blend, and the artifacts from each step vary widely in practice; however, whether each step is implicit or explicit, the step occurs in one way or another.

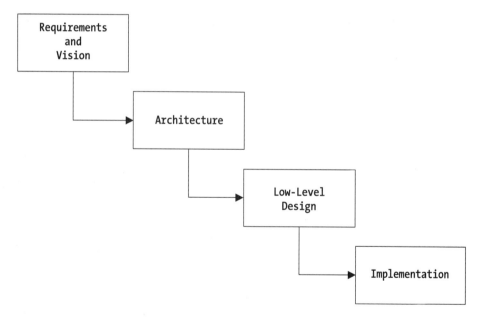

Figure 1-1. A typical software cycle

Different problems and challenges exist in each step of the software cycle. As you encounter problems and challenges along the way, there is a 90 percent chance that someone else has encountered the same problem. During the requirements-gathering process, it is common that architects and the product marketing area have difficulties gathering proper requirements and formulating them into reasonable architectural requirements. In this case, you would look for patterns for requirements gathering.

During architecture, groups of requirements and business drivers generate use-cases and system structures. Often, given a requirement such as "The user-interface for the product shall integrate with other applications via portal standards" leads to an off-the-shelf system structuring to ensure user-interface integration with a portal. At a higher level yet, business requirements often lead directly to system structures and decision points. For example, knowing that becoming part of an integrated value chain will drive revenue for your company will drive a decision to go with Web Services to open up your own application.

Once in a design phase, patterns become more pervasive and formal. Thousands of software design patterns document the common problems encountered by software designers and generic solutions for those problems. For example, an architect may give a system structure that identifies a point in the system where an object change drives listeners to make changes in their own state, or the change kicks off a business process. In these cases, a designer can look and determine that the Publish/Subscribe or the Observer pattern can fulfill the requirements and constraints an architect put on the design. Once identification of patterns is complete, the generic structure given in a pattern drives the design of the particular system structure.

After design, programmers must develop the code that implements the design. Programmers are bound to a computer platform and language that typically do not bind the designer. Idioms are best practices for implementing a design in a specific language or platform.

Understanding Web Service Patterns

Patterns apply to Web Services in several ways. First, the Web Service paradigm builds on a variety of patterns. Second, Web Service implementations can benefit from existing patterns. Finally, some patterns that seemed incidental in an object-oriented paradigm are useful, educational, and more important in a Web Service paradigm than in an object-oriented paradigm.

Learning About Web Services

You will start your look at patterns with three that help illustrate Web Services. The following patterns look at how Web Services implement the service-oriented architecture, how service implementations interact with the Web Service environment, and how to locate and use Web Services:

Service-Oriented Architecture: The Web Services environment is an architecture implementation known as the *service-oriented architecture*. There are several different implementations of the service-oriented architecture with Web Services having the most penetration in the industry to date. Implementations of service-oriented architectures stress two attributes: implementation transparency and location transparency. Implementation transparency requires a common system structure that applies equally to all possible underlying service implementations and a neutral mechanism for describing services. Location transparency requires the use of agnostic interfaces. You will dissect the Service-Oriented Architecture pattern to learn about the foundations of Web Services.

Architecture Adapter: This pattern expands on the GoF Adapter pattern. Although the GoF Adapter pattern resides in object-oriented programming as a way to adapt an exposed interface from a component to an expected dependent interface from another component, the Architectural Adapter pattern is responsible for allowing two completely separate architectures to interoperate.

Service Directory: In statically bound systems, and even in many dynamic systems, companies assume that their choices for the purchaser of software are the right choices. The Web Service paradigm challenges this tradition. Instead, by creating detailed metadata about a service, a service user should be able to locate your service and use it without application modification. The metadata in a service-oriented architecture includes its interface, location for binding, mechanism for communication, and information about the business that created the service. This pattern goes into depth on the Service Directory patterns that are inherent in the leading service architectures and that you will encounter in Web Services.

With these patterns and the sample implementations that go along with the patterns, you should have a good understanding of the Web Service environment. Further, the examples and samples in the text use the Apache Axis Web Service environment, so you will also have a good understanding of this environment after you finish the patterns.

Adapting to Web Services

The next four patterns walk through a typical progression of thought refinement as object-oriented programmers adapt to Web Services. These patterns illustrate various business concepts with the sample implementations showing how to deploy them as Web Services. These patterns are examples of patterns taken for granted in an object-oriented environment but that become interesting in a Web Service environment. First, the patterns illustrate a typical learning curve in Web Services, and the patterns give insight into the Web Service environment. Second, the patterns give insight as to how business concepts embody themselves in Web Services:

Business Object: This pattern discusses the typical structure and contents of a single business object. Although the frequency that you will use a single business object for deployment is low, there are substantial lessons you can learn from the exercise of deploying a business object. As with the first three patterns, this pattern is heavy in discussion around the Web Service environment and lessons you can learn from deploying relatively simple objects.

Business Object Collection: In business, you will rarely find business objects that are not collected. Like the business object itself, handling collections with Web Services yields substantial instructional substance as you learn more about the Web Service environment.

Business Process (Composition): Business systems today revolve more around business processes than around supporting business objects. A business process does not necessarily correlate to a single business object but is more abstract in nature. This pattern looks at business processes and lays a general framework for exposing them as Web Services. The business process is also a form of composition. To achieve a business process, multiple business objects and, often, other business processes and activities must run.

Asynchronous Business Process: A world where all business processes are synchronous would be a fine world to live in for programmers. Unfortunately, most important business processes are not synchronous. Even the most basic business processes, such as fulfilling a book order, run into asynchronous complexities. In introducing the Asynchronous Business Process pattern, you will find many similarities to the relationship between business objects and business object collections.

Determining When Changes Occur

These patterns are most interesting in what they teach you about the Web Service environment. The next three patterns introduce practical mechanisms to determine when changes occur to a Web Service. The first is a commonly used pattern in business applications when you deal with services that did not predict you would care to be notified when a change occurs to the internal state of a Web Service. The latter two patterns implement existing patterns within the Web Service paradigm to illustrate mechanisms that can aid clients in determining when data changes occur within your Web Service:

Event Monitor: Often, the burden of determining when events occur in a service lies with the client. There are a variety of reasons for this, such as the service not having a reasonable publish/subscribe interface or the client desiring control of the event determination. This is a common, and relatively simple, design pattern to implement that has well-established roots throughout software history.

Observer: Rather than leaving a client to determine when data changed on a server, it is often more efficient to have the server component tell interested clients when data changes. This is especially true when the server component has a low frequency of updates compared to the frequency that clients will want to check. The Observer pattern formalizes the relationship between one or more clients and a Web Service that contains interesting state. The Web Service delivers events to interested clients when an interesting change occurs. The Gang of Four documented the Observer pattern. This implementation is similar to the original documentation of the pattern, with necessary information about Web Services.

Publish/Subscribe: The Publish/Subscribe pattern [Buschmann] is a heavily used pattern in EAI software as well as in many distributed programming paradigms. The Publish/Subscribe pattern is interesting in the context of the definition of Web Services as application components. Using a topic-based mechanism common in very loosely coupled architectures, you create a stand-alone event service that is, in effect, an application component. The event service forwards published events to subscribers without awareness of the application components that use the event service.

The Observer and Publish/Subscribe patterns introduce an interesting issue. The subscriber to Web Service events must, itself, be a Web Service. Web Services are, by definition, application components. Instead of an application component, event subscribers are a part of another application that requires up-to-date information on changes to a target Web Service. In other words, subscribers by their nature are not stand-alone application components.

Refining the Structure of Your Web Services

The next two patterns address this issue in radically different ways, one by embracing the Web Service paradigm and the other by pretending to embrace the Web Service paradigm:

Physical Tiers: Throughout the book and the sample implementations in the chapters, you will use a simple Java-based deployment mechanism built into Apache Axis. Therefore, your components live entirely within the process space that Apache Axis uses. This is not an optimal model for enterprise applications. The model discourages runtime reuse and creates a larger footprint than is necessary. Further, the event patterns produced some interesting challenges for a Web Service environment. A client interested in events from a Web Service often exists in its own process. This pattern discusses Web Service implementations that must, and often should, communicate to other processes for their implementation behavior.

Faux Implementation: One of the most fascinating pieces of the Internet is the ability of someone or something to be able to pretend to be something they are not and actually get away with it. As long as an interface and the behavior of a service implementation is what others expect, there is no way to tell what drives the behavior of the service implementation. The Observer and Publish/Subscribe patterns require clients to implement a Web Service to receive event publications. The Faux Implementation pattern shows that as long as the behavior fulfills the contract, there is no reason you have to implement a service with traditional mechanisms.

Creating Flexibility in Your Web Services

The final three patterns give some additional mechanisms to bring flexibility to the Web Service paradigm. The first brings flexibility to clients who want to leverage a Web Service that exhibits a particular behavior. The last two provide mechanisms to streamline client interactions with Web Services:

Service Factory: Class factories are common in Java programming. A class factory gives a mechanism to bind to a class implementation at runtime rather than compile time. The same capability is possible with service implementations. For example, there is no reason that a company must use a single package shipper for all shipments. Instead, the service factory illustrates how your application can determine what service to use at runtime.

Data Transfer Object: The Data Transfer Object pattern originated with Java 2 Enterprise Edition (J2EE) patterns. When you move from a single process application to a distributed application, calls between participants in the distributed architecture become more expensive in terms of performance. By giving clients mechanisms to get groups of commonly accessed data in single operations, you can streamline clients and lower the number of accesses necessary to your Web Service.

Partial Population: The Data Transfer Object pattern passes fully populated data structures between programs. This is a great paradigm but creates a proliferation of data structures and relegates the service implementation to determining what the most likely groups of accessed data will be. Partial population takes a different approach to data transfers; it allows clients to tell the server what parts of a data structure to populate. In this way, you can lighten the burden on the communication mechanism as well as the query in the server object. This technique is especially useful for services that contain complex, nested data structures (not something you will typically find in a Web Service environment).

Overall, the 15 previous patterns run the gamut from patterns that help understand the Web Service environment to patterns that optimize Web Service implementations. The organization of the patterns in the book starts with patterns to help understand Web Services and moves slowly to patterns that apply to relatively complex service implementations.

Using the Sample Code

This book's source code and working samples are available in the Downloads section of the Apress Web site (`http://www.apress.com/book/download.html`). This source is as presented in the text—potential bugs and all. (Refer to Appendix A for instructions on how to install and run the code samples.)

A working copy of the P.T. Monday application presented in this book is available in the Web Service Design Patterns in Java project on SourceForge (`http://sourceforge.net/projects/websvcdsnptn/`). This project is active, and the source contains bug fixes and evolutionary changes to the patterns and classes presented in the text. You are also welcome to join the project and contribute to the application in this book. You could build a user interface to it, contribute more robust Java Data Objects (JDO) code, or test new Web Service design patterns and specifications.

Finally, I am always available for feedback at `pmonday@apress.com`. I try to get to all of my email and am relatively humble about the code I produce and writing I do, so I will be glad to discuss a pattern or two with you.

Summary

This chapter briefly reviewed some notable changing points in the history of networked computers. It laid the groundwork for Web Services through brief discussions on the Internet, Moore's Law, and the ability of technology to overcome the seeming chaos that the disruptive technologies cause. Integrated value chains, with FedEx and other shipping companies leading the charge, and disparate architectures within companies are two of the first problems for which Web Services play a critical role.

Next, the chapter discussed patterns and their contribution to the software industry. Following this brief discussion, you saw a preview of the patterns that this book introduces to the Web Service paradigm. Three of the patterns—the Observer, Publish/Subscribe, and Data Transfer patterns—exist in common books but are introduced in this text to illustrate their usefulness in the Web Service environment. The other 12 patterns have their roots in various business problem solutions. In all of the cases, the patterns apply to other environments than Web Services, though they are mechanisms that will aid in your own Web Service applications.

The next chapter discusses the architecture and design for a company's application that leverages Web Services. The case study is not a complete architecture and design, but rather, it is enough detail so that the application can provide context for all of the patterns documented in this book.

Additional Reading

- Alur, Deepak; Crupi, John; Malks, Dan. *Core J2EE Patterns: Best Practices and Design Strategies.* Prentice Hall, 2001.

- Buschmann, Frank et. al. *Pattern-Oriented Software Architecture, Volume 1: A System of Patterns.* Jon Wiley & Sons, 1996.

- Gamma, Erich et. al. *Design Patterns: Elements of Reusable Object-Oriented Software.* Addison-Wesley, 1995.

- Schmidt, Douglas C. *Pattern-Oriented Software Architecture, Volume 2: Patterns for Concurrent and Networked Objects.* Jon Wiley & Sons, 2000.

CHAPTER 2

Introducing the
P.T. Monday Case Study

THE APPLICATION OF PATTERNS occurs early in the architectural process and continues throughout application design and well into the implementation stages.
In order, you would apply architectural patterns, design patterns, and idioms to
the stages of development. An *architectural pattern* guides the structure of a system from the user through the database and any layers that make up the
application structure. *Design patterns* guide the structure or mechanics of
classes and components within an architectural subsystem. *Idioms* are common
techniques within a particular technology or language.

Patterns and catalogs of patterns are best understood if they all relate to
a common application. This book uses a simplified case study that lays out a
company vision and a variety of common requirements that the application
must fulfill as a basis for the patterns. Throughout the text, the patterns and
examples fill in the architectural and design details to complete core portions of
the case study.

The case study introduced in this chapter is the P.T. Monday Coffee
Company. The company roasts and delivers coffee beans to individuals and
restaurants. The P.T. Monday Coffee Company exists as a part of a value chain.
The end of the value chain for direct customers is the delivery of the beans to the
customer. The P.T. Monday Coffee Company owns the entire value chain and
leverages other companies to fulfill portions of the chain. For a restaurant pur-
chasing beans, the end of the value chain is actually the purchase of a cup of
coffee by a customer. In this case, a large portion of the value chain actually
exists outside of the company, and the P.T. Monday Coffee Company merely
enables a portion of the value chain that the restaurant originates.

Your goal will be to get the P.T. Monday Coffee Company "online" as efficiently as possible and support the company's vision. In building the online
system, you want to create room for flexibility within the application. For example, the P.T. Monday Coffee Company today uses a single shipper for all orders;
there are many reasons that shipping decisions should be more dynamic than
this. Instead of creating a static shipping decision, you will use the Service
Factory pattern to ensure the application is flexible enough to withstand different decisions in shipping that occur after completing the application.

It is important in any architecture to start with a vision. In this case, you need to understand the vision of where the company should be within the next five years. You also need to gather the proper functional and nonfunctional requirements and start fulfilling them with the architecture and design process. This chapter covers the common architecture patterns that the system uses.

Understanding the Current State of the Business

The P.T. Monday Coffee Company roasts and delivers, or has delivered by a shipping company, hundreds of pounds of coffee per week. The company takes orders off the Internet for direct customer sales as well as sales to cafés and delis that resell the P.T. Monday coffee and brew it in their own stores. The current Web site consists of static Web content and a simple form that customers submit to place an order. The form ends up in an email message to the secretary for the P.T. Monday Coffee Company after a Perl script processes the form. Although customers can submit orders, the secretary ends up handling the back-end work of fulfilling orders and taking care of credit card orders. There is no customer database; instead, the company retains paper records of the transactions.

As for order fulfillment, there are times when there are not enough coffee beans to fulfill the outstanding orders. This leads to some problems with customer satisfaction. Luckily, current customers are loyal to the company because of its local roots and friendly delivery people. The P.T. Monday Coffee Company relies on a single grower of coffee but would like to find additional growers. By keeping their options open with growers, the company can alleviate some of their order fulfillment problems.

Despite the weaknesses, the P.T. Monday Coffee Company has a loyal and increasing following. The company achieved coolness in Milwaukee, Wisconsin, through their coffee delivery service and unique designs for the delivery vans.

Understanding the Company Vision

The company has built an aggressive business plan that calls for 40-percent increases in year-to-year sales over the next five years. Resellers are the keys to fueling growth, as well as the expansion of delivery services into nearby Chicago, Illinois. The company's goals are to sell coffee to one regional chain in the next year and one national chain in the next five years. With a correctly worked partnership deal, the company wants to dramatically expand direct customer sales to correspond with the expansion of restaurants offering the coffee.

The owners of the company realize that the key to their aggressive expansion requires a sound, Internet-based application that integrates a new ordering system from the P.T. Monday Coffee Company with its customers' systems.

Further, the P.T. Monday Coffee Company's systems need to integrate with its partners' systems to quickly locate a partner with excess coffee beans in the event that the P.T. Monday Coffee Company runs out of beans from its default supplier.

The company also needs to expand its direct sales Web site to better facilitate customers and enable the company to reach out to existing customers with special offers, especially when there is excess capacity in terms of beans and roasters. Further, the site has to retain valuable customer information to personalize the site and make it easier for customers to place additional orders.

Gathering Application Requirements

A part of creating the architecture is the act of gathering and distilling requirements for the application. In general, you work from four types of requirements:

- **Business requirements:** The reasons your business needs this application going into the future

- **User requirements:** The behaviors and qualities that users of the application request

- **Functional requirements:** The behaviors that the application needs to embody

- **Nonfunctional requirements:** Application requirements that do not correlate directly to a function of the application, such as performance

You will use only a partial list of requirements for the P.T. Monday Coffee Company's new application. It is not my intention to build and deploy an entire operations site, only portions of the infrastructure relevant to the Web Service patterns. Further, I only list those requirements that relate to those patterns. This approach should simplify and shorten the requirement lists substantially.

Gathering the Business Requirements

Table 2-1 lists the business requirements for the new application. The business requirements, in many cases, restate the company vision and direction.

Documenting and capturing business requirements are a vital portion of architecture, so those requirements placed on the system can correlate directly to a business reason.

Table 2-1. Business Requirements

ID	BUSINESS REQUIREMENT
B1	The application shall have the ability to integrate into the reseller's value chain.
B2	The application shall have the ability to integrate bean suppliers into the company's value chain.
B3	The application shall enable the company to decrease its dependency on individual bean suppliers.
B4	The application shall increase direct customer service without contacting a customer service representative.
B5	The application shall decrease the manual processing of customer information and orders.
B6	The application shall increase the ability to manage seasonal fluctuations through better price management.
B7	The application shall provide the ability to manage a remote distribution company for a separate locale.

Often, you represent business requirements in use-case diagrams that both summarize the requirements and graphically represent them for easy access. Figure 2-1 shows a use-case diagram with the proper actors and summarized requirements.

Several of the business drivers for the system point you toward Web Services. The key word to look for is *integration*. This application needs to work with partner computers in a variety of ways. Your direct partners could be influenced to go toward a proprietary or platform-specific solution, but the unspecified restaurant chains that you will work with are different. It is unlikely that as the P.T. Monday Coffee Company grows it will have the influence to alter a large chain's computing directions away from open standards, such as Web Services. There will be additional reasons to select Web Services as the integration technology as you move through the functional and nonfunctional requirements of the system.

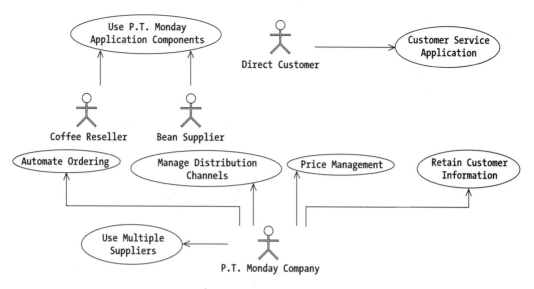

Figure 2-1. Business requirements for the P.T. Monday Coffee Company application

This application facilitates direct sales by retaining and accessing personalization information and exposing the order-to-fulfillment process to the direct consumer. The application aids resellers with a programmatic interface to ordering and various business processes in addition to the advantages given by the direct sales improvements. Internally, process improvements occur in the order fulfillment arena through increased ability to automate the coordination and purchase of unroasted coffee beans from growers. Enhancements extend to the shipping department to help plan and automate distribution through the local truck routes and third-party shippers. Finally, the management staff gains increased visibility to the business processes, their status, and quicker exposure to weaknesses in the value chain (such as a decrease in demand resulting in excess beans).

Gathering the User Requirements

User requirements give a concrete list of behaviors and functionality that users within the company, as well as external users such as direct Web purchasers, expect to see from your application. A comprehensive list of user requirements would take pages for the application. Table 2-2 lists the requirements that you will focus on throughout the book.

Table 2-2. User Requirements

ID	REQUIREMENT	USER
U1	The application shall have Web-based access to the customer profile for update directly by customers.	Direct/Reseller
U2	The application shall allow customers to access the current order status through a programmatic mechanism and through a user interface.	Direct/Reseller
U3	The application shall enable a customer to access product catalog and sale information through a user interface and programmatically.	Direct/Reseller
U4	Customers shall be able to view current invoices and payment schedules.	Direct/Reseller
U5	Customers shall be able to change billing options and make payments through a Web-based interface.	Direct/Reseller
U6	Direct orders from customers shall require credit card information.	Direct
U7	Approval and authorization for credit card usage shall be required for the placement of direct sales orders.	Direct
U8	Customers shall have the option of automated and manual selection of the shipping method.	Direct/Reseller
U9	The application shall notify management when the outstanding quantity of orders for beans exceeds the amount of beans in the warehouse.	Management
U10	The application shall notify management when there is a substantial amount of excess beans in the warehouse.	Management
U11	Managers shall have the ability to run monthly and weekly reports on throughput.	Management

Like business requirements, use-case diagrams help depict the web of user requirements. Figure 2-2 shows the user requirements.

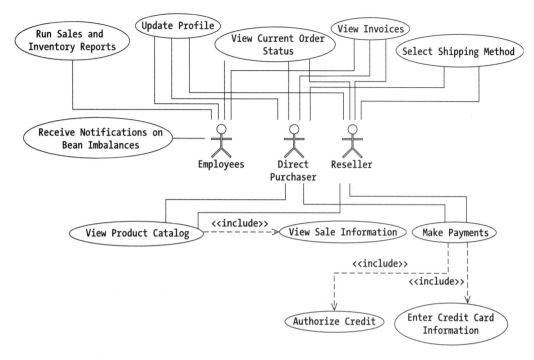

Figure 2-2. User requirements for the P.T. Monday Coffee Company application

Considering that Table 2-2 is just the tip of the iceberg for user requirements, it does provide a glimpse into some of the challenges the application faces. For example, several processes require both Web-based access and programmatic access from customers. Further, there are several dynamic processes identified in the latter portion of the table, such as the ability to automate the selection of a shipping company and the ability to automate a bean-ordering system.

Gathering the Functional Requirements

Functional requirements for an application capture the intended behaviors of the application. These requirements show the application capabilities that are required to fulfill the user requirements. Although this section does not express all of the application's functional requirements, it expresses enough for you to continue on the course of your application architecture. Table 2-3 lists some of the functional requirements.

Table 2-3. Functional Requirements

ID	REQUIREMENT
F1	The Web-based forms shall provide a secure mechanism for updating customer personalization information.
F2	The Web-based forms shall be accessible from Internet Explorer, Personal Digital Assistants (PDAs) that run Microsoft operating systems, and cell-phones that have Web Markup Language (WML)-compliant functionality.
F3	The application shall provide programmatic access to submit orders, observe the fulfillment process, and pay invoices.
F4	The Web-based forms shall provide a secure mechanism for invoice payment.
F5	The Web-based forms shall provide a secure mechanism for placing direct sales orders with immediate payment and scheduling direct sales orders with an automatic payment mechanism.
F6	The Web-based forms shall provide a personalized order history.
F7	The Web-based forms shall provide access to order status.
F8	The external Application Programming Interface (API) to the system shall be accessible to all current programming languages and platforms.
F9	The inventory management system shall automatically request additional beans from suppliers based on management-configured parameters for the definition of low supplies and grower preferences.
F10	The inventory management system shall notify management via email when either excess roasted and unroasted beans are available or a low-inventory situation occurs.
F11	The inventory management system shall notify management via email when a low-inventory situation is resolved or if manual intervention is required.

Several of the functional requirements fall into the category of business processes. These business processes are often viewable by application users. For example, a customer that orders several pounds of coffee would often like to know when its order is roasted and shipped. This response mechanism should aid the company in reducing curiosity calls to the customer service department. In a more advanced system, you could add business intelligence to predict the expected shipment date. The Ship Order and the Generate Delivery Route processes could use third-party services from the shipper and an Internet-based route finder.

Gathering the Nonfunctional Requirements

Table 2-4 lists the qualities and constraints of your application in the form of nonfunctional requirements. There are always some nonfunctional requirements that you can assume to be in existence, but for this case, many of these assumptions are actually lower priorities than the business, functional, and user requirements. Although it is true that you want your system to perform well, performance is well below the need to embrace open standards for integration points. Integration with external systems and flexible business processes are also priorities in the final application. For succinctness, I omitted several of the obvious requirements and retained those that stand out in this application.

Table 2-4. Nonfunctional Requirements

ID	REQUIREMENT
NF1	The application shall embrace open standards for the external API.
NF2	The application shall not require duplicated logic within the application.
NF3	The application must choose low-cost options and open-source software whenever that software does not compromise the stability of the application.

These requirements should not leave any doubt that there is a place for Web Services in your application. As with the other requirements included in the text, I have omitted the bulk of the nonfunctional requirements.

Making High-Level Application Architecture Decisions

Application architecture has somewhat fuzzy lines drawn with respect to where application architecture leaves off and where application design starts. In this chapter, you will create a simple system structure and make specific technology decisions based on the gathered requirements. By the end of this chapter, you should have a general understanding of your overall architecture direction but have questions about the details of the architecture.

Making Technology Choices

Architecture goes through *micro-iterations* during which you choose and recommend technologies for system implementation. In the process of choosing those technologies and components, you make slight revisions to interfaces for the various subsystems of your application. Instead of portraying micro-iterations in text, which is a difficult thing to do, I simply list the technology choices before showing the structure of the application. Remember that even though these technology decisions are set early in the text, technology choices should minimally impact your overall application architecture.

Table 2-5 contains a list of decisions and the simplified reasons for those decisions. In many cases, the decisions are based on deeper requirements or experience that is not portrayed entirely in the requirements listed.

Table 2-5. Technology Choices

TECHNOLOGY	DESCRIPTION
Java Platform	The Java Platform is ideal for deploying Web Services because of its maturity and first-class integration into most Web Service platforms.
Java Data Objects (JDO)	The persistence mechanism to use from the Java platform is a difficult choice. There will always be programmers who can handle databases through the JDBC Data Access API, but you are looking for a more natural programming environment. The JDO specification and implementations give you a natural and relatively simple mechanism to leverage the object-oriented environment of Java in concert with persistence without adding complex database code to your classes.
Apache Tomcat	The Apache Tomcat application server is free, mature, and common in the business world. That combination creates a competitive environment for hosting your Web Service technologies.
Apache Axis	Although not as mature as Apache Tomcat, Apache Axis is shaping up to be both competitive and robust in terms of supporting different programming environments. Apache Axis will be your choice for the Web Service environment. It also plugs nicely into Apache Tomcat.
MySQL	Choosing a database is a tricky proposition. You need it to be robust and manageable while maintaining a low total cost of ownership. MySQL is an open-source and free database. Because most of your access to the database will be through JDO, you will be able to avoid most direct database interactions, and the lack of development tools for MySQL does not hurt you badly. Another equally valid choice is PostgreSQL.
MM.MySQL	This is a JDBC driver for MySQL. JDO uses a JDBC driver for accessing the database.

Choosing the Java platform and JDO as the internal service implementation and persistence model is difficult to legitimize without completely exposing the requirements and architecture process. The primary reason for the selection is the open and accessible standards through the Java Community Process (JCP), coupled with the experience of the person implementing the solution.

Determining the Application Structure

The high-level application structure you use is an important place to start the application case study. The requirements of the application help to determine the structure of the application. Fortunately, where requirements leave off, architectural patterns begin. Three architectural patterns are of interest as you get started. The Layers pattern [Buschmann] gives you guidance on how to deal with a separation of concerns that will aid you in development of your application. The N-Tier Architecture pattern is a derivative of the Layers pattern with more specificity applied. Finally, the Java architecture blueprint gives a concrete example of an n-tier architecture.

After reviewing each of these important architectural patterns, you will finally produce the overall architecture of the P.T. Monday Coffee Company application. The basic architecture presented is a derivative of the patterns presented in the next three sections.

Introducing the Layers Architectural Pattern

The Layers architectural pattern is basic in nature but important in practice. The essence of the pattern is that you should design applications in layers, with each layer representing a group of related concerns. Each layer contains related classes and components and has a structured interface and communication mechanism to access capabilities within the layer.

Layers typically stack on top of one another, building capabilities of the overall application, as shown in Figure 2-3. It is common that each layer accesses only the layer underneath, though layers often have to access multiple layers in practice.

The most difficult part of working with layers is determining what layers to separate and how to embody the separation between the layers. The layer separation should make sense from a technical grouping standpoint as well as an organizational structure standpoint. Keep in mind that the technical content will outlast your personnel structure, so be careful to consider technical merit as the primary organizational principle. Typical layers are the presentation layer, the business content layer, the persistence layer, and the client layer. For example, the concerns of presentation to a browser are radically different from the concerns of persistence to a database.

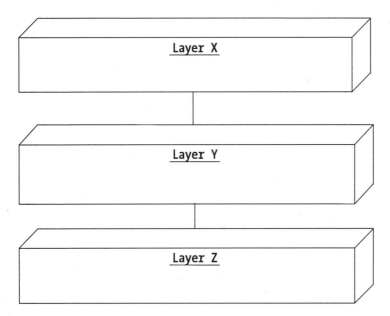

Figure 2-3. Layers architectural pattern

You can create separation between layers in different ways. It is entirely possible to implement architecture with layers yet have the entire application run
within a single physical process. In this scenario, you only leverage the layered
approach at development time, not at deployment time. You can also separate
layers by process on a single computer or by process on separate computers.
This technique introduces performance penalties in terms of intercomponent
communication, but you may be able to compensate for the performance loss
by the flexibility in which you can deploy each layer. Further, each layer can
focus on optimization within their own components as long as they adhere to
the layer interface.

Just stating that your architecture adheres to the Layers pattern is not
enough for developers and designers. You must go further to explain the content
of the layers in the architecture as well as a sampling of components in the layers. The next two patterns dig deeper into specific examples.

Introducing the N-Tier Architecture Pattern

The N-Tier Architecture pattern is a generalization of a three-tier architectural
pattern. The three-tier architecture consisted of a workstation presentation, the

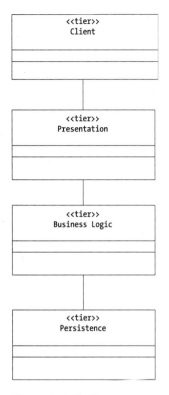

Figure 2-4. N-Tier Architecture pattern

business logic, and a database and the logic to support it. In today's component architectures, including Web Services, a three-tier architecture simply does not properly portray the flexibility with which you can use a component architecture.

A description of the tiers as well as a description of how the tiers communicate typically accompanies identification of the n-tier architecture. Figure 2-4 shows an example that contains a client tier, a presentation tier, a business logic tier, and a persistence tier. Communication between the client tier and the presentation tier occurs over Hypertext Transfer Protocol (HTTP), communication between the presentation tier and business logic tier occurs with Remote Method Invocation (RMI), and communication between the business logic tier and persistence tier occurs with JDBC.

Looking back at the case study requirements (including B1, B2, F3, and F8), you can see that there are multiple access points to your system. Users can access your system through a visual interface, and programs can access your system through a programmatic API. You do not necessarily know how your customers will use your business logic; they may have their own logic tier or a process tier with yet another presentation tier on top of that. Screen scrapers can add additional presentation tiers on top of your own, and you can even help them by introducing an API to your presentation tier to send and retrieve forms.

By locking yourself into a three-tier architecture, you may inhibit your flexibility to create a malleable system that fulfills as many requirements and scenarios as possible. The n-tier architecture will suit your requirements and give developers and designers a better place to start than simply identifying the Layers pattern.

The J2EE architectural blueprints expound further on n-tier architectures. The more detail and examples that you, as architects, can give to designers and developers, the better off you will be by the time implementation of the architecture gets started.

Introducing the J2EE Application Architecture

Examples of J2EE application architecture are excellent examples of an n-tier architecture in practice. The J2EE documentation calls an n-tier architecture a *multitier* architecture. The primary architectural blueprint appears as a three-tier architecture, but the flexibility of the architecture turns it into an n-tier architecture.

The three-tier J2EE base implementation consists of a client tier, a middle tier, and an enterprise information services tier, as shown in Figure 2-5. The middle tier is more complex than a traditional middle tier and facilitates both rendering for clients and business logic accessed by the presentation. In essence, the middle tier contains layers within the tier. The middle tier layers get physically deployed into two containers: an EJB container and a Web container. The containers separate the operating environments and give a single point of control for container configuration that applies to the components residing within each separate container. In J2EE, the tiered representation implies more of a deployment model than a logical development model. You can think of the development model as a four-tier, or more, architecture.

Variations of the J2EE architecture include the insertion of additional tiers between the middle tier and the client tier. For example, a Webtop (a thin client that contains a Java operating system) inserts an additional Webtop server tier between the middle tier and the client tier. To facilitate this additional tier, you have to ensure that the middle tier has acceptable interfaces on which clients can rely.

One of the problems with layered architectures comes in the development of a product on top of a layered architecture. Business logic developers adhering to the strict definition of tiers or layers will want to build interfaces agnostic of the tiers above them. Developers of the presentation tier will want tiers below them to fulfill only their requirements and optimize the interface to business logic for the presentation tier's use. The reality is that developers must compromise reality and purity. The primary use of the business logic will be through a presentation tier; making it work in an optimal way for customers is a priority for the business logic tier developers. On the other hand, business logic developers must push back as presentation concepts creep into the business logic tier because there is no guarantee that outsiders will use a presentation tier on top of the logic.

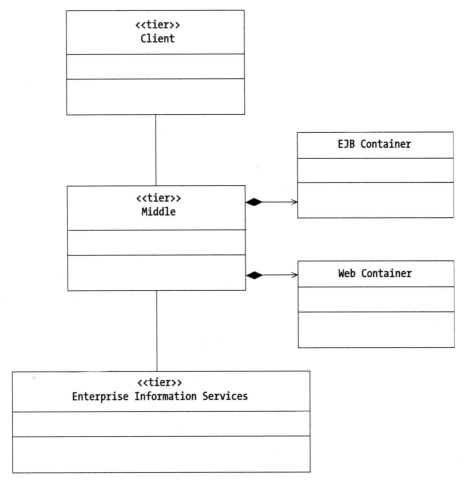

Figure 2-5. J2EE architectural blueprint

Determining the P.T. Monday Application Structure

The P.T. Monday Coffee Company application structure follows directly from the N-Tier Architecture pattern and the J2EE architecture blueprint. Figure 2-6 shows the high-level structuring of the application and platform. In it, you see a classic n-tier structure that is common in today's Web-based applications and that is derived from the Layers architectural pattern. You also see many attributes of the J2EE architecture, with a formal breakdown of the Web tier and the business logic tier.

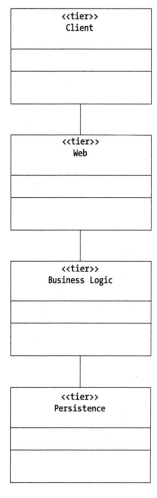

Figure 2-6. High-level application structure

The application structure consists of the following:

Client tier: This tier contains the different devices and mechanisms your customers will use to access the application. Your two primary accessors are users accessing the application from a browser and other computers accessing the Web Services that you expose. The primary support protocols are Extensible HTML (XHTML) over HTTP and Simple Object Access Protocol (SOAP) over HTTP. Your implementation must be flexible enough to adapt to other channels of access, perhaps with the addition of a tier to support the other access channel, such as the Webtop in the J2EE example.

Web tier: This tier has two responsibilities: accepting requests from browser-based clients and accepting requests from other business logic tiers accessing logic through a programmatic API. Both types of requests forward business logic to the business logic tier for processing, and the Web tier handles any presentation or request/response transformations.

Business logic tier: This tier contains the logic that the application must use to fulfill user requirements. There are cases when business logic to fulfill a particular process actually exists *outside* of your application. In this case, the business logic tier contains the logic required to integrate the external logic into your own application.

Persistence tier: The ever-present database makes up the persistence tier. Although no explicit coding is required in the presentation tier because of the technologies in use, it is important to acknowledge its existence up front so that you can consider it during deployment.

Although the client tier and the persistence tier are relatively straightforward and are *considered* but not *built*, there are some additional architectural details to consider when looking at the Web and business logic tiers.

Exploring the Web Tier

The Web tier facilitates the connection between client requests and the business logic that fulfills the client requests. There are a variety of ways to structure the Web tier depending on the types of clients it facilitates. The Web Service path facilitates the programmatic access to business logic, and a path with Java Server Pages (JSPs) and servlets facilitates the browser-based entry to the Web tier.

There are two paths through the Web tier, as illustrated in Figure 2-7. Programmatic clients work through the Web Service interface. Tomcat routes requests against a Web Service to the Axis Web Services engine running within the Tomcat process. Tomcat routes requests for views, typically from a browser, to a Front Controller [Alur]. The Front Controller facilitates a Web-based Model-View-Controller paradigm for presentation.

This book does not cover the presentation path and the Front Controller pattern; see the "Additional Reading" section for more details on the presentation path. Your concern is the Web Service path through the Web tier. This book looks at how clients interact with business logic, how you leverage the Web Service environment in the Web tier, and how you structure business logic for access through the Web Service environment.

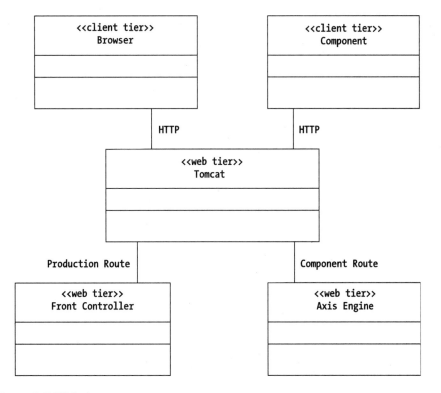

Figure 2-7. Web tier components

With respect to how the Apache Axis Web Service environment runs, you have some interesting issues. These issues are not fully addressed until Chapter 13, "Exploring the Physical Tiers Pattern." In short, there are different mechanisms for deploying a Web Service using the Apache Axis engine. Using the Java 2 Standard Edition (J2SE) and the simplest mechanism for developing Web Services with Axis, your business logic tier gets instantiated directly inside of the Web tier process. Although not a violation of your tiered approach to architecture, it is worth keeping in mind as you develop services throughout the book and up to Chapter 13. Chapter 11, "Implementing the Observer Pattern," and Chapter 12, "Implementing the Publish/Subscribe Pattern," finally push your architecture over the edge, so you must know the Physical Tiers pattern to create physical separation between the tiers.

Exploring the Business Logic Tier

The business logic tier handles the processing of all business logic and behavior that is not concerned with client interaction. You should consider the two types of interaction—programmatic and visual—while developing your interfaces. In fact, the visual presentation programmers should inspect and codevelop the business logic interfaces whenever possible. Considering the Web Service interface to the business logic forces your presentation components to compromise on the content of the interfaces.

In your application, you should be concerned with two types of business logic:

- Objects that represent a physical business domain.

- Objects that represent processes that your business logic must carry out. In many ways, business processes compose interactions between other business processes and activities as well as the objects that represent the physical business domain.

Depending on the type of technical infrastructure you use, there are additional forms of logic, such as declarative business rules, that help facilitate replacing behavior in one of the two primary categories of logic. This book does not focus on the more advanced systems and mechanisms for altering behaviors.

J2SE is the language of choice for implementing business logic in your application. Evolving Web Service standards could replace Java as the language of choice for complex business processes. Although it is important to keep track of these standards, they do not change the overall concepts behind what a business process is. Further, because this book focuses on Java, it leaves the topic of advanced business process metadata for your own extracurricular activities.

Four chapters discuss business object and business process structuring for Web Services. Although these patterns are fairly well known and taken for granted in pure object-oriented systems, it is important to understand how they interact with the Web Service paradigm.

The J2EE architecture blueprint represents its logic tier with Enterprise JavaBeans (EJBs). By nature, EJBs run within their own container (a manageable context that applies to all of the classes running within it). By choosing to stay with J2SE technologies, you do not have the benefit of a first-class container mechanism, nor is it necessary for the concepts introduced in this book. I strongly suggest you take some time to understand the idea of a container [Volter] and the advantages that a container yields. The Physical Tiers pattern (see Chapter 13, "Exploring the Physical Tiers Pattern") yields more information on using a container mechanism, such as EJB or your own self-constructed container.

Taking the Next Steps

The next steps for application development involve digging deeper into the architectural patterns that form the basis of Web Services. Only by understanding the core elements of Web Services will you be able to leverage the environment adequately. The patterns documented in this book illustrate the Web Service environment (the Service-Oriented Architecture, Architecture Adapter, and Service Directory patterns) and are important outside of the Web Service environment as well.

After the three Web Service patterns, you will spend the rest of the book on various patterns that help form the structure of your business logic tier and how clients access the business logic through Web Services. Starting with Chapter 6, "Exploring the Business Object Pattern," you will look at common structures that exist in Java and get used within a Web Service environment. These help illustrate many of the adjustments you must make to account for the Web Service environment while you build an interface to a business logic tier.

If you are a reader that uses code and likes to play with the application as you go, refer to Appendix A for instructions on how to install and run the code samples in the book. You will find running code for every chapter in this book. All of the code assumes you use the Apache Axis Web Service environment.

Summary

This chapter discussed an imaginary company and its business, user, functional, and nonfunctional requirements, which drive the application. You will build this application throughout this book. Large portions of the application center on its ability to integrate with other businesses and applications through an external API and through, possibly, external user interface integration techniques.

You briefly saw the high-level architecture of the application and its structuring into an n-tier application that includes the client tier, Web tier, business logic tier, and persistence tier. Leading up to the decision to structure the application in this way, the chapter discussed two existing architectural patterns—the Layers and N-Tier Architecture patterns—and the J2EE architectural blueprint. The chapter expanded on the Web tier to discuss the two users of the Web tier—users who access the tier through a presentation client and users who access the tier programmatically. The chapter also discussed how the business logic tier must facilitate both types of clients as well as the business object and business process content of the tier.

The architectural depiction of the application did not go to a deep level as the patterns presented in the next chapters will drive out more details of the architecture and design. Further, up until now you have worked with a high-level definition of Web Services and an implicit decision as to the use of Web Services throughout the application. The next chapters discuss the Web Service architecture using three patterns (the Service-Oriented Architecture, Architecture Adapter, and Service Directory patterns) and clear up the motivation and architecture details around embracing the Web Service architecture.

Additional Reading

- Alur, Deepak; Crupi, John; Malks, Dan. *Core J2EE Patterns: Best Practices and Design Strategies*. Prentice Hall, 2001.

- Buschmann, Frank et. al. *Pattern-Oriented Software Architecture, Volume 1: A System of Patterns*. Jon Wiley & Sons, 1996.

- Singh, Inderjeet; Stearns, Beth; Johnson, Mark. *Designing Enterprise Applications with the J2EE Platform, Second Edition*. Addison-Wesley, 2002.

- Völter, Markus; Schmid, Alexander; Wolff, Eberhard. *Server Component Patterns: Component Infrastructures Illustrated with EJB*. John Wiley & Sons, 2002.

CHAPTER 3

Exploring the Service-Oriented Architecture Pattern

UNTIL WEB SERVICES BECAME a reality, making applications communicate across the Internet was a serious challenge to application programmers. Predating Web Services are three techniques, each of which vied for programmer's attention but none of which achieved ubiquity for communicating across the Internet:

- You could choose to implement your services using a particular platform, such as the Java 2 Standard Edition (J2SE) with its Remote Method Invocation (RMI) capabilities as the mechanism for communication.

- You could choose a heavier-weight standardized model, such as the Common Object Request Broker Architecture (CORBA).

- You could roll your own service access and usage protocol.

Each of these techniques (and others like them) has dramatic downsides, as well as some benefits. With Java's RMI mechanism, a client to your service is bound to being a Java program itself. Using CORBA creates a barrier to entry to your service in terms of complexity and nonconventional knowledge, yet it loosens the requirement on a particular implementation language. In fact, components and clients can freely mix implementation languages with CORBA mechanisms, facilitating the communication between the different languages. Both RMI and CORBA have a common theme: They extend the object-oriented paradigm to a distributed system. Finally, rolling your own service communication protocol is always exciting, but the clients to your service must learn your communication protocol in addition to the Application Programming Interface (API) you are surfacing. This technique is fine if you use a single service, but imagine trying to integrate 100 services from different people who chose to implement their own protocol.

Web Services embody an important shift in computing. They stress standardized communication between services above the particular platform and implementation of services. To achieve a common communication mechanism that all languages and platforms can use, Web Services rely heavily on standardized Extensible Markup Language (XML)-based mechanisms for exchanging information.

Five years ago, the requirement to move into and out of XML for every request would have brought performance to a crawl. Today, the increase in computing power and network bandwidth (through Moore's Law) makes it reasonable to insert conversions between XML and a platform language to both ends of a communication path. Further, over the past five years, XML parsing and standard document definitions have matured to a point where most programmers have some understanding of XML document parsing and the ability to understand document definitions, if necessary.

The basis of Web Services is the service-oriented architecture. This architecture pattern outlines a simple, yet effective, set of components, responsibilities, and collaborations that promote implementation and location transparency. The Web Service architecture is an implementation of the service-oriented architecture. Taking the time to understand what a service-oriented architecture is helps to understand Web Services and how you can apply Web Services to the integration scenarios in the P.T. Monday Coffee Company application.

In this chapter, you will see the Service-Oriented Architecture pattern in detail. You also will look at how Web Services embody this architecture and get your first look at the Apache Axis environment, which is an implementation of the Web Service environment. All of these topics give a foundation for how you will use Web Services and Apache Axis in the P.T Monday Coffee Company application.

Defining the Service-Oriented Architecture

To understand service-oriented architecture, it is important to understand a few important definitions as well as the goals for service-oriented architectures.

In short, the *intent* of building a service-oriented architecture is to provide location and implementation transparency for services. Location transparency is the ability to locate and use a component that exists anywhere in a network without having to modify your program based on where the component exists, including within your own process space. Implementation transparency is the ability to use a component without regard to the language or mechanisms used to fulfill the components public interface or behavior specifications.

There are many definitions for a service in texts and on the Internet; the one that the Openwings project (see the "Additional Reading" section for more details) provides is perhaps the best:

A service is a contractually defined behavior that can be implemented and provided by a component for use by any component, solely based on the contract.

The interesting portion of this definition is its partitioning of the behavior contract and interface contract from the provider of the behavior. This separation of contract from implementation plays an important role when you understand the deeper motivations for the service-oriented architecture.

Using the Service-Oriented Architecture

The computing ecosystems of today are complex in terms of both the software and the hardware that drives the software. The complexity arises from the gradual acquisition and evolution of software and hardware that run a business as well as the competitive nature of selling into a business. For example, a small business that grows into a large business adds functionality as it becomes more successful. A small business may not require a distribution management application whereas a large business can optimize and leverage distribution applications to trim costs and compete against other businesses. As the small company grows, it may want to add distribution applications to its existing business infrastructure.

Businesses need some of the following capabilities in the architecture to help tame their computing ecosystem:

- Allow computers to share their computing power.

- Create dynamic applications that span networks.

- Provide well-encapsulated pieces of logic for use by a variety of applications.

- Allow application behavior and content to vary without redeployment or rebuilding of any application components.

- Allow applications to coexist with each other without regard for their implementation language, platform, or architecture.

In short, these capabilities add up to a component-oriented architecture with location and implementation transparency as primary goals of the architecture. The Jini platform is a service-oriented architecture that fulfills all of these goals, except the last-implementation transparency. Over time, it became apparent that the Jini implementation actually required implementation transparency. This was necessary because small devices, a primary target for initial Jini marketing campaigns, could not support a full Java environment and therefore could not participate in a Jini network. The Jini team corrected the oversight through the addition of the Surrogate architecture, but the fact remains that the base Jini architecture is natively Java. Programmers must acquire additional knowledge and expertise to adapt their services to other languages. Had the Jini architecture originally added implementation transparency in such a way that it was robust and easy to facilitate, this book could be about the Jini platform instead of Web Services.

Today's large business applications are a mix of technologies and programming languages. In many cases, access to the Java language would be difficult and simply unrealistic. Further, there does not appear to be a time in our lives where there will be a single programming language. Just as Java passed 50 percent of new implementations, Microsoft's C# became available, so the battle for a *de facto* programming language is starting to heat up.

Web Services implement both location transparency and implementation transparency in the primary architecture. Interestingly, the core pieces of the service-oriented architecture are the same from a high level—thus the development of a pattern to address the service-oriented architecture.

Service-oriented architectures are useful in a variety of scenarios:

Two or more separate architectures or programming platforms need to leverage functionality from each other: In this scenario, the service-oriented architecture is an integration point for the different architectures and platforms.

You want to expose services to the others, but you are not in control of the architecture or platform from which they will access your service: In this case, the service-oriented architecture can simplify others' jobs of using your service.

You build applications that can dynamically expand, contract, and change in terms of the functionality that they provide or represent: Hardware-based scenarios are easy to visualize using this scenario. Consider storage management applications that need to be aware of available storage devices and have policies to manage the available storage. In this case, the application needs to be immediately aware of the addition of storage devices. Further, replaceable management policies are well suited to the service-oriented architecture.

You build an application that leverages functionality available across the Internet and/or from multiple providers: A credit check authority is a great example of this capability. Several businesses can provide credit-checking capabilities to your application; each one uses similar databases of information. In this case, you may want the ability to switch providers based on price point and availability rather than being statically bound to a provider at design time.

Service-oriented architectures are useful in many other scenarios. In all cases, your application will be network based and dynamic in nature.

Understanding the Structure of the Service-Oriented Architecture

The high-level depiction of service-oriented architecture contains three components: the service, the directory, and the client. Three collaborations take place between the components: locating services, publishing services, and communicating between services and a client. Some service-oriented architecture descriptions include the act of binding to a service as a fourth operation. Figure 3-1 shows the components and operations.

Each implementation of service-oriented architecture is responsible for dictating how the three operations take place as well as the design of the components that make up the architecture. Some implementations could stress the dynamic capabilities of the architecture and sacrifice ease of implementation transparency, such as the Jini platform. Other implementations may choose to stress implementation and location transparency and sacrifice unique attributes that a particular programming language may have. This second approach is the one Web Services take; if you are a Java programmer, you will notice many sacrifices that Web Services make to achieve implementation transparency when you relate the feature and functions to native Java capabilities.

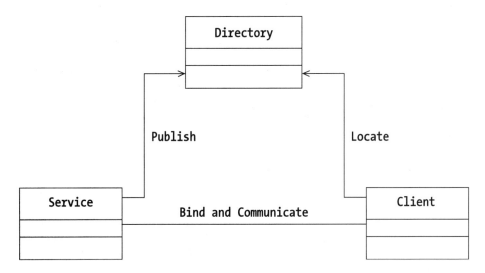

Figure 3-1. Architectural structure of the service-oriented architecture

Understanding the Components of a Service-Oriented Architecture

The three types of components in the service-oriented architecture divide responsibilities between services and clients to services. The directory facilitates physical separation between the client and the service. The three components are as follows:

> **Service:** Any number of services participate in service-oriented architecture. Each service embodies a particular function that is available to other services and clients. Examples of services are a credit authorization service or a sales order entry service.

> **Directory:** There is typically one directory within service-oriented architecture (unless the application considers fail-over or load-balancing scenarios). The directory retains information about businesses and the services that each business publishes. The directory also contains information about how to communicate with each service in terms of its location, interface, and details about communication protocols.

> **Client:** Clients use the directory to locate services and then use the services themselves to fulfill business needs. A client could be another service, or it could be a full Web-based or fat client. In the former case, an order placed through a sales order entry service may call out to a credit authorization service to validate that the user has enough credit to make the purchase. In the latter case, a Web-based client may use a stock ticker service to display up-to-date information, or a portal may collect information and forward it to a service for processing. Depending on how the service gets used, you could view a service as an extension, albeit a physically separated extension, of a client's business logic tiers. A client could also use an aggregation of services as its only business logic tier and place user interfaces directly on top of the services.

Architecturally, the division between the three components is clean. In reality, different architecture implementations, such as Web Services or the Jini platform, use different techniques to implement the architecture components. For example, Web Services use a two-part service implementation, one half to receive and parse a request, the other to fulfill it in a first-class programming platform such as Java. On the other hand, a Jini platform service directly receives and fulfills a service request using Java's RMI. The "Introducing Web Services, and Implementing the Service-Oriented Architecture" section discusses the Web Service environment and how it builds on top of and extends the base service-oriented architecture.

Understanding the Collaborations in a Service-Oriented Architecture

The collaborations that occur in service-oriented architecture are, frequently, the most important aspect of the architecture. By standardizing how collaborations take place, the architecture bypasses the underlying implementation of the service, client and directory. The collaborations that occur in a service-oriented architecture are as follows:

Publish: A component publishes a service, making it available to others via the publishing interface of the directory. Publishing a service involves placing information about the service's interface and additional service details depending on how much information particular directory implementations require. Once published, other clients and services can locate the service via the directory.

Locate: Potential clients of services locate the services via the directory. Clients can locate specific instances of services or look for a match based on search criteria that a particular directory implementation supports. The directory returns to the client information about how to bind to a service, the service interface, and any other information that the client may have requested.

Communicate: The client makes requests of the service via the network protocol specified in the service's directory information. The service fulfills the request and returns the information to the client.

Like the components that make up Services-Oriented Architecture, there is a lot of room for the implementations to innovate and cater to particular needs for the implementation. The Jini platform uses Java's RMI as the primary mechanism to communicate with a service, and Web Services use XML-based mechanisms for the primary communication method. Each has their advantages—speed vs. broad support. And each has their setbacks—closed protocol standard vs. performance overhead.

A client has a simple sequence of operations, from a design perspective, to use the components of the design. The client makes a request of the service directory to look up a particular service. The lookup call typically contains some criteria about the service that the client wants. The service information returned helps the client bind to the service and call an operation against the service.

Figure 3-2 shows a typical sequence, ignoring some intermediate steps that may occur depending on the service-oriented architecture implementation.

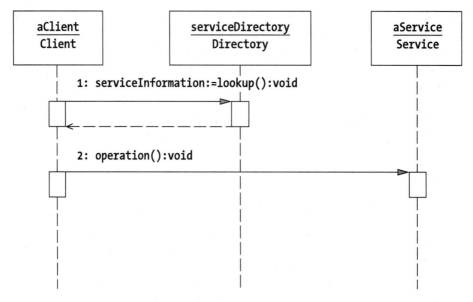

Figure 3-2. Collaborations from client to service

Conceptually, service-oriented architectures are simple. As they say, the devil is in the details.

Preparing to Implement a Service-Oriented Architecture

Whether you are choosing an implementation of service-oriented architecture or building your own implementation, it is useful to know some of the details about implementing service-oriented architecture. Web Services embody most of these practices:

> **Standardize the communication paths to achieve implementation transparency:** Service-oriented architectures stress the ability to communicate with a service regardless of its implementation or location. In this sense, the service-oriented architecture is all about communication, not implementation. The more open the communication mechanism is, the more open the service-oriented architecture will be. For example, by

implementing a simple XML communication protocol based on TCP/IP, you allow most languages, platforms, and architectures to participate in your service-oriented architecture without work. XML parsers are essentially ubiquitous, as is the TCP/IP communication stack.

Provide a standardized directory interface that can provide business information as well as programmatic information: Service-oriented architectures provide ideal platforms for implementing business processes. A well-implemented directory structure can allow a client to locate not only a suitable service, but also an ideal service for use. Unfortunately for programmers, more than just the interface of the service is necessary for choosing a proper implementation. The selection of a proper service may include the business name, the location of the business, the target market for the business, and more. This information must be standardized or "generally accepted" for it to be useful. For example, consider an enterprise IT shop ordering 1,000 development computers. You would not want to waste the time of the ordering process in locating a local computer repair store that also sells refurbished computers. Even if the programmatic interfaces match, the target business market for the local refurbished store is not the enterprise business.

Provide a mechanism for strong, standardized contracts and interfaces: Just like it is important to provide standardized information about business information, it is important to provide strong contracts and interfaces for services. Without a mechanism to fully define contracts and interfaces, a simple parameter such as *name* can be confusing when calling one service or another. For example, does the service require the first name, last name, or both? It seems trivial, but these are computers that cannot always interpret the context for a piece of information. For this reason, it is best to use standard business interfaces for individual business processes. The service-oriented architecture should provide a mechanism for defining and using a well-known interface.

The Web Service implementation of the service-oriented architecture illustrates most of these attributes. There is one glaring oversight in Web Services: the standardization of contracts and interfaces. Other architecture implementations do attempt this standardization, such as ebXML and CORBA. Unfortunately, ebXML and CORBA fall short in terms of other attributes and, especially, in mindshare. Creation of a standard cannot occur if you do not have mindshare and market presence to enforce the standard.

Introducing Web Services, and Implementing the Service-Oriented Architecture

From a high level, the Web Service architecture is a textbook implementation of the Service-Oriented Architecture pattern. It provides a directory—most often Universal Description, Discovery, and Integration (UDDI)—service implementations, and clients to the services. All components communicate via an XML-based protocol to publish, locate, and communicate. Figure 3-3 shows the overall Web Service architecture.

In reality, at the next level of architectural detail, you find that the Web Service architecture is simply a layer on top of the underlying service implementation architecture. A client interacts with Web Services over an XML communication mechanism, SOAP. The Web Service implementation translates the request into the service implementation's architecture. In this case, the Web Service implementation talks to a service implementation over a Java protocol. In this sense, a service actually consists of two parts: the service interaction implementation and the service behavior implementation (see Figure 3-4).

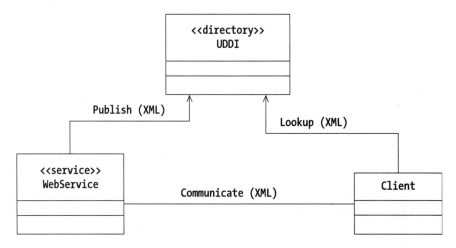

Figure 3-3. Web Service conceptual design

> **NOTE** *No part of the Web Service specification mandates that you write service implementations in Java. The service implementation could just as easily be in C or Perl, as long as the Web Service knows how to communicate with the service implementation over the native protocols of the language.*

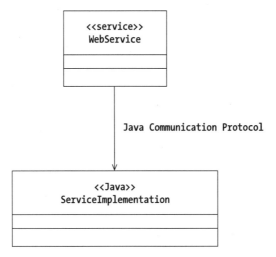

Figure 3-4. Two-part service implementation

Each major component of the Web Service architecture uses this two-part pattern implementation; the next chapter discusses a pattern for this type of implementation: the architecture adapter. Even the directory holds conversations using the XML-based communication protocol. The implementation of UDDI translates the XML-based message to the native implementation of the UDDI directory.

For the remainder of this chapter, you will see a simple service implementation and its conversion to a first-class Web Service. The simple service implementation is a single business object, a company with a name attribute. The Java implementation of the service is a JavaBean with get and set methods for the name attribute, as shown in Listing 3-1.

Listing 3-1. A Simple Service Implementation

```
public class SmallCompanyImpl {
    public String getName(){
            return name;
        }

    public void setName(String name){
            this.name = name;
        }

    private String name="P.T. Monday Coffee Company";
}
```

Notice there is no knowledge of Web Services in the Java class itself. With this service implementation completed, you have to deploy it to a Web Service implementation that handles the Web Service calls for you and turns them into calls to an instance of your Java class. After that, you can communicate with the service using SOAP. You can also publish your service to a directory to make it available for others to use. You will briefly see these pieces of Web Services to help clarify the environment and the pattern.

Deploying a Service

Consider that Web Services deal with how services communicate and that there is no standard underlying language for implementing a service. I chose to implement the SmallCompanyImpl class using the Java language; this class forms the behavior of a Web Service. Service implementations, such as SmallCompanyImpl, do not typically process messages directly; instead, they rely on the Web Service environment, such as Apache Axis, to route the message to the service implementation and return a response in the proper format to the client. Depending on the Web Service platform you choose, there will be a variety of different ways to deploy your service.

In this section, and throughout the book, you will rely on the Apache Axis service that plugs into the Apache Tomcat servlet engine. The Apache tools are nice because they are both free and widely used in the field.

You will concentrate on a *very* simple example of deployment to the Apache Axis environment. In the next chapter, you will spend much more time learning how the adaptation of a Java class to the Web Service's environment occurs.

Deploying Services Using Apache Axis

Tools in Apache Axis simplify the deployment and usage of your service implementation. As long as you can describe how to connect to your service, Apache Axis generates the half of your service that communicates through the Web Service environment. After compiling the SmallCompanyImpl class using the Java compiler, you copy it to the Axis deployment directories.

Next, you supply Axis with enough information so that it can route requests to an instance of the class. For Axis, you build a Web Service Deployment Descriptor (WSDD) that gives Axis the necessary information. Listing 3-2 illustrates a simple WSDD file.

Listing 3-2. Apache Axis WSDD

```
<service name="SmallCompanyImpl" provider="java:RPC">
  <parameter name="className"
    value="com.servicefoundry.books.webservices.entities.SmallCompanyImpl"/>
  <parameter name="scope" value="Application"/>
  <parameter name="allowedMethods" value="getName setName"/>
</service>
```

In the WSDD file, Axis requires several critical pieces:

- The first line of Listing 3-2 contains the service name and the provider that Axis should use to hold a conversation with the service implementation. A *provider* is the Axis mechanism for holding a conversation with a service implementation.

- The second line contains the Java class name for your service implementation.

- The third line contains the lifecycle of the service implementation. By specifying Application, you tell Axis that any Web Service access for this class can use this single service implementation; other values allow only a session to use the object instance or to create a new instance for each request.

- The final parameter line in the WSDD file identifies what methods Axis will elevate through the Web Service interface.

With this information, Axis can properly route SOAP requests through a series of handlers and into an instance of your service implementation. After Axis calls the requested operation on your service implementation, the method response returns through the handler chain until it reaches the client that invoked the service. You submit this information to the Axis administration client via a simple call to the administration client shown here:

```
java org.apache.axis.client.AdminClient deploy.wsdd
```

At this point, the service is available for clients to access as a Web Service.

Every Web Service platform is different with respect to how to deploy a service and the required information to accompany the service registration. The important thing to realize is that tools will ease the adoption of a service implementation into a Web Service platform.

Using the Web Services Description Language (WSDL)

Web Services Description Language (WSDL) describes the interfaces and binding mechanisms for particular services. WSDL is an XML-based language similar in nature to CORBA's Interface Description Language (IDL). It is a platform-neutral and language-neutral mechanism for describing the interface and the location of a particular Web Service. There is a subtle difference in a WSDL from a common interface language; the WSDL contains the network address information for the Web Service as well as the protocol used to access the service.

With Apache Axis, as well as with most Web Service platforms, the Web Service platform generates WSDL files from the service implementation interface and input to a tool. This is a bit different, as you would expect the interface to be a prerequisite to deploying a service implementation. WSDL files are important not so much for describing a runtime interface to a service but for allowing potential clients to generate and understand how to package data to send to the service. Most often, a Web Service platform tool will consume the WSDL file. For example, the WSDL2Java tool in Apache Axis reads a WSDL file and builds a proxy to a remote service for Java clients to use.

Another scenario is the case where you would like to implement a service implementation that adheres to a particular standardized interface, given to you in a WSDL file. In this scenario, you use a tool, WSDL2Java again in Axis, to generate stub implementation in the language you want to use for the service implementation.

WSDL files are large and complex, even for the simplest services. A WSDL file consists of data type definitions, message descriptions, port types, binding descriptions, and the service type and location. The data type definitions use XML Schema to define any data types that are not native to Web Services. For your `SmallCompanyImpl` class, all data types are native to Web Services, so there is no data type section.

Message descriptions define the documents that Web Services pass in a network to make a request and return a response. For each method exposed on a class there is request and response message. For the `getName` method on the `SmallCompanyImpl`, the request and response pair is relatively simple. Recall that the `getName` request uses no parameters, and the response returns a `String` to the caller. The fragment of WSDL in Listing 3-3 shows the pair of `getName` message definitions in the WSDL file.

Listing 3-3. WSDL Message Definition

```
<wsdl:message name="getNameResponse">
    <wsdl:part name="return" type="xsd:string" />
</wsdl:message>
<wsdl:message name="getNameRequest"/>
```

Port types describe the operations offered by a service. The operations are similar to the methods offered by a service and put in terms of the messages (defined previously) that facilitate the operation. The getName operation on your Web Service consists of the request and response messages defined in the message definition section of the WSDL, shown in Listing 3-4.

Listing 3-4. WSDL Port Type Definition

```
<wsdl:portType name="SmallCompanyImpl">
    <wsdl:operation name="getName">
        <wsdl:input message="intf:getNameRequest" name="getNameRequest"/>
        <wsdl:output message="intf:getNameResponse" name="getNameResponse"/>
    </wsdl:operation>
</wsdl:portType>
```

The binding descriptions for a service move the generic interface described thus far to an implementation level of how a particular Web Service will accept messages intended for the interface. For example, some of the binding information about getName includes treating the request as a Remote Procedure Call (RPC) and using SOAP messages transported across HTTP to access the service. Further, a binding will give specific encoding styles for requests and responses. This expansion of the interface to binding information will give service callers no room for ambiguity about how to call particular operations on the service. Listing 3-5 shows the binding information for your service.

Listing 3-5. WSDL Binding Information

```
<wsdl:binding name="SmallCompanyImplSoapBinding"
        type="intf:SmallCompanyImpl">
    <wsdlsoap:binding style="rpc"
        transport="http://schemas.xmlsoap.org/soap/http" />
        <wsdl:operation name="getName">
            <wsdlsoap:operation soapAction=""/>
            <wsdl:input name="getNameRequest">
                <wsdlsoap:body
                        encodingStyle="..."
                        namespace="..."
                        use="encoded" />
            </wsdl:input>
            <wsdl:output name="getNameResponse">
                <wsdlsoap:body
                        encodingStyle="..."
                        namespace="..."
                        use="encoded" />
            </wsdl:output>
        </wsdl:operation>
</wsdl:binding>
```

Finally, the WSDL file contains information about how to access a particular service, shown in Listing 3-6. Starting from this point in the file, you could chain all the way back up through the file to obtain the operations on a service as well as the semantics for how to have a conversation with the service.

Listing 3-6. WSDL Service Definition

```
<wsdl:service name="SmallCompanyImplService">
    <wsdl:port
        binding="intf:SmallCompanyImplSoapBinding"
        name="SmallCompanyImpl">
        <wsdlsoap:address
        location="http://localhost:8080/axis/services/SmallCompanyImpl" />
    </wsdl:port>
</wsdl:service>
```

The casual reader receives no joy from reading WSDL files. They are complex and, frequently, very large. Luckily, tools consume the WSDL, not humans. In the next chapter, you will see how WSDL facilitate the creation of architecture adapters, the portion of the Web Service that translates the Web Service request to the Java method call, for clients to access a service.

Communicating Using Simple Object Access Protocol (SOAP)

SOAP is an XML-based communication protocol that fulfills the requirement of implementation independence for communication between services and clients. Any platform and language that can build an XML document or translate an XML document to its own mechanism for fulfilling functionality can participate in Web Service implementations. The ubiquitousness of XML capabilities in computing languages makes participation in the Web Service implementations possible from almost every platform and language, including Perl, C, C#, Java, Python, and more.

There are two considerations to keep in mind while using Web Services: one is the content of messages passed between services, and the other is how delivery of messages occurs. The level of detail in the following sections is relatively coarse in nature. Although it is important to understand what is happening with SOAP messaging, you will learn in Chapter 4, "Exploring the Architecture Adapter Pattern," that your application will not directly access XML from code. Instead, architecture adapters generated by tools build and send SOAP messages for you.

Understanding SOAP Message Structure

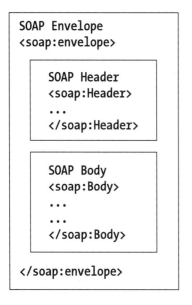

Figure 3-5. SOAP message structure

SOAP messages are simple and generic in structure. The key to SOAP, as with any XML-based schema, is that both ends of a conversation understand the content of a particular message. The root node of a SOAP message is the envelope. Within an envelope are a header and a body. The SOAP header contains header blocks that have information about the message, meta-information. Receivers of the message determine how to process the message or what to do with the message by using the meta-information. The SOAP body contains the message itself. The body contains subelements that are the information sent between the sender and the receiver. Both ends of the conversation must understand these subelements. Figure 3-5 shows the encapsulation of the SOAP content within the envelope.

It is important to understand that SOAP messages are simply XML-based documents. The power of SOAP is not in its ability to represent an RPC and subsequently make that call; rather, the power is in the versatility of the document. SOAP message deliveries typically go through HTTP, but even Simple Mail Transfer Protocol (SMTP) or any other network protocols can carry SOAP documents for processing by the destination.

Understanding SOAP Message Content

Clients use SOAP to make requests of Web Services. Web Services then return data to the caller using SOAP. A Web Service call consists of two separate SOAP documents, a request document and a response document, as defined by the WSDL file.

Recall that the request message for the getName operation on the SmallCompanyImpl Web Service did not contain any parameters but does have a response. The SOAP request message, shown in Listing 3-7, contains only information about the operation, so the body of the SOAP message is simple, a getName tag.

Listing 3-7. SOAP Request Message

```
<?xml version="1.0" encoding="UTF-8"?>
<SOAP-ENV:Envelope
    SOAP-ENV:encodingStyle="http://schemas.xmlsoap.org/soap/encoding/"
    xmlns:SOAP-ENV="http://schemas.xmlsoap.org/soap/envelope/"
    xmlns:xsd="http://www.w3.org/2001/XMLSchema"
    xmlns:xsi="http://www.w3.org/2001/XMLSchema-instance"
    xmlns:SOAP-ENC="http://schemas.xmlsoap.org/soap/encoding/">
  <SOAP-ENV:Body>
   <getName/>
  </SOAP-ENV:Body>
</SOAP-ENV:Envelope>
```

Upon receiving the SOAP request message, Apache Axis instantiates `SmallCompanyImpl` and converts the SOAP message to the `getName` Java method call on `SmallCompanyImpl`. Next, Axis receives a response from the method and converts the response back into a SOAP response message that Axis returns to the caller. The response message is slightly more complex because it is returning a `String` to the caller that contains the name of the company. The body to the SOAP message, shown in Listing 3-8, conforms to the WSDL interface described earlier. The body identifies the `getNameResponse` message, and it contains the `getNameReturn` data of type `String`.

Listing 3-8. SOAP Response Message

```
<?xml version="1.0" encoding="UTF-8"?>
<soapenv:Envelope
    xmlns:soapenv=http://schemas.xmlsoap.org/soap/envelope/
    xmlns:xsd=http://www.w3.org/2001/XMLSchema
    xmlns:xsi="http://www.w3.org/2001/XMLSchema-instance">
    <soapenv:Body>
        <getNameResponse
                soapenv:encodingStyle=
                "http://schemas.xmlsoap.org/soap/encoding/">
                    <getNameReturn xsi:type="xsd:string">
                        P.T. Monday Coffee Company
                    </getNameReturn>
        </getNameResponse>
    </soapenv:Body>
</soapenv:Envelope>
```

The most important aspect of the SOAP communication in Listing 3-8 is the flexibility that this paradigm offers. The document driven concept allows requests and responses to be delivered in any way that a service provider can handle, SMTP, HTTP, socket connections, and so on.

Delivering the Request Message to the Proper Location

With the flexibility of document delivery, it is important to understand that creation of the request document is separate from the delivery of the request document. Looking one more time at the WSDL file, you will see that there is an *end point* in the service definition that you can deliver the document to for each port defined in the WSDL. For the request document in Listing 3-8, you will deliver it to the address defined in the WSDL document:

```
<wsdlsoap:address
location="http://localhost:8080/axis/services/SmallCompanyImpl"/>
```

Upon delivery of the message to the Uniform Resource Indicator (URI) identified, Axis uses the information from the WSDD file to convert the message to the proper service implementation and gather the response for return to the caller.

Publishing a Service with Universal Description, Discovery, Integration (UDDI)

With the service available via Apache Axis, and your knowledge of how to communicate with the service via SOAP messages, you could go ahead and register it with a directory so that others can locate the service. There are many available public UDDI registries: IBM, HP and Microsoft each have registries you can use. Registration with a directory is a purely *optional* step when using services. Without using a registry, potential service clients have to be in possession of the interface information for your service, the WSDL file.

Although you can register with a public directory or with no directory at all, there is a third option of deploying a private registry for your own application usage. As lightweight directories become more common, this is becoming a simple and powerful mechanism for maintaining the benefits of service-oriented architecture without the public implementation of services.

If you do want the benefits of registering your services in a registry, there is some basic structural information that you will want to understand about a registry. The Service Directory pattern (described in Chapter 5, "Exploring the Service Directory Pattern") gives more information about service registration and the directory implementation.

Leveraging Web Services in the Case Study

Web Services should be an integral part of your strategy for communicating outwardly from your system as well as allowing clients to communicate with functionality within your system. The Web Service environment exposes much of your business logic tier to the outside world. Clients are still responsible for adding a presentation tier to the functionality you provide. Also, clients will most likely have to build out the rest of their own business logic tier; your services will merely fulfill critical pieces of their own requirements.

You saw in this chapter that Web Services only aid you in communicating between services and clients wanting to access services. Therefore, your base assumption that Java forms the root of the service implementations still holds. You publish each Web Service in a public UDDI directory. This act of publishing makes your services available for the outside world to access.

Identifying Important Classes and Files in the Case Study

Table 3-1 identifies the primary code discussed in this chapter, as well as related files from the downloaded samples.

Table 3-1. Sample Location

FILE	LOCATION	DESCRIPTION
SmallCompanyImpl.java	\src\com\ servicefoundry\ books\webservices\ entities	This is the small company service implementation illustrated in Listing 3-1.
DirectSOAPTestClient.java	\src\com\ servicefoundry\ books\webservices\ tests	A simple program that uses SOAP to directly communicate with the Web Service deployed through Apache Axis. This code was not discussed in the chapter because you are not focusing on using SOAP from the client; instead, you rely on adapters into the Web Service environment, presented in Chapter 4, "Exploring the Architecture Adapter Pattern."
SmallCompanyImpl.wsdl	\descriptors	This is the WSDL file generated by Axis after the deployment of SmallCompanyImpl into the Web Service environment.
services.wsdd	\descriptors	This is the WSDD file used in every chapter that contains deployment descriptors for all Web Services in the book.

Using Ant Targets to Run the Case Study

Table 3-2 gives the targets to run for the ant environment to see the programs and chapter samples in operation. Before running any samples, be sure you read and perform all of the install steps in Appendix A.

Table 3-2. Ant Targets

TARGET	DESCRIPTION
DirectSOAPTestClient	Uses SOAP structures to communicate directly with the SmallCompanyImpl Web Service deployed in this chapter

Summary

This chapter dissected Web Services and the architectural pattern that Web Services use as a basis, the Service-Oriented Architecture pattern. The chapter began with a discussion on the generic service-oriented architecture and then showed how Web Services build out the basic architectural pattern and how Web Services function in a real environment. Although it did not discuss details of specific services in this chapter, it is apparent that Web Services play an important role in how your application will interact with the outside world.

The next two chapters continue to dissect Web Services and some of the generic patterns that Web Services leverage—specifically, the Architecture Adapter pattern and the Service Directory pattern. These chapters stay relatively abstract so that you have a complete understanding of your application environment before diving into specific structures that you will build underneath Web Services and expose through Web Services.

Related Patterns

The following patterns relate to this chapter's discussion of the Service-Oriented Architecture pattern:

Architecture Adapter: The Architecture Adapter pattern separates the service-oriented architecture and the underlying service implementation architecture, allowing them to vary independently of each other.

Service Directory: This is the pattern used for publishing information about a service and the business that owns the service. This information is vital to the consumption and usage of your service or to selecting and consuming a service.

Faux Implementation: This chapter showed heavyweight and common ways to implement Web Services through a complete Web Service environment. Because Web Services enforce strict SOAP semantics and interfaces, you can choose instead to implement a lightweight Web Service that sits on a socket and reads data. Although you lose a lot of the robustness of your Web Service environment, you also lighten the burden on a client installation that needs to surface a Web Service.

Additional Reading

- Web Service specification documents and related information: http://www.w3c.org/

- The Jini technology: http://www.jini.org/

- The Openwings technology, a service-oriented architecture based on Jini: http://www.openwings.org/

CHAPTER 4

Exploring the Architecture Adapter Pattern

THE PREVIOUS CHAPTER EXPLAINED the Web Service architecture in terms of the Service-Oriented Architecture pattern. Web Services implement the service-oriented architecture using Simple Object Access Protocol (SOAP) as a communication mechanism between services and Universal Description, Data, and Discovery (UDDI) as a directory implementation. Web Services Description Language (WSDL) describes the interface to a Web Service. Web Services do not support inheritance or polymorphism, and they do not delve into the service implementation techniques. On the other hand, Web Services build on such a small set of primitive types and concepts that you can use virtually any semi-modern programming language to build service implementations.

In the beginning days of Web Services, Java programmers coded socket listeners that received SOAP messages, parsed them, and called the proper code in the Java language. There are significant challenges to writing the code that converts between the Web Service implementation of a service-oriented architecture and the Java platform. Thankfully, tools, such as some of the tools included with Apache Axis, automate the creation of this code that converts data from the Web Service architecture to the Java architecture. At design time, it is easy to wrap up the responsibilities of this conversion from Web Services to Java in a simple design pattern: the Architecture Adapter pattern.

In this chapter, you will look at the architecture adapter as a generic pattern. You then dissect the architecture adapter in terms of service deployment in Apache Axis and service consumption from Java.

Facilitating Communication Between Architectures

Before digging too deeply into the architecture adapter, it is worth taking a few moments to discuss exactly what is the true nature of architecture. Once you have an understanding of some of the highlights of architecture, you can explore the issues surrounding Web Services and the Java platform.

What Is Architecture?

There are many definitions of architecture, and there are many interpretations of those definitions. The architecture of a system, in general, discusses its structure through a set of the following:

- Architecture components that describe the core blocks of a system

- Connectors that describe the mechanisms and expectations on communication paths between components

- Task flows that illustrate how an application uses the components and connectors to fulfill a requirement

The architecture of a system becomes very complex very quickly, especially for an enterprise-class application. Architecture documents usually consist of 100 or more pages.

For this discussion, you need to focus on the content of the architecture with respect to the components and connectors. Typically, at the root of architecture are an architectural style and a variety of architecture patterns. Style is somewhat difficult to describe. When you think of an architectural style, you can compare it to physical building architecture. In the physical world, an architectural style dictates the dominant feel of a building. Typically, neighborhoods all contain the same architectural style. Unique architectural styles, such as Western Indian architecture, have elements that make it unique. For the Western Indian architectural style, one thinks of Islamic-style domes, ornate columns, and marble building blocks. The Taj Mahal in India is a perfect example.

Compare the Western Indian style with Frank Lloyd Wright's prairie architectural style, recognized as one of the first original American architectural styles. The Prairie style contains dominant horizontal lines; includes large, sweeping roofs; and weaves common Japanese architectural styles. The style attempts to connect the structure itself with the dominant Midwest prairie landscape.

Now, imagine placing the Taj Mahal next to a home built in the prairie style. The two architectures are fundamentally different, and only a master landscaper could make the transition from one structure to the other structure appear seamless and be functional. The transition contains elements of both architectural styles, yet blends its own techniques to help the transition between the two dominant styles. This transition landscaping is an architecture adapter.

Common elements of software architecture styles include the following:

The dominant communication style: Two common communication styles are *message-based communication* and *call-return communication*. The former is similar to today's message services, such as the Java Message Service (JMS), that provide loose coupling and that lend themselves well to asynchronous communications. Java's method call mechanism is an example of the call-return communication mechanism. In call-return communication, the thread of control originates with and returns to the method caller.

The dominant structuring technique for the functional implementation: Component and object-oriented styles are common in architecture. A component architectural style indicates a tendency toward the loose coupling of components and a high degree of cohesion within the components. This style is valuable when you want to create boundaries between components and allow programmers to easily restructure applications, acquire new units of functionality, and replace pieces of functionality. Object-oriented styles do not stress loose coupling as much. Often, if you want to take an object and use it in another application, you bring many other classes and dependencies with you. In a component style, the act of reusing functionality in an entirely different program is trivial.

No inherent problems exist with either type of architecture. The strengths and weaknesses balance out and often reflect preferences and experiences of the senior architecture staff. Once an architect promotes a particular architectural style, it permeates the entire application implementation.

Using Web Services and Java

Web Services and the Java platform have dramatically different architectural styles. The Web Service architecture, based on the service-oriented architecture, has its roots in the component-based architectural style, and it facilitates all of the dominant communication architectural styles: message-based and call-return. The Java platform is a classic embodiment of the object-oriented architecture style with a call-return communication style.

Java interacts with Web Services in two scenarios:

- Java serves as the platform for writing a service implementation that turns into a Web Service at deployment time.

- A Java program needs to use one or more Web Services.

The first scenario deals with how to represent programmatic function written with object-oriented techniques into an architecture that minimizes dependencies and does not stress or allow rich class hierarchies. The second scenario deals with representing loosely coupled and relatively flat structures in a rich, object-oriented environment. The communication mechanisms also differ between the two architectures. Either of the two scenarios requires a conversion from Java's call-return communication style to the Web Service dominant message-based communication style.

The challenges in combining the two architectural styles is not as difficult as putting a Prairie style home next to the Taj Mahal, but it is a significant challenge rife with minute details that take several iterations to get correct. As you architect and design your system, it is important that you isolate the component responsible for making the conversion between the architectures. The root motivation of the architecture adapter is to isolate this conversion process out of the primary business components and logic.

Understanding the Structure of an Architecture Adapter

A convenient representation for an architecture adapter is a single component with a set of requirements on it and the boundary interfaces that the requester expects to see. This leaves the details of the mediation between the two architectures to a lower level of design and implementation (see Figure 4-1).

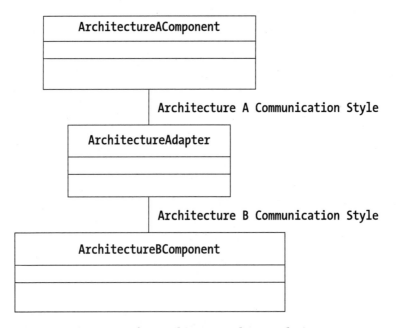

Figure 4-1. Structure of an architecture adapter solution

The low-level design and implementation of an architecture adapter is a bit more involved. Designs will be radically different based on the architectures involved, how reusable and generic the architecture adapter will be, and the facilities readily available for doing the necessary conversions between the architectural styles. The closer the match between the source and target architectures, the thinner and easier it is to write the architecture adapter. Conversely, the further apart that the source and target architectures are, the more complex and difficult it is to write the adapters.

Understanding Components of an Architecture Adapter

Three components make up the structure of a complete solution. A single component, the ArchitectureAdapter, holds the responsibilities of mediating between the two architectures involved. The three components are as follows:

ArchitectureAComponent: The A component implements functionality in a particular architectural style. For example, it may implement its functionality using the Java platform and, therefore, use an object-oriented, call-return architectural style.

ArchitectureBComponent: The B component implements complementary functionality in a different architectural style than the A component. Most likely, the complementary functionality did not occur in a preplanned fashion. Instead, the A and B component are often purchased functionality in different software upgrade cycles. For example, a company purchased the A component as it installed an Enterprise Resource Planning (ERP) system and purchased the B component when it decided it needed a Customer Relationship Management (CRM) solution to facilitate its growing customer base.

ArchitectureAdapter: The architecture adapter mediates between the two architecture styles inherent in the ArchitectureAComponent and the ArchitectureBComponent. To mediate properly, the adapter must offer a natural interface to both components, regardless of the complexities of mediating the service interaction. The implementation must convert one component's architecture entirely to the other component's architecture and maintain the behavior and expectations of both clients. To do this, data styles must be mapped properly, differences in the behavior of communications must be mapped properly, and even such complexities as converting a rich object hierarchy to a flat component interface must be achieved gracefully.

Frequently, the architecture adapter splits into two halves, one that communicates directly with the A component and one that communicates directly with the B component. The two halves then implement their own architectural style to communicate with each other, as shown in Figure 4-2.

In Figure 4-2, ClientAdapterA and ClientAdapterB make up the entire functionality of the ArchitectureAdapter. By splitting the ArchitectureAdapter into halves, it becomes easier to add a third component type into the mix. Without the intermediate architecture style, you must build two new architecture adapters—one to communicate with each of the existing components. With this modified design, you can build a single adapter to communicate into the intermediate architectural style. Welcome to one of the primary motivations for the Web Service architecture: a mechanism to provide mediation between different architectural styles. Web Services implement the Architecture Adapter pattern in such a way that it is simple to mine differing architectures for functionality.

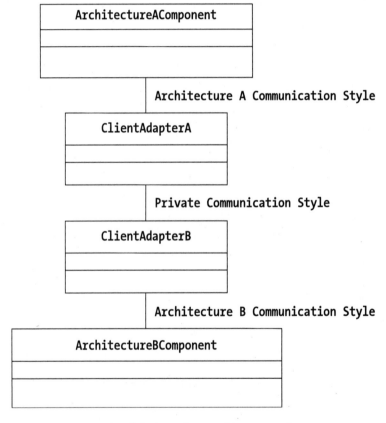

Figure 4-2. Lower-level design of an architecture adapter

Understanding Collaborations Between Architecture Adapter Components

The interesting part of the collaborations between components is in the call style and the data structures passed between components. Instead of using the first structuring from Figure 4-1, I use the second structuring from Figure 4-2 to show a sequence that more closely resembles a Web Service scenario. Figure 4-3 shows the sequence of operations for component A to make a call against component B.

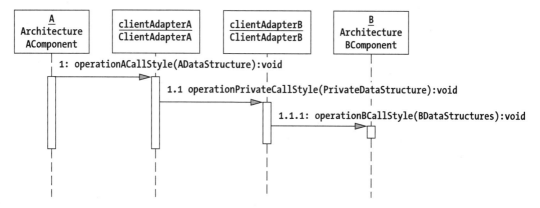

Figure 4-3. Sequence of operation calls between architectures

The call between component instance A and clientAdapterA takes place in the operational call style inherent in the A architecture and with data structures native to the A architecture. The first client adapter converts the call to a neutral third architectural style and makes a call in this third style with the appropriate data structures to the second client adapter. This second client adapter converts the operation to B's architectural style and makes the call to the B component with data structures and a call style native to the B architecture.

Preparing to Implement Architecture Adapters

The Architecture Adapter pattern isolates complexity to the adapter and away from client and target service code. When implementing the Architecture Adapter pattern, you should follow a few general rules. Specific scenarios, such as Web Services to Java, drive more implementation details based on the architectural styles involved:

Establish a common pattern for traversals between architectures and build reusable adapters whenever possible: If you traverse between architectures once in a program, you will probably do it repeatedly. There are likely common serialization and de-serialization techniques for moving data into and out of the architectures. Encapsulate these techniques. Reusable adapters will also include a generic dispatcher or mapping table to select the proper target service and invocation method.

Architectures that use different programming paradigms are more difficult to adapt than similar programming paradigms: Architecture adapters between object-oriented languages will usually be much easier to write than an architecture adapter between an object-oriented language and a procedural language. Although the architectural details may appear simple, leave enough time to address design and implementation complexities for the adapters.

Plan for performance concerns: Serialization and de-serialization of data takes time. Be aware that the adapter route can never perform as well as code that is entirely native to an implementation. For example, calling a C function from Java to calculate the first five prime numbers would be wasteful because of the adapter overhead. Calling a C function to locate the 10,679[th] prime number would likely pay off in terms of performance.

Architecture adapters should decrease the complexity within a component for accessing functionality in a different architecture: Using an architecture adapter in a component should allow client programmers to program in a single language with method calls that appear as if the programmer is simply calling another class or procedure. Isolating this complexity should make the primary code line easier to read and maintain.

Use prebuilt architecture adapters and platforms, such as Web Services, whenever possible: If you plan, there are few reasons to build your own architecture adapters. The Java Native Interface (JNI) and Web Services are two excellent technologies for allowing Java to utilize other architectures. These layers can be difficult to get right, so try to reuse whenever possible.

Understanding Architecture Adapters in Web Services

To understand how architecture adapters facilitate better and easier programmer practices, you will look at a slightly more complex Web Service scenario than the previous chapter. You will also fully leverage the facilities in Apache Axis so that you do not have to manually build the architecture adapters. In fact, from here on out, Apache Axis tools allow you to be entirely SOAP ignorant. Instead, you access Web Services from Java method calls using architecture adapters generated from the WSDL interface of a service, as illustrated in Figure 4-4, a sequence diagram based on Figure 4-3.

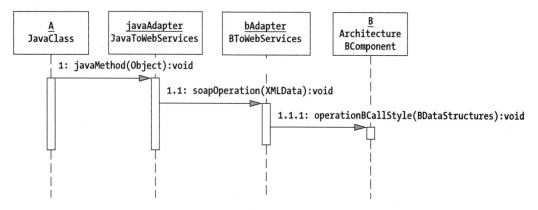

Figure 4-4. Java to Web Service sequence diagram

In Figure 4-4, I took liberties to place the expected Java method call, to the conversion to SOAP, and, finally, to a third, unknown architecture—the mysterious architecture B.

To illustrate the facilities of Apache Axis for building architecture adapters, you use a set of classes that make up the beginnings of a customer database. Figure 4-5 shows the diagram for the primary classes involved in making up a collection of customers. As you can see, a single class, CustomerCollectionImpl, contains the customer object query methods. Customer data comes from a CustomerImpl class containing basic information, such as their address, and more advanced information, such their primary credit card and Internet address information, which is separated into the CustomerInformationImpl.

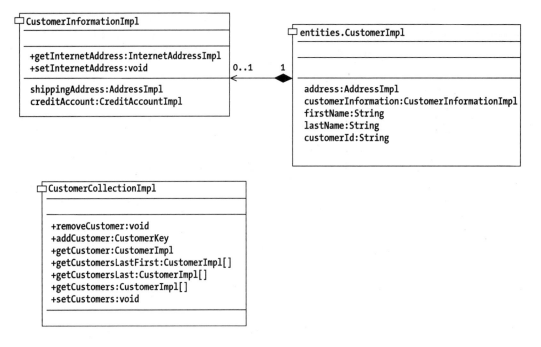

Figure 4-5. Customer collection class diagram

Several important design principles within these classes make the transition to Web Services easier:

- The customer data classes adhere to the JavaBeans contracts.

- There is no operation overloading.

- Methods return arrays where multiple values are possible.

The reasons to apply these principles are to create predictability and avoid exploitation of the object-oriented paradigm. In turn, these things are important to help ease the transition from the rich object-oriented paradigm of Java to the flatter component model of Web Services. Although it is possible to build an architecture adapter that makes the transition between architectures possible, the more you exploit one architecture, the more difficult the adapter will be to write. As tools become more advanced, the level of support for conversion between architectures will grow and the complexity of the classes can increase.

As far as the code goes, the most interesting part of the code is the implementation of the CustomerCollectionImpl class. In Figure 4-5, you will notice that there is no explicit containment of `CustomerImpl` classes from the `CustomerCollectionImpl` class. This technique is a reflection of using Java Data Objects (JDO) for the persistence mechanism underneath your classes. The `CustomerCollectionImpl` class uses a series of queries against a `CustomerImpl` extent rather than explicitly loading the collection and sorting through the objects each time a client requests a single customer.

In terms of architecture adapter responsibilities, Apache Axis uses an inbound/outbound division of labor. One adapter set takes care of Web Services to Java conversions (or to another language), and another adapter takes care of the Java to Web Service conversion. The former takes SOAP messages and converts them to Java method invocations on proper object instances. The latter takes Java method invocations, converts them to SOAP messages, and routes them appropriately.

Creating a Web Services to Java Service Implementation

Apache Axis is, essentially, an implementation of the Architecture Adapter pattern taken to an extreme. Using tools, you can generate an architecture adapter that allows you to call methods in Java and convert them to a Web Service call using SOAP; this is the A architecture adapter from the pattern structure. This SOAP message is received by an Apache Axis implementation running within a Web application server that parses the SOAP message and makes the appropriate method call to the target service. The receiving end is the B architecture adapter from the pattern structure.

These processes form the core of the architecture adapter between SOAP and the target service, or Web Services and the target service, depending on your perspective. Rather than creating a custom adapter for each target service, Apache Axis uses a single generic adapter that leverages plug-in message processing chains and message dispatchers. The entire design is online at the Apache Axis homepage. You are going to view the design from the perspective of a user of Apache Axis.

You deployed a small Web Service in the previous chapter, but it did not have the complexities of the customer collection that you will deploy in this chapter. Recall that the Web Service Deployment Descriptor (WSDD) tells Axis the details about a particular service so that Axis can route messages to the service implementation. This process sets up a generic architecture adapter with specific information about your service. The generic architecture adapter in Axis requires you to give the following:

- The service name (call the service `CustomerCollection`)

- The provider (use the Axis built-in Java RPC provider)

- The class name of the target service implementation
  (`com.serviceroundry.books.webservices.entities.CustomerCollectionImpl`)

- The methods to turn into service targets (expose all methods on the
  `CustomerCollectionImpl` class by using *)

- Complex data types necessary for a user to access the exposed service

The only significant difference from the previous chapter is the addition of
tags to identify the complex data types. Listing 4-1 illustrates a `beanMapping` tag to
identify the `AddressImpl` JavaBean as a complex data type. Recall from Figure 4-5
that the `CustomerImpl` class contains a reference to a customer's address. Axis
requires the bean mapping tag to have additional data for the Web Service architecture that does not exist in the architecture supported by Java. You must add
information about the namespace that the address resides in—which is a similar
concept to packages—but not enough to allow the engine to use the package
name as is. You also must tell the deployment tool the language that the complex
data type uses—in this case, Java. Finally, you could give the Axis engine information about special serializers (Java classes adhering to an Axis class interface)
that you write to help move a bean or class from one architecture to the other. In
this case, you use the basic JavaBean patterns, and there is not special handling
for your classes, so a serializer is unnecessary. In fact, you will not use serializers
throughout this entire book.

Listing 4-1. WSDD File for `CustomerCollectionImpl`

```
<service name="CustomerCollection" provider="java:RPC">
// . . .
<beanMapping qname="myNS:Address"
xmlns:myNS="urn:CustomerCollection"
languageSpecificType=
"java:com.servicefoundry.books.webservices.entities.AddressImpl"/>
// . . .
</service>
```

Using the Apache Axis administration tool (as shown in the previous chapter), submit the file to Apache Axis for proper configuring of the Axis server-side
engine, otherwise known as an architecture adapter.

Consuming Web Services with Apache Axis

Without architecture adapters, consuming Web Services would be a difficult and tedious job. Most likely, you would end up writing the architecture adapters yourself as you learned the patterns that your language uses to build SOAP messages and submit them to the Web Service. Fortunately, you do not have to build your own. WSDL's Extensible Markup Language (XML)-based representation and strict definition allows tool vendors to write language-specific tools that build the architecture adapter. The tools convert WSDL into interface and code to turn the language-specific request into a SOAP request to a specific Web Service.

Apache Axis comes with WSDL2Java, a tool that converts a WSDL to a Java interface and architecture adapter implementation; a programmer's job in consuming Web Services just got a lot easier. Instead of constructing SOAP messages, covered in the previous chapter, a consumer manipulates Java classes and objects directly, which then interact with the Web Service environment. Listing 4-2 shows how to create a customer object from a Java program that accesses the Web Service deployed in the previous section. Access occurs through an architecture adapter built using WSDL2Java.

Listing 4-2. Customer Creation Through the Client-Side Architecture Adapter

```
CustomerCollectionImplService service = new
CustomerCollectionImplServiceLocator();
CustomerCollectionImpl port = service.getCustomerCollection();

Address ai = new Address();
ai.setAddressLine1("Web Service Line 1");
ai.setAddressLine2("Web Service Line 2");
ai.setCity("Highlands Ranch");
ai.setState("CO");
ai.setZipCode("80129");
Customer ci = new Customer();
ci.setAddress(ai);
ci.setFirstName("Paul (Web)");
ci.setLastName("Monday");
port.addCustomer(ci);
```

Out of the code, the only slightly abnormal calls are the first two lines of code. These lines retrieve the customer collection service offered previously in this chapter. Listing 4-2 is far easier than constructing a SOAP document and submitting it to the customer collection Web Service, and it is much more natural for a Java programmer to manage. In this case, I put the cart before the horse; I decided to illustrate how you use the architecture adapter before show-ing you how to build the architecture adapter.

Constructing the architecture adapter for a particular Web Service with Apache Axis is as simple as obtaining a WSDL representation of the Web Service and running a tool against the WSDL. It is important to realize that although your service implementation is in Java, the WSDL does not expose any syntax or fea-tures that are unique to Java; instead, the WSDL is a pure Web Service construct.

The complete WSDL for the CustomerCollectionImpl is too large to show in this chapter, but Figure 4-6 is a graphical depiction of the WSDL file contents at a high level of abstraction. In it, you should see that the customer collection interface, detailed in Figure 4-6, forms the Web Service itself with the customer data described as a series of data type definitions.

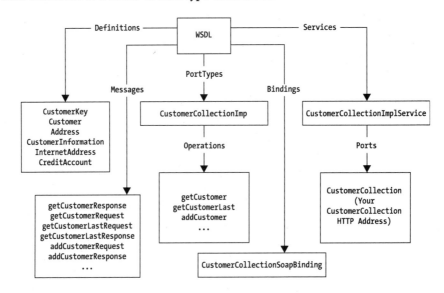

Figure 4-6. WSDL high-level depiction of a customer collection

The data type definitions from the WSDL turn into JavaBeans for use in con-junction with the Web Service. Your client may construct the JavaBeans to pass as parameters to the customer collection Web Service, or the JavaBeans are data returned from method calls on the Web Service.

The WSDL file necessary to generate the architecture adapter gets generated when you access the Web Service with the ?wsdl parameter on the end of the Web Service's URL (http://localhost:8080/axis/services/CustomerCollection?wsdl). To have Axis generate the Java-side architecture adapter, run the Apache Axis WSDL2Java tool against the CustomerCollection.wsdl file. The output from the tool is a set of classes that you import into your application if you want to access the Web Service.

WSDL2Java creates several classes that act as the adapter between Java and the Web Service, as well as any classes that are required to interact with the Web Service, such as parameters and return types. The classes include the following:

- **CustomerCollectionImpl:** An interface representing the port types on the CustomerCollection Web Service.

- **CustomerCollectionImplService:** The service interface for a class factory responsible for creating the architecture adapter for the customer collection.

- **CustomerCollectionImplServiceLocator:** The implementation of the service locator that builds an implementation of the customer collection using the location of the service identified in the WSDL as a default or the location identified as a parameter to the creation method.

- **CustomerCollectionSoapBindingStub:** The `CustomerCollectionSoapBindingStub` is an architecture adapter that the service locator returns to the requesting client. This adapter generates SOAP messages based on the methods and data that are set using the methods in the interface `CustomerCollectionImpl`.

- **Address, Customer, CustomerInformation, CustomerKey, InternetAddress:** These classes are JavaBeans that represent customer data types in the WSDL file. The `CustomerCollectionImpl` class serializes these to SOAP contents when the architecture adapter moves information from the client to Web Services.

Early in the chapter, you saw code that creates a new customer. Operations on individual JavaBeans, such as `Address` and `Customer`, have no effect on the actual values that the Web Service represents; only operations on the retrieved `CustomerCollectionImpl` object instance affect server-side data.

Leveraging Architecture Adapters in the Case Study

The P.T. Monday Coffee Company application uses architecture adapters only when interfacing with Web Services. Further, Axis generates the architecture adapters, and they have no impact on developers in terms of coding responsibilities. On the other hand, the build environment is definitely more complex with the extra generation steps. Direct usage of architecture adapters occurs in three places:

- When service behaviors require interactions with external Web Services

- When you expose service behaviors as Web Services

- When service behaviors must interact with the service directory to publish or locate a service

In the case of interacting with the service directory, you use an off-the-shelf package, UDDI4J, to interact with the service directory. The client-side class library handles service interactions. It is likely that developers built much of the client-side access library with a tool similar to the Apache Axis WSDL2Java tool.

Generation of the architecture adapters that connect SOAP messages to the service behaviors occurs upon deployment of a service through the administration facilities of Apache Axis, as discussed in this chapter and the previous chapter. Generation of the architecture adapters from WSDL files, for your service behaviors to access outside Web Services, occurs using the WSDL4Java tool at build time for your application.

Identifying Important Classes and Files in the Case Study

Table 4-1 shows the primary code discussed in this chapter that you should browse in the downloaded source code.

Table 4-1. Sample Location

FILE	LOCATION	DESCRIPTION
CustomerCollectionImpl. java	src\com\servicefoundry\ books\webservices\ entities	The primary Java class that becomes a Web Service by using the Apache Axis deployment mechanisms. This class uses JDO as a persistence mechanism.
CustomerImpl.java	src\com\servicefoundry\ books\webservices\ entities	A class whose object instances represent customers in your application. In this chapter, the customer implementation is not a Web Service; however, the customer collection implementation does serialize instances of customers to your client application.
CustomerInformationImpl. java	src\com\servicefoundry\ books\webservices\ entities	Additional information about customers, such as credit card numbers. Like the customer, this class is not a Web Service, though the customer collection ends up returning instances of the customer information indirectly through the customer instances.
TestCustomerCollection WebService	src\com\servicefoundry\ books\webservices\tests	A client-side test program that uses the client-side architecture adapter to access the customer collection Web Service.

Using Ant Targets to Run the Case Study

Table 4-2 describes the targets to run for the ant environment to see the programs and chapter samples in operation. Before running any samples, be sure you read and perform all of the install steps in Appendix A.

Table 4-2. Ant Targets

TARGET	DESCRIPTION
testcustomercollectionwebservice	This runs the `TestCustomerCollection` `WebService` program. You must have deployed the Web Services according to the instructions in Appendix A.

Summary

The architecture adapter is a powerful pattern that allows you to treat two architectures and the communication between them as a single component. You are able to place specific responsibilities and expectations on a construct, the architecture adapter, that allows designers to concentrate on how to best facilitate the mediation between two different architecture styles.

Web Services with Java use architecture adapters in two locations: from the client Java program to SOAP and from SOAP to the Java service implementation. Of course, you need to keep in mind that once the Java service implementation is a Web Service, there is no requirement that you use the service from Java. Architecture adapters for C#, COBOL, or any other language are possible with the communication facilitated through the third architectural style embodied in Web Services.

You saw the design of the architecture adapters built into Apache Axis for offering Web Services, as well as the architecture adapters that Apache Axis' WSDL2Java tool builds for Java clients of Web Services. The client-side and server-side adapters are similar in design and serve reverse needs, one adapting Java to Web Services, the other adapting Web Services to Java. You deployed and used services through the architecture adapters to show the simplicity that isolation of architecture conversions to a single pattern brings to the programming environments.

At this point, you should have an adequate understanding of the mechanisms you will use to expose application functionality to the outside world. You have not spent considerable time on the service directory that your partners use to locate your services. In the next chapter, you will learn about service directories and the patterns inherent in them. Chapter 5, "Exploring the Service Directory Pattern," wraps up the discussion of Web Service foundation patterns, so you can move on to designing specific entities and constructs for use with Web Services.

Related Patterns

The Architecture Adapter pattern relates to all of the example code in this chapter. This is simply because the client code is all written in pure Java using the client-side architecture adapters generated by Apache Axis. Pattern-wise, the Architecture Adapter pattern is most closely related to the following pattern:

- **Service-Oriented Architecture:** The service-oriented architecture uses architecture adapters to help with implementation transparency, one of the primary characteristics of the architecture.

Additional Reading

- Apache Axis Architecture Guide: `http://xml.apache.org/axis/`

- Gamma, Erich et. al. *Design Patterns: Elements of Reusable Object-Oriented Software.* Addison-Wesley, 1995.

CHAPTER 5

Introducing the Service Directory Pattern

THE PREVIOUS TWO CHAPTERS showed the generic Service-Oriented Architecture pattern and the Architecture Adapter pattern. These patterns illustrated the primary communication paths between services. There was a notable piece of the service-oriented architecture missing from both chapters—an in-depth look at the service directory. The service directory facilitates location transparency in service-oriented architectures. Without the service directory, Web Services appear similar to what Java's Remote Method Invocation (RMI) has to offer: a way to communicate between services using remote protocols.

The combination of the communication protocols and a standardized directory could make Web Services as ubiquitous as the Web is today. Web Services can achieve this ubiquity by giving common locations to find services and robust interfaces to look up the exact service you want. In essence, a standardized service directory and the Web Service communication protocols and techniques give you a similar model to the Google search engine with Hypertext Transfer Protocol (HTTP) and Hypertext Markup Language (HTML) for locating and using published content.

Web Services and service-oriented architectures use the service directory much as you use the *Yellow Pages* to locate businesses that fulfill your needs. For example, if you need to find a place that can sell you coffee beans in Milwaukee, Wisconsin, it is worthwhile to first check the Milwaukee phone book's *Yellow Pages*, probably under the heading *Coffee*. Using better search criteria and depending on how much information a seller placed in the phone book, you can get closer and closer to the exact phone number of a business that can sell you unroasted coffee beans.

This chapter first looks at how you can use a service directory to help your P.T. Monday Coffee Company application, as well as how service directories get used in today's applications. You will then look at a generalized service directory structure that forms the basis of the Service Directory pattern. The bulk of this chapter discusses the Universal Description, Discovery, and Integration (UDDI) service directory interface. The UDDI service directory structure has not only gained acceptance, but it continues to gain dominance over other service directory implementations for the Web Service environment.

Seeing the Service Directory in Practice

It is important that you do not limit your business to a single provider in any part of the business. For example, you do not want to get into a situation where a supplier of raw coffee beans is a bottleneck to order fulfillment. For this reason, you want to have multiple bean suppliers as well as a way to locate new suppliers at a moment's notice. Further, the status of coffee bean suppliers is always changing because of economic and environmental shifts. Your application must adapt quickly based on the following:

- Changes in coffee bean suppliers (new suppliers as well as those that go out of business)

- Changes in companies that can fulfill your shipping needs (small companies that grow into an ability to fulfill the large orders as well as large companies that become bottlenecks)

- Shifts in the number of coffee beans that you need to keep your business growing

The first two requirements affect your ability to deliver on your value; the final factor affects your ability to continue the aggressive growth curve that you set forth in the company's vision statement (see Chapter 2, "Introducing the P.T. Monday Case Study"). Web Services with a robust service directory implementation can help facilitate the type of dynamic application you need to adjust quickly to the changing business environment.

A service directory helps your application by giving you a single, Internet-based location to look up services using standardized search and listing criteria. For example, companies must list their information using standardized business codes. This requirement helps you locate potential partners quickly from thousands of companies that will eventually post Web Service implementations for use by partners or potential partners.

This ability to locate partners in a service directory can help potential partners find your business services as well as allow you to locate potential partners. Ideally, a restaurant that needs roasted coffee beans could simply locate your roasted coffee bean listing in the service directory, bind to your Web Services, and determine if you can fulfill their needs.

In today's world, the process of finding a new supplier uses phone books, customer calls, and contacts made at industry trade shows. Increasingly, businesses turn to the Internet to locate information on potential suppliers. With Web Services, computers rather than people locate suppliers and place orders.

Understanding the Structure of a Service Directory

Service directories are flat structures with deep associated structures that represent the data they store about a service. Depending on the amount of data a service directory chooses to store, the structure may become complex underneath the service interface. An essential point to remember about a service directory is that it too is a service; therefore, the directory lies underneath a single point interface.

Figure 5-1 illustrates the participants in a service directory. The ServiceInformation is the most volatile part of the design diagram. Requirements and designs of different Service-Oriented Architectures drive different designs for the service information.

The structure and operations on a service directory make it similar to a database structure. Interestingly, if you consider the service directory as a participant in a service environment that exhibits both implementation and location transparency, it is not important what architecture you use to implement a service directory.

The ServiceInformation association to the ServiceImplementation contains an interesting twist in the world of Service-Oriented Architectures. This association does not have to be a classic aggregation or composition relationship between the components. Instead, the ServiceInformation must contain enough information for an application to bind to and communicate with the real service implementation.

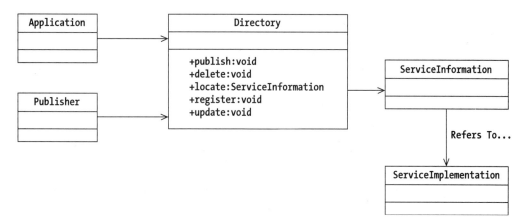

Figure 5-1. Service directory class diagram

Understanding the Components of a Service Directory

You need to consider five major components in a service directory and the context for the service directory. Two components, `Directory` and `Service Information`, are a part of the formal directory. The `ServiceImplementation` may or may not reside within the `Directory` itself. The following are the service directory components:

Directory: The service directory is the primary point of contact for publishing, locating, registering for notifications, and maintaining directory entries. To a component on the outside of the service directory, the directory appears to be persistent and always available. Service publishers determine the contents of the service directory, and applications locate service information through the same interface.

ServiceInformation: Service information is the core asset of the service directory. There are zero to n pieces of service information associated with a service directory. Actual contents of the service information vary based on the particular Service-Oriented Architecture implementation. For example, Jini registries have proxies to the services published within the directory. Web Service directories only contain information about how to bind to and communicate with a service, not a service or proxy to the service. Common types of information are the service interface, information about any standards that the service adheres to, what business owns the service, and additional information about the service itself.

Application: An application uses the location and registration operations on the service directory. Applications leverage the directory to locate suitable implementations of business processes. Applications use the notification methods to wait for specific services to enter the directory or to make sure they get notified if there is a change in an implementation or status of a service.

Publisher: The service publisher is an intermediate component that leverages the publishing operations on the directory to publish information about a service. Occasionally, the service itself acts as the service publisher, but considering the components separately allows a decoupling of the service implementation from the particular service directory implementation.

ServiceImplementation: The service itself never directly interacts with the service directory (unless it is a self-publishing service). A service information component resides in the directory that represents information about the location and interface to the service as well as any additional contextual information about the service. Frequently, the service does not know the contextual information or its own location.

Of the previous components, the ServiceInformation component is the most volatile of the high-level design components. The "Using Universal Description, Discovery, and Integration (UDDI) for Web Services" section discusses a concrete example of the primary service directory used in a Web Service environment, UDDI.

Understanding Service Directory Collaborations

Most collaborations within a service directory are similar to those you would see on a database (create, read, update, and delete). Advanced service directories, such as UDDI version 3, go further than the original versions to support the ability to register for changes within the contents of the directory. The primary collaborations in a service fall into two categories: service users who want to locate particular services and components that publish information about a service. The collaborations are as follows:

Publish: A Publisher pushes information about a particular service through the Directory interface. Often, the service publisher creates an instance of ServiceInformation and passes it directly to the Directory for publishing.

Delete: A Publisher can delete service information out of the service directory by invoking the delete operation and identifying the proper service information to remove.

Update: A Publisher can update service information through the service directory interface. Service publishers use the update operation to change and add company information (such as contacts), change the location of services, or change some status information about the service.

Locate: An application locates one or more service information objects through the locate interface on the service directory. The application passes a filter to the service directory, and the directory uses the filter to select appropriate service information objects for return to the application. The service information objects returned to the application contain all of the information that a user requires for contacting a service directly.

Register: An application registers with a service directory to receive updates based on some filter criteria. The filter can apply to updates to the service directory that do not correspond to a single existing service information object, or the filter can apply to a specific service information object. The former would capture service directory changes such as the publishing of a service information object; the latter would capture an update to a service information object.

Notify: The `Directory` notifies all registered application components when publishing, creating, or updating service information. The notification occurs based on filter criteria set by the service user. Filters could apply to changes to the service directory or to changes to specific-service information objects.

From all of the previous collaborations, not even one has to interact directly with the service. The `ServiceInformation` object serves as the information someone needs to bind to and communicate directly with the service. Web Services give you the interface for the service as well as the location and communication protocol to use to contact the service. Different designs and contents of the `ServiceInformation` class enable different approaches.

Figure 5-2 illustrates the basic sequence of events, ignoring temporal aspects of the sequence. A publisher creates a service information object and publishes it to a directory. Some point after that, an application uses the directory to look up a service. The directory returns the service information object to the application. The application creates a representation of the service to use in their process, such as a proxy or full-blown architecture adapter, and then communicates directly with the service.

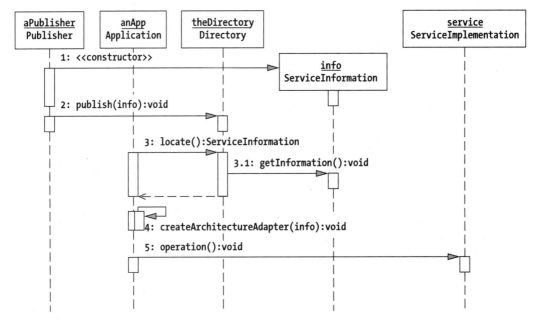

Figure 5-2. Collaborations between directory components

It is important to remember that upon publishing, the information about your service leaves your control. Once in a public directory, your service is available for any number of productive or nonproductive uses. It is important to prepare for thousands of users, and it is important to prepare for people who may misuse your service.

Preparing to Implement a Service Directory

The primary point of variance in directory implementations is the ServiceInformation class. Determining what information that a service directory should keep and what is irrelevant is somewhat difficult without knowing every type of user and publisher that will use the directory. The following implementation details may help shed more light on service directories before dissecting the service directory implementation:

Determine what information the directory needs to hold in the ServiceInformation class: If a company uses a private service directory, putting details about the company implementing each service in the service directory seems like a bit too much information because it will always be the same company. On the other hand, this information could play a vital role in a directory that services the world. Some applications may want to choose a business process implementation on company information.

Determine if it is appropriate to hold onto a service's proxy in the ServiceInformation class or whether binding information and the interface to the service is sufficient: Jini uses a model that pushes a proxy to a service into the directory. For Jini this is a good decision because programmers write the bulk of Jini applications using the Java platform and can therefore use the proxy downloaded from the service directory. On the other hand, you design Web Services in such a way that any language or platform can access the service directory. There is not a lot of use in putting a Java RMI proxy into the service if clients to your Web Service want to use Python.

Plan for performance concerns: The Application is the most likely component to be using the directory in the context of a larger, performance-critical operation. A directory will likely perform a lot like one of the common Web search engines. There will be frequent bursts of usage, but in general, the performance will be good. Nonetheless, be wary of *expecting* good performance from a service directory all the time. Applications should cache service information locally whenever possible.

Plan for scalability: Specifically, plan for scalability concerns in terms of both the number of service users and publishers that will use the service directory as well as the number of service information objects that will reside in the service directory. Both numbers will be unpredictable. An interesting aspect of the number of service information objects is that the directory will more likely increase over time than decrease. After all, how many Web pages exist on the Web that are no longer maintained but still clutter up search engines (I would guess millions).

Plan for an explosion of listings in common directories: As volume increases, it will become harder to separate legitimate services from imposters or services that represent businesses that cannot fulfill your needs. Either tight regulation of the service directories or strong self-policing of the directory space will be required. In either case, you will likely want to have an approved list of services that you allow your application to use. You can generate this list through a combination of automation and footwork. Using the directory notification mechanisms, your application can notify you when it finds a new match for a potential business partner. After you check out the potential business partner through traditional means, you should enter the information into an approved list of partners for the application to use.

Consider the service directory a service with a well-known address and binding type: There is no reason that directories should not be first class services in the Service-Oriented Architecture. In fact, the latest versions of UDDI contain Web Service Description Language (WSDL) files that developers can take off the shelf to build interfaces for the directory in their own languages.

Using Universal Description, Discovery, and Integration (UDDI) for Web Services

UDDI is the most pervasive directory mechanism for Web Services. Implementations of UDDI are Web Services and, therefore, are accessible from any language or platform. UDDI is unique in terms of the service implementation in that it is not location transparent; you need the address of a directory to access the directory. There are two major scenarios for UDDI:

- A software package delivers a private UDDI directory within an intranet for use with its own products or within a company.

- Applications use an Internet-based UDDI directory to collaborate with business partners or potential business partners.

IBM, Microsoft, and others have UDDI directories available on the Internet for access and tests. These directories can stay in sync with each other through the notification Application Programming Interfaces (APIs) built into the later versions of UDDI. The hope is that businesses can publish their information in the public directories for other businesses to find, much like you would locate a business using Google. There are two major differences between Google and UDDI. The first difference is that you will only be dealing with businesses returned from a search, without the wealth of nonbusiness content. The second difference is that the information is supposed to be highly standardized, so searches are more effective.

In many cases, standardization of information about businesses that implement a service already exists in the industry. There are several different classification systems for businesses; I use the North American Industry Classification System (NAICS) in this chapter, a standard that was available in the late 1990s before Web Services burst onto the scene. NAICS is a substantial evolution of an even older classification system that started in the 1930s: the U.S. Standard Industrial Classification (SIC) system.

Perhaps more troublesome than standardizing how to represent metadata about companies will be the problem of how to standardize service interfaces in Web Services. In my opinion, standardized interface development will be the most difficult achievement in Web Services simply because service interface agreement is not a technical achievement, it is a social achievement.

Service information structures change between different directory implementations, so you will spend some time dissecting the service information that UDDI holds. Rather than using SOAP structures to manipulate UDDI structures, you will use a UDDI client-side architecture adapter provided by the UDDI4J (UDDI for Java) package. As a result, all of the code presented in this chapter is in Java.

Understanding UDDI Service Information Structures

The information stored in UDDI is complex for beginners with Web Services. In fact, much of the information stored in UDDI does not even relate to Web Services. UDDI is simply a business-centric information repository.

In UDDI, four structures form the published business and service information:

Business Entity: This represents information about a business, such as the name, description, and any human contacts within the business. The business entity contains one or more business services.

Business service: This represents information about the services that a particular business offers. You would expect these services to represent Web Services, but they do not have to represent them. A service simply is a standard mechanism for describing how to access the services that a business offers, whether they are programmatic interface services or services you would access using your Web browser. Deleting a business entity deletes all of its business services.

Technical model (tModel): Technical models are specifications that elements in the directory can share. Business entities do not own or indirectly own tModels. A tModel exists in its own lifecycle; thus, deleting a business entity does not delete associated tModels. Contents of a tModel include a reference to a WSDL file if the tModel represents a Web Service.

Binding template: The binding template is an association between a service and a tModel. Consider the case where a tModel exists and represents a particular standard, such as UDDI. The tModel contains a reference to the standardized UDDI interfaces. The existence of the tModel does not imply the existence of an implementation of the tModel; instead, a specific business must give an implementation of the standard, thus the binding template and the independent lifecycle of the tModel. The binding template associates a business service (owned by a business entity) with a technical specification. The binding template gives information on how to access a particular service that adheres to the definition given in the technical specification.

The business entity, business service, and binding template nest within each other whereas the tModel stands on its own. A business entity contains one or more business services. A business service contains one or more binding templates. Each binding template refers to a tModel that is the specification of a service and forms the bridge between the nested business entity structure and the technical specification given in the tModel. Figure 5-3 shows the structure of the base structures that reside within a UDDI implementation.

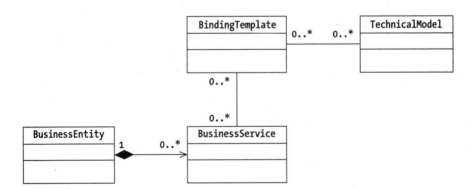

Figure 5-3. UDDI service information

The complete UDDI specification is amazingly powerful and versatile. Consider UDDI the next generation of the phone book. Using the phone book, you will not only be able to locate any business, but you can locate a business based on the services it can offer you rather than on a broad category of services. Using today's *Yellow Pages*, you can easily locate a mechanic for your car, but you cannot tell whether that mechanic can offer you detailing and neon lighting. Correct usage of UDDI allows you to search for companies based on the services they have to offer, the technical specifications they adhere to, or even the company name and contacts available at a company.

Publishing Business Entities

The structure of a business in UDDI starts with the business entity. The business entity contains all of the information that a person or a program needs to locate your business. An interesting note is that UDDI renders the case study in Chapter 3, "Exploring the Service-Oriented Architecture Pattern," virtually irrelevant, except for its illustration of core Web Service attributes. The ability of UDDI to represent your company information makes the information available through the SmallCompany Web Service duplicate functionality.

A reason to use the UDDI representation of your company is the considerable amount of analysis that goes into the company representation. As an architect or designer, you can always benefit from independent analysis. You will not fully leverage the business representation in UDDI in this book, but you will see a few of the important pieces that help you locate businesses programmatically.

To build a UDDI business entity, you first construct a local version of the BusinessEntity and its contents. There are two parameters on the constructor, the business entity key and a name for the business entity. All primary constructs including the business entity, the business service, the binding template, and the tModels have unique keys associated with them. Passing a zero-length string tells the UDDI directory to create the unique identifier for you. After calling the constructor, you set the default description in code, as shown in Listing 5-1.

Listing 5-1. Creating a New Business Entity

```
BusinessEntity newEntity =
    new BusinessEntity("",
        "P.T. Monday Coffee Company");
    newEntity.setDefaultDescriptionString(
        "P.T. Monday Coffee Company Business Description");
```

At this point, your business entity resides within your own process. You still have a considerable amount of work to do to publish the information in UDDI.

Exploring the UDDI *Yellow Pages*

Once created, you want to ensure people and programs can locate your business through a standard classification system. UDDI supports many common standards; you will use the NAICS to identify the P.T. Monday Coffee Company as a Coffee and Tea Manufacturing business. Code 31192 identifies the business. You also want to identify the unique identifying key for the tModel (discussed in the section "Publishing tModels") that represents the NAICS codes; this key is UUID:C0B9FE13-179F-413D-8A5B-5004DB8E5BB2. The only way to find much of this information is by browsing an existing UDDI directory, such as the IBM test directory at `http://www-3.ibm.com/services/uddi/`.

You place this information in a category bag within the new business entity. A *category bag* is simply a structure that contains zero or more references to other structures, usually in the form of a structure known as a *keyed reference*. Each business categorization is a keyed reference that consists of the tModel key, the name of the key, and the value of the key. The tModel key is a reference to the governing structure for this particular type of code. In this case, the tModel keys reflect a reference to the NAICS business identification system. Listing 5-2 shows how to create the category bag and insert a keyed reference, and it shows the subsequent placement of that reference into the entity. This information represents a way to look up the business as if it were in a *Yellow Pages* directory.

Listing 5-2. Categorizing Your Business Entity with a NAICS Identifier

```
CategoryBag catBag = new CategoryBag();
KeyedReference naicsRef = new KeyedReference();
naicsRef.setTModelKey("UUID:C0B9FE13-179F-413D-8A5B-5004DB8E5BB2");
naicsRef.setKeyName("naics: Coffee and Tea Manufacturing");
naicsRef.setKeyValue("31192");
catBag.add(naicsRef);
newEntity.setCategoryBag(catBag);
```

> **NOTE** *There are several references to obtain NAICS identifiers. One location is* `http://www.census.gov/epcd/www/naics.html`; *this is a U.S. Census Bureau Web site. You can also look up NAICS keys at UDDI registries, such as IBM's test registry at* `http://uddi.ibm.com/testregistry`.

Exploring the UDDI White Pages

Business entities also contain information about specific contacts at a business. Contacts contain names, physical addresses, email information, and more. One interesting twist on White Pages information is the way the address class holds address lines. Managing an internationalized structure for address information is difficult. An evolving standard exists in the UDDI community, but I do not use it in this section because of a lack of available information at the time of writing. As the information for internationalized addresses becomes widely available, I highly recommend using it.

Creating a contact is straightforward, and you will not have a problem reading Listing 5-3 to create a new contact and insert it into a business entity. This information corresponds to an address book's *White Pages*, information about people, and their locations. Typically, you would not look up a business by the people in it, but this is useful information after you locate a business to find people you can contact directly for information.

Listing 5-3. Adding Contacts for a Business Entity

```
Contacts contacts = new Contacts();
Contact primaryContact = new Contact("Paul Monday");
Vector addresses = new Vector(1);
Address address = new Address();
Vector addressLines = new Vector(4);
AddressLine ad1 = new AddressLine("500 Eldorado Boulevard");
AddressLine ad2 = new AddressLine("Broomfield");
AddressLine ad3 = new AddressLine("CO");
AddressLine ad4 = new AddressLine("80021");
addressLines.add(ad1);
addressLines.add(ad2);
addressLines.add(ad3);
addressLines.add(ad4);
address.setAddressLineVector(addressLines);
addresses.add(address);
primaryContact.setAddressVector(addresses);
Vector emailVector = new Vector(2);
emailVector.add(new Email("pmonday@attbi.com"));
emailVector.add(new Email("pmonday@hotmail.com"));
primaryContact.setEmailVector(emailVector);
contacts.add(primaryContact);
newEntity.setContacts(contacts);
```

At this point, you are still operating against a locally constructed business entity. You still have to save this information to a public location before others can access it.

Saving the Business Entity to the UDDI Directory

You now have the bare minimum of information regarding your business. This information resides in a local set of classes. You now want to save this information to the UDDI directory you have chosen. Before calling the function to create the entity, you built a proxy to represent the UDDI directory using the UDDI4J package. It is a straightforward process, and you can browse the downloadable code for more information on this process. The uddi object instance represents the architecture adapter that converts the business entity (along with some authorization information in the authInfo instance variable) to a SOAP message and makes the service request of the target Web Service. The save_business method receives a vector of business entities so that the UDDI directory can build them all with a single service call (see Listing 5-4).

Listing 5-4. Saving the Business Entity to UDDI

```
Vector newEntities = new Vector(1);
  newEntities.add(newEntity);
  BusinessDetail business =
      uddi.save_business(authInfo, newEntities);
```

Once built, anyone can locate your business using the NAICS code or business name and subsequently locate contact information for the company. You can also look at the business detail returned from the call to the UDDI proxy to obtain the unique identifier created by the UDDI directory for your service.

Most UDDI registries allow you to look up businesses from a Web page. Try out IBM's test registry at http://uddi.ibm.com/testregistry (if they moved the site, do not panic; be sure to use IBM's search engine to locate it).

Exploring the UDDI Green Pages

In addition to the *White Pages* and *Yellow Pages* in the UDDI directory, there is the concept of the *Green Pages*. The *Green Pages* hold technical information about a business, such as the business processes that a business supports, operating platforms, communication mechanisms, and more. There are two parts to a business service that represents this information: information about the service and a binding template that allows traversal to the information. The former describes the business service in enough detail that a business entity can be located based on the services it provides, and the latter binds a service to a technical service implementation. In this section you will look only at the information you provide with a service so that it can be located in the UDDI directory; the next section introduces tModels, and then you will look at how to create a populated binding between the service and tModels.

Listing 5-5 contains the simple code that creates the business service. The service contains a name, an empty binding template, and a business key, which is obtained from the created service in the previous section (the downloaded code contains information on how to retrieve the key from the business detail returned from the call to the UDDI proxy). You can associate category bags that contain keyed references, similar to the NAICS code associated with the business entity, to further identify the service as a standardized service that adheres to a known definition. These keys make it easier to search for a service based on a standard understanding of where a service gets used.

Listing 5-5. Creating a Business Service in UDDI

```
BusinessService bs = new BusinessService();
Vector names = new Vector(1);
names.add(new Name("Product Collection"));
bs.setNameVector(names);
bs.setBusinessKey(businessKey);
bs.setServiceKey("");
Vector templateVector = new Vector(0);
BindingTemplates bindingTemplates = new BindingTemplates();
bindingTemplates.setBindingTemplateVector(templateVector);
bs.setBindingTemplates(bindingTemplates);
Vector services = new Vector(1);
services.add(bs);
rtrnValue = uddi.save_service(authInfo, services);
```

The empty binding template created in Listing 5-5 is simply a placeholder for the binding template you have yet to create. When creating a business service in a normal scenario, the tModel usually already exists. As a result, you create the binding template at the same time as the business service. I have chosen to place the business service creation before the tModel creation so you can understand the nesting of the business entity and business service structures. You will come back and populate the business service with a binding to a tModel after you create the tModel in the "Publishing tModels" section.

Publishing tModels

tModels represent the technical specification of a service in the UDDI directory. Businesses do not own tModels; rather, they associate various elements to tModels. For example, a NAICS identifier is merely a key that a tModel specifies. Recall that upon creating your business entity, you identified your business as a Coffee and Tea Manufacturing business and associated the code for this business to your business entity. Further, upon creating the code, you also identified the technical specification that originates the code. By specifying the tModel, the directory can validate the code when you create the business entity.

Similarly, you can create your own tModels by publishing a reference to a service interface within UDDI. A tModel does not equate to an implementation of the model, just a specification. Listing 5-6 shows how to create a tModel for your product collection. It is similar to the creation of the business entity, so I will not go into many details. The important pieces of the code are the overview document specifying the location of the ProductCollection WSDL file and the subsequent identification of the overview document as a standard WSDL file. You identify the overview document as a WSDL file by creating a keyed reference and setting the tModel key to the UUID associated with the WSDL tModel.

If you used a standard other than WSDL, the keyed reference would point to a different technical specification. As with the business entity, a category bag holds onto the keyed reference. The final step to create the tModel and publish it is to use the uddi proxy to submit the locally built tModel to the Web Service.

Listing 5-6. Creating the tModel in the UDDI Directory

```
TModel tm = new TModel();
tm.setName(Publish.PRODUCT_COLLECTION_TMODEL_NAME);
tm.setTModelKey("");
OverviewDoc od = new OverviewDoc();
od.setOverviewURL(
    "http://localhost:8080/axis/services/ProductCollection?wsdl");
tm.setOverviewDoc(od);
Vector keyedReferences = new Vector(1);
KeyedReference kr1 =
    new KeyedReference("uddi-org:types", "wsdlSpec");
kr1.setTModelKey("UUID:C1ACF26D-9672-4404-9D70-39B756E62AB4");
keyedReferences.add(kr1);
CategoryBag cb = new CategoryBag();
cb.setKeyedReferenceVector(keyedReferences);
tm.setCategoryBag(cb);
Vector tModels = new Vector(5);
tModels.add(tm);
TModelDetail tmodelDetail =
uddi.save_tModel(authToken, tModels);
```

By running Listing 5-6, you have a business entity, a business service within the business entity, and a separate technical specification for a product collection. There is *no* established link between the tModel and the business service. It is important to realize that the tModel exists for businesses to share. You want your partners to use the same technical specification as yours. Companies relying on the same tModels reference the published tModels by binding to them with a UDDI binding template.

Binding Services to tModels

Creating a binding between business service and a tModel allows the UDDI directory to show that you use an open technical specification for a particular service. In theory, there will be a day that everyone uses the same tModels to implement similar business behaviors; however, that day may be some time from now.

Creating a binding between a service and a tModel is similar to the processes you have already seen. The important steps are setting the business service key that UDDI created for you earlier in the chapter, identifying the access point for the service, and identifying the tModel instance that the service implements. There does appear to be some duplicate identifying information in Listing 5-7—specifically the overview document created for you by the binding template. This overview document is in the same location as the technical specification. Keep in mind that this may not be the case because another party could create the tModel.

Further, UDDI allows you to identify more than one tModel with the binding to the service, in which case you would have a unique WSDL file to associate with your service.

Listing 5-7. Binding a Service to a tModel

```
BindingTemplate bt = new BindingTemplate();
bt.setServiceKey(businessServiceKey);
bt.setBindingKey("");
AccessPoint ap = new AccessPoint();
ap.setURLType("http");
ap.setText(
    "http://localhost:8080/axis/services/ProductCollection");
bt.setAccessPoint(ap);
OverviewDoc od = new OverviewDoc();
od.setOverviewURL(
    "http://localhost:8080/axis/services/ProductCollection?wsdl");
InstanceDetails instanceDetails = new InstanceDetails();
instanceDetails.setOverviewDoc(od);
TModelInstanceInfo tmii = new TModelInstanceInfo(tModelKey);
tmii.setInstanceDetails(instanceDetails);
Vector tmiiv = new Vector();
tmiiv.addElement(tmii);
TModelInstanceDetails tmid = new TModelInstanceDetails();
tmid.setTModelInstanceInfoVector(tmiiv);
bt.setTModelInstanceDetails(tmid);
Vector entities = new Vector();
entities.addElement(bt);
rtrnValue = uddi.save_binding(authInfo, entities);
```

You now have a complete canonical description of your business and the services it implements. Figure 5-4 gives an overview of the complete UDDI structure you just created. The diagram itself is a physical containment relationship between all of the different structures in the service directory. It relates back to Figure 5-3 in terms of the containment relationships and associations, but its intent is to represent the physical containment of the structures with data instances rather than a diagrammatic representation of classes and instances.

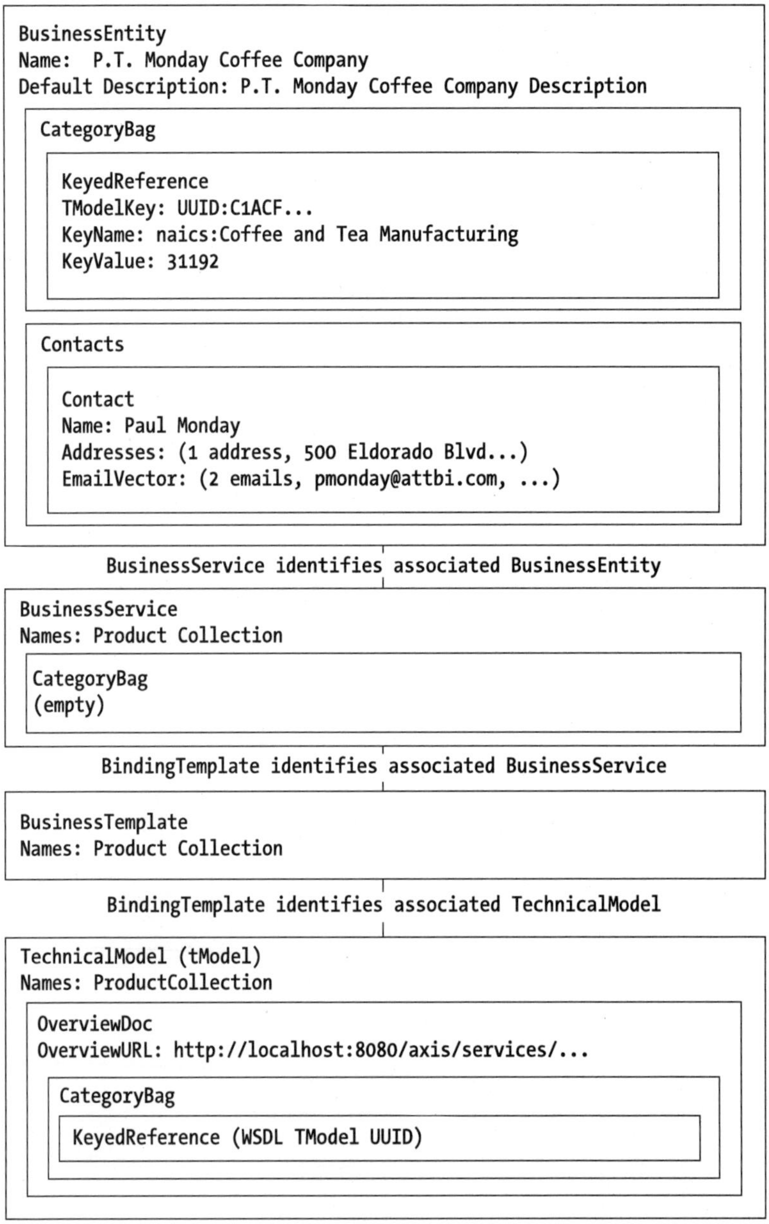

```
BusinessEntity
Name:  P.T. Monday Coffee Company
Default Description: P.T. Monday Coffee Company Description

    CategoryBag

        KeyedReference
        TModelKey: UUID:C1ACF...
        KeyName: naics:Coffee and Tea Manufacturing
        KeyValue: 31192

    Contacts

        Contact
        Name: Paul Monday
        Addresses: (1 address, 500 Eldorado Blvd...)
        EmailVector: (2 emails, pmonday@attbi.com, ...)
```

```
        BusinessService identifies associated BusinessEntity

BusinessService
Names: Product Collection

    CategoryBag
    (empty)
```

```
        BindingTemplate identifies associated BusinessService

BusinessTemplate
Names: Product Collection
```

```
        BindingTemplate identifies associated TechnicalModel

TechnicalModel (tModel)
Names: ProductCollection

    OverviewDoc
    OverviewURL: http://localhost:8080/axis/services/...

        CategoryBag

            KeyedReference (WSDL TModel UUID)
```

Figure 5-4. The P.T. Monday Coffee Company UDDI structure

The structure contains all of the information under a single representation, but recall that someone else could own the tModel itself, or others could be referencing your tModel as an open standard. The entire structure gives programs and people many different ways to locate your business: through the NAICS identifier, through the tModels you implement, through people employed by your company, or any number of other criteria or combination of criteria you have created here.

Locating Information in UDDI

Most of this chapter discusses the publishing model of UDDI. You have learned about the business entity, business services, tModels, and the service bindings that form the basis for UDDI contents. Although there was a lot of code and explanations, you have really just scratched the surface of the different types of content that UDDI stores at your request. You typically publish information only a few times, but you want it to be located many times in the course of its life.

UDDI supplies a robust query mechanism that allows you to search on any type of information in a variety of combinations and with a variety of different ways to manage the data that returns from the query. The query mechanism is not as generic as Structured Query Language (SQL) or an Object Query Language (OQL) implementation, and it is not as flexible. You will be able to specify different structures and keys to search for without having to start from the top of the hierarchy, the business entity. You can also specify combinations of keys to look for in the directory.

For this example, consider the case where you want to locate all of the businesses in the coffee industry that implement the technical specification for product collections (that you published). This will be of extreme value as you attempt to locate businesses that you can interact with programmatically and integrate into your value chain.

Your query should return results that fill both of the following criteria:

- All businesses in UDDI that use the NAICS code 31192 to classify themselves

- All businesses that offer a product catalog that uses your technical specification for the interface

Recall that you published your own company with similar code to Listing 5-8 for identifying yourself as part of the coffee industry (the category bag instance variable name is changed). Listing 5-8 shows the code for creating the category bag again.

Listing 5-8. Setting Up the Query Criteria for the NAICS Code

```
CategoryBag categoryBag = new CategoryBag();
KeyedReference naicsRef = new KeyedReference();
naicsRef.setTModelKey("UUID:C0B9FE13-179F-413D-8A5B-5004DB8E5BB2");
naicsRef.setKeyName("naics: Coffee and Tea Manufacturer");
naicsRef.setKeyValue("31192");
categoryBag.add(naicsRef);
```

Next, you assume that you have a string that contains the tModel key that the business must implement for the product catalog. You can obtain this key in a variety of ways (manually searching, storing the tModel key from when you created it, querying for it using name and category criteria for tModels). Listing 5-9 shows how to create a tModel bag for use in the query criteria. The bag contains the key of the tModel obtained when you created the model in a previous section; this is the tModelKeyString instance variable.

Listing 5-9. Setting up the tModel Key on Which to Query

```
TModelBag tModelBag = new TModelBag();
TModelKey tModelKey = new TModelKey(tModelKeyString);
tModelBag.add(tModelKey);
```

Finally, you can use the architecture adapter, stored in the uddi instance variable, to submit the query and obtain query results in the form of a business list. All of the parameters on the method call in Listing 5-10 are either null or contain no list items except for the tModelBag and categoryBag.

Listing 5-10. Submitting and Processing the Results of a UDDI Query

```
BusinessList businessList = uddi.find_business(names,
                            discoveryURLs,
                            identifierBag,
                            categoryBag,
                            tModelBag,
                            findQualifiers,
                            5);

BusinessInfos businessInfos = businessList.getBusinessInfos();
System.out.println("Located the following businesses...");
for(int i=0 ; i<businessInfos.size() ; i++){
    BusinessInfo bi = businessInfos.get(i);
    String name = bi.getNameString();
    System.out.println("\tName="+name);
}
```

Upon return from the location method, you loop through the returned businesses and print their names. There are many different processes you could do besides printing their name based on the information contained in each business. For example, because you know the product catalog interface, you could generate your own product catalog for the other business or do comparison shopping with the other product catalog. You could also automatically go to their Web page or locate contacts in the business to call on the telephone or send emails.

The query mechanisms in UDDI are robust and versatile. If you know the data contained in the various UDDI constructs from different businesses, you can construct a query to locate the information you need, when you need it.

Leveraging Service Directories in the Case Study

The concept of a service directory is central to the concept of sharing your application and locating other potential partners. Your application will be ready for the day that you can allow your program to locate new business partners without intervention from management, but you will not push forward to deploy such grandiose mechanisms. More important than technical coolness is a dose of reality and simple pragmatic deployment. Your company will enter business partner query criteria by hand and only allow your program to select known business partners for now.

From the requirements presented in Chapter 2, "Introducing the P.T. Monday Case Study," the service directory fulfills only a couple of key requirements, shown in Table 5-1.

Table 5-1. Business Requirements

ID	REQUIREMENT
B2	The application shall have the ability to integrate bean suppliers into the company's value chain.
NF1	The application shall embrace open standards for the external API.

All of the Web Service infrastructure pieces build up only a few essential requirements of system integration with external business partners. Only when you start building business objects and processes can you see how your application fulfills the concrete requirements, such as providing notifications or access to particular types of data.

Identifying Important Classes and Files in the Case Study

Table 5-2 shows the primary code discussed in this chapter that you should browse in the downloaded source code.

Table 5-2. Sample Location

FILE	LOCATION	DESCRIPTION
Publish.java	com\servicefoundry\ books\webservices\util	This program contains the UDDI code presented in this chapter. The program publishes, queries, and deletes UDDI information from the IBM test registry. You must obtain a user ID from the IBM test registry and replace the uddiUserId and uddiPassword properties in the build.properties file.

Using Ant Targets to Run the Case Study

Table 5-3 describes the targets to run for the ant environment to see the programs and chapter samples in operation. Before running any samples, be sure you read and perform all of the install steps in Appendix A.

Table 5-3. Ant Targets

TARGET	DESCRIPTION
publish	Publishes entries to the UDDI directory and tests that the entries can be subsequently located using the UDDI query mechanisms
unpublish	Removes entries from the UDDI directory

Summary

This chapter, and the Service Directory pattern presented in it, is the final pattern that specifically addresses Web Services, their design, and how to use the Web Service environment. In this chapter, you learned about the uses and capabilities that service directories offer. You also looked at a specific service directory implementation, UDDI, to examine how it fills out the generic Service Directory pattern.

UDDI presents a robust mechanism for representing business entities, as well as the business services that a business entity offers. You spent most of the chapter discussing how to publish information in UDDI and some time discussing how to locate information in UDDI. Because of the robust set of mechanisms to represent businesses and services, it is useful to understand the data structure within UDDI because the location operations on UDDI simply allow you to combine the data structure elements into queries and extract the information based on the portions of the data structure that you specify.

For the case study, you published a business entity that represents the P.T. Monday Coffee Company and a business service that represents the product collection. You also published a tModel to describe the product collection. You associate the business service with the tModel through a binding template. Others can use the tModel to implement their own product collection; this reuse makes it easier to integrate systems from different vendors.

UDDI is not a part of the Apache Axis Web Service environment. Axis gives your applications the infrastructure that you need to communicate between Java programs and Web Services and from Web Services to service implementations. A broader community supports UDDI. You used the UDDI4J package from IBM and the IBM UDDI test registries to play with service directories. Before you can successfully deploy the sample applications, you must register with the IBM test registry, located at `http://uddi.ibm.com/testregistry`, and alter sample code to use your user ID and password.

Starting with the next chapter, the book discusses specific ways to offer and consume Web Services with the assumption that you know enough about Web Services to understand the mechanics behind them.

Related Patterns

The primary relationship for the directory within the context of the book is the Service-Oriented Architecture pattern:

Service-Oriented Architecture: The service directory is a component of a service-oriented architecture. The Service Directory pattern serves as the basis for UDDI and the Jini Lookup Service. It is also similar in nature to most distributed component registries that are not full-blown service-oriented architectures.

Additional Reading

- Universal Description, Discovery, and Integration (UDDI):
  http://www.uddi.org/

- U.S. governmental site on NAICS:
  http://www.census.gov/epcd/www/naics.html

- UDDI for Java (UDDI4J):
  http://www.uddi4j.org/

CHAPTER 6

Exploring the Business Object Pattern

THE PREVIOUS THREE CHAPTERS worked through the base patterns at the heart of Web Services:

- The Service-Oriented Architecture pattern forms the architectural pattern of Web Services.

- The Architecture Adapter pattern showed the mechanism for translating Web Service interactions into underlying service implementations.

- The Service Directory pattern showed the mechanism for retrieving meta-data about a Web Service, and that metadata resides in the Universal Description, Discovery, and Integration (UDDI) directory typically used with Web Services.

Because Web Services are the integration technology of choice for the P.T. Monday Coffee Company application, it is critical that you understand these base Web Service patterns to some level of detail. With this knowledge, you become more effective at creating your Web Services and even designing your service implementations.

Starting with this chapter, you will look at traditional object-oriented structures and how they translate into the Web Service environment. For the next four chapters, you will increase the complexity and responsibilities of the structures that you represent to external users. This chapter starts with a relatively simple concept of a business object; by the end of Chapter 9, "Exploring the Asynchronous Business Process Pattern," you will be dealing with the basics of business processes and the orchestration of the underlying business objects and business activities to fulfill a business task.

Business objects typically embody a business concept from the real world, such as a customer, a company, an order, or a product. Business objects are natural constructs in an object-oriented world. The power of inheritance, whether by interface or implementation, can play a large role in modeling business concepts. For example, products that a company sells all have certain characteristics, such as a Stock Keeping Unit (SKU) unique identifier, a weight, and some inventory information. Products also have extended information, such as the roast of a particular bean and the roasting date. In this sense, products are good candidates for object-oriented techniques. Web Services are not an object-oriented architecture; instead, they exhibit a component structure, which is less complex on the outside than a business object. The paradigm shift from an object-oriented paradigm to a Web Service paradigm makes the business object, business object collections, business processes, and asynchronous business processes worth examining. These patterns can teach you a great deal about the interactions between the Web Service environment and Java service implementations. Further, the P.T. Monday Coffee Company surfaces several business objects through Web Services, typically through a business object collection.

This chapter looks at stand-alone business objects and how they translate into the Web Service paradigm as an exercise to understand the patterns in Java that most effectively translate into Web Services and custom types. Although you will use this pattern infrequently in a live application, it does give you valuable, repeatable practices for more common patterns, such as business object collection and business process.

Seeing Business Objects in Practice

The intent of a business object is to represent a highly cohesive business concept, such as a sales order, a business contact, or a company. A business object is singular in nature but is often collected in groups, such as a collection of sales orders. Representation of business concepts through Web Services often starts by defining the object in Java. The business object is often a convenient metaphor for a physical concept from the business domain, such as a bag of coffee or a warehouse that stores the coffee. If you develop an application with the primary interface to the business concepts being Web Services, you could just as easily start by modeling the Web Service interfaces and subsequently implementing the service implementations in Java. In fact, this alternate approach will yield a more usable Web Service. Unfortunately, you will have a less object-oriented application infrastructure. By the end of this chapter, you should learn a few of the complexities that lead to this observation.

In the early object-oriented programming days, the business object also encapsulated complex logical operations. Over time, business objects encapsulate less complex logic and, instead, contain only data access operations. One can debate whether this style of programming has merit. From an object purist point of view, this style reverses one of the fundamental underpinnings of object-oriented computing—that objects encapsulate both behavior and data.

From a practical development perspective, this style shows more and more promise. Two major data points back up the separation of data objects from process objects:

- Data objects easily relate to the relational databases tasked with storing persistent representations of the objects.

- New techniques and standards, such as Business Process Execution Language (BPEL), move complex business process logic into metadata rather than leaving it in a proprietary language.

Adhering to the separation of business objects from business processes, you will define your business concepts to be the data required for representation of a business concept as well as the operations that occur directly against the data, such as update and deletion operations. Chapter 8, "Exploring the Business Process Pattern" discusses business processes in more depth.

Understanding the Structure of Business Objects

Designing business objects in Java, you rely heavily on the JavaBean patterns to represent interfaces relating to data. The JavaBean patterns encompass several standards, including method signature patterns and patterns for observing state changes within a bean. Typically, as is the case in this chapter, relying on JavaBean patterns refers to the method signature patterns inherent in JavaBeans. The method signature patterns, in short, include the concept of a property that is simply a piece of data or calculated data. A property contains accessor methods, get methods, and set methods (otherwise known as *mutators*). Properties of type boolean can use an is prefix for the accessor methods.

Listing 6-1 shows an example of the JavaBean patterns in practice. In the listing you see two attributes, test and debug, each with their associated method accessors. The debug property is a read-only property; thus there is an accessor with no mutator. If debug was a read/write property, you would add a setDebug(boolean inDebug) method to the class.

Listing 6-1. JavaBean Example Class

```
public class JavaBeanExample {
    private String test = null;
    private boolean debug = true;
    public String getTest() {
        return this.test;
    }
    public void setText(String inTest) {
        this.test = inTest;
    }
    public boolean isDebug() {
        return this.debug;
    }
}
```

The choice of JavaBeans heavily influences the structure and representation of a Web Service that represents a business object. There are two primary reasons for relying on JavaBeans in business objects:

- Using the predictable JavaBean patterns simplifies the generation of architecture adapters for tools that enable Web Services.

- Java object/relational mechanisms often rely on the JavaBean patterns—again, for their predictability—when generating the persistence mappings.

Using the JavaBean patterns applies to the service implementation interface itself and the complex properties that the service implementation surfaces. Figure 6-1 illustrates a simple, generic pattern for designing business objects implemented in Java.

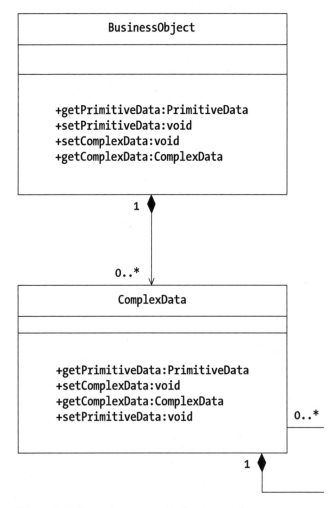

Figure 6-1. Generic pattern for business objects

Using JavaBeans, it is possible to build a rich business object domain by nesting the complex data types. Interestingly, this is in direct conflict with the flat nature of Web Services. Because the Web Service architecture derives many of its attributes from a component-oriented architecture, the focus is on loose coupling of components, not on the ability to create a versatile and flexible object paradigm. Often, loose coupling goes against the nature of rich object-oriented structures. The pattern in Figure 6-1 is purely generic in nature, but you should understand the potential richness of the structure. Not pictured in Figure 6-1 is the potential for inheritance in an object-oriented paradigm. Because inheritance *does not* translate at all to many programming platforms, it makes sense to leave inheritance out of the generic pattern. On the other hand, rich data structures, such as the one portrayed in Figure 6-1, do typically translate to other programming platforms, thus its inclusion in the diagram.

Understanding the Business Object Structure

There are two primary components of a business object structure: the BusinessObject and the ComplexData structure:

BusinessObject: This is a representation of a top-level business concept, such as a sales order, customer, or product. The business object surfaces only properties or, in more complex business objects, operations against multiple properties. Properties can represent primitive data, such as a string, integer, or boolean value. You also treat complex data, described next, as a property on the business object.

ComplexData: You can think of complex data as a subcomponent of a top-level business concept that is more complex than a primitive type of data. For example, a primitive type may be the last name of a person represented as a string, whereas the address a person resides at is a complex data type. In this case, the complex data type gets built from multiple primitive data types and is a separate concept from the primary business object of a person. Complex data can contain additional complex data types, such as the case of a company containing employees who, themselves, have addresses.

This chapter does not cover the components that act on the business object. Occasionally the actors are part of a pattern, but in this case, the actors are irrelevant.

The structure of the business object is relatively straightforward. The number of properties and complex data types that a business object contains can vary greatly. The important part of the design of business objects is not the number of properties but that the properties on a business object all belong together. In other words, the business object must be highly cohesive.

Understanding Collaborations with a Business Object

Clients of a business object expect to be able to retrieve and change data residing in the business object. The business object also, typically, gates access to the complex data contained within it. Figure 6-2 illustrates a scenario where an application first retrieves some complex data and then changes a property on the complex data. In most business object scenarios, the client changed a local copy of the complex data, not the real instance of the complex data. The application must submit the change back to the business object to change the business object's copy of the data.

The key interaction between the business object and application, the call to the getComplexData() method, returns a copy of the complex data to the client application. This allows the business object to retain ownership of the data but, in turn, forces a second interaction with the business object to change the data owned by the business object.

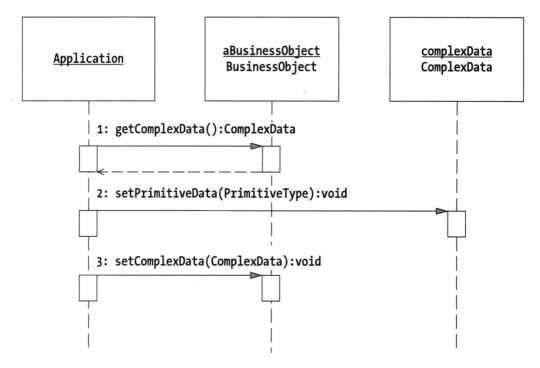

Figure 6-2. Retrieving and changing complex data in a business object

Preparing to Implement Business Objects

Business objects can quickly scale in complexity, especially in a true object-oriented model. Containment relationships mingle with implementation and interface inheritance to make a complex web of objects. A few simple implementation details can help maintain the business object in the long term and help guide how you think about business objects:

Flat business object structures translate to other representational models better: In enterprise systems, your object-oriented application is not the only application deployed. Frequently, legacy applications that do not employ object-orientation are in play. Often, the mechanism for communicating with these applications will be through the database. Although database systems are not necessarily equivalent to flat object-oriented structures, they are also not as rich with inheritance. Keeping alternative representations of your data in mind will help with integration scenarios. Although object purists will cringe when I say this, acknowledging the relationship between relational models and object-oriented systems is important. If you have trouble representing your objects in a relational database model, your structure is probably too rich for an environment where you have to integrate your application with other platforms.

Most business objects have an element of persistent data. The reality of persistence is often that the structure of a business object can hurt performance and make the administration of the data relationships to the objects difficult to maintain. Be cognizant of the model you will use and the impact on performance that your design decisions will have.

You should offer interfaces on the service implementation for all contained and indirectly contained data. Further, rather than exposing the implementation details of a particular complex data type, it is typically easier and better to offer a set and get method for the entire complex type (setJavaBean, getJavaBean). This technique allows the JavaBean to change structure without affecting the operations on the service implementation if you had elevated the JavaBean properties into the service implementation interface. For example, you may be inclined to add methods such as setAddressLine1 on the business object instead of a single method that sets the entire address. The latter is a better way to handle the interface modification.

Implementing Business Objects

The business object structure translates into Web Services using tools from Apache Axis. In the P.T. Monday Coffee Company application, all of the business object structures are collected, a topic covered in Chapter 7, "Exploring the Business Object Collection Pattern." Still, the Business Object pattern teaches you many things about the Web Service environment, so this will be a bit of a contrived sample, knowing that you will replace it with a more appropriate sample in the next chapter.

This example revolves around allowing customers to retrieve data about your company. You create a business object to represent your company and then expose the business object as a Web Service. This second step allows any type of client to access your company information.

The CompanyImpl class contains complex data in the form of an AddressImpl class, as well as simple primitive data, such as the name of the company. The classes adhere to the JavaBean semantics by surfacing get and set methods for primitive and complex data. The address implementation does not contain any additional complex data. Figure 6-3 shows the structure of the Java business objects.

In addition to the company business object, the conceptual Web Service diagram overlays the conventional Java business object implementation. For Web Services, CompanyImpl is the service implementation for a Web Service, which you simply call Company. Of interest is that the CompanyImpl signatures become the operations on the Web Service; the address class becomes complex data surfaced by the Company Web Service.

Different Web Service implementations expose the service implementation and the contained complex types in different ways, but for simple deployment, the business object interface becomes the Web Service interface. Apache Axis leverages the JavaBean semantics to determine the contents of the SOAP messages that move between a client and the Web Service. Axis has built-in serializers and deserializers that convert a JavaBean from the native Java class representation to the proper format for transfer via Simple Object Access Protocol (SOAP).

The next sections, "Deploying the Service Implementation" and "Using the Business Object," illustrate details of the deployment and usage of the Company Web Service that connects to the CompanyImpl service implementation. It is important to understand that not all Web Service implementations use the same techniques for exposing and consuming Web Services. On the other hand, all Web Service implementations must understand the SOAP messages (described briefly in "Understanding the SOAP Message Structure") and the Web Services Description Language (WSDL) files. The conversion from Java to the Web Services architecture illustrates many of the complexities of managing the

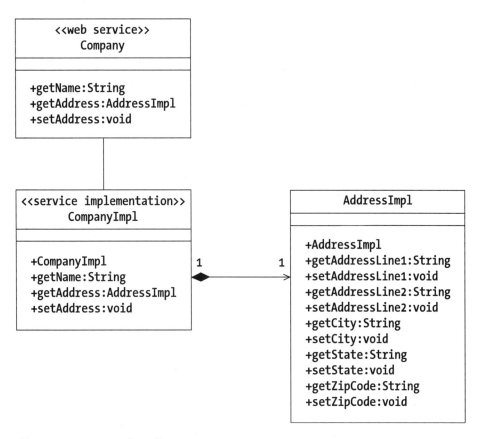

Figure 6-3. Company *class diagram*

architecture mismatch. The most complex details of the conversion between architectures is left to Apache Axis and other Web Service environments, as detailed in Chapter 4, "Exploring the Architecture Adapter Pattern."

Deploying the Service Implementation

From the Java classes detailed in Figure 6-3 that define the business object domain, you can directly deploy CompanyImpl as a Web Service. To do so in Apache Axis, you have to define the service as well as any associated complex types on which the service implementation relies. In this case, the CompanyImpl class forms the Web Service interface; any JavaBeans used by the Web Service become the additional complex types identified by a beanMapping tag. Listing 6-2 shows the Web Service Deployment Descriptor (WSDD) file used to deploy the CompanyImpl class to Apache Axis.

Listing 6-2. Company *WSDD*

```
<service name="Company" provider="java:RPC">
  <parameter name="className"
    value="com.servicefoundry.books.webservices.entities.CompanyImpl"/>
  <parameter name="scope" value="Application"/>
  <parameter name="allowedMethods" value="*"/>
  <beanMapping qname="myNS:CompanyAddress" xmlns:myNS="urn:Company"
      languageSpecificType=
      "java:com.servicefoundry.books.webservices.entities.AddressImpl"/>
</service>
```

In Listing 6-2's beanMapping tag, notice the qualified name (qname) of
CompanyAddress associated with the Company namespace. Also, notice the mapping
you create to the AddressImpl class that implements the complex type. Using the
WSDD file in Listing 6-2, you deploy the Web Service to a running Apache Axis
instance.

After deployment, the WSDL file generated by Apache Axis exposes the
address class as a complex type represented in the wsdl:types portion of the file.
This portion of the file precedes specific operation definitions and can become
extremely complex based on the nesting and richness of the object model within
the service implementation. The Extensible Markup Language (XML) in
Listing 6-3 identifies the CompanyAddress complex type and each of the elements
that make up the CompanyAddress, including addressLine1, city, state, and more.

Listing 6-3. Address Complex Type XML Definition

```
<complexType name="CompanyAddress">
<sequence>
  <element name="addressLine2" nillable="true" type="xsd:string" />
  <element name="addressLine1" nillable="true" type="xsd:string" />
  <element name="city" nillable="true" type="xsd:string" />
  <element name="state" nillable="true" type="xsd:string" />
  <element name="zipCode" nillable="true" type="xsd:string" />
</sequence>
</complexType>
```

Notice the correlation between the complexType name and the qualified
name in the WSDD file. Also, notice that you did not explicitly identify the
address interface and properties to Apache Axis; instead, Axis used reflection
and the JavaBean patterns to determine what elements make up the
CompanyAddress type.

This technique within Axis works for an extremely high percentage of JavaBean classes. There are also techniques for deploying special classes to aid in the serialization and deserialization of JavaBeans with special needs or classes that do not adhere to the JavaBean semantics, such as a java.util.Vector. I have chosen to avoid the complex objects and the objects unique to Java, which results in easier consumption by platforms other than Java. Unfortunately, you constrain yourself from leveraging all of the facilities of the Java platform for classes that become Web Services.

Using the Business Object

At this point, you have deployed an available business object with a Web Services interface. You can access it through constructing SOAP messages, binding to the deployed Company Web Service, and sending the SOAP messages. As discussed in earlier chapters, it is easier for the client to access the Web Service through architecture adapters generated by Apache Axis.

When you use Apache Axis to build Java adapters to SOAP using the WSDL2Java tool, you see a similar class hierarchy as the original that forms the service implementation. Be careful about getting used to the end-to-end Java with the Web Services as a remote proxy. It is critical you always remember that your Web Service does not require Java to access it. In fact, for a pure Java scenario, you would be far better off using Remote Method Invocation (RMI).

As previously mentioned, it is extremely important to note that instances of the CompanyAddress (the class representing the AddressImpl service-side class after a transformation through the Web Services environment) JavaBean reside *only* in the client's workspace. Changes to complex types using the mechanisms described in this chapter will only affect the address in the client's environment. To change the actual address implementation, you have to call the setAddress() method on the CompanyImpl class. This method call creates a SOAP message and deserializes the address into the proper XML representation that resides within the SOAP operation.

In Listing 6-4, the Java client-side code creates a representation of the Company Web Service for use by the Java program. Next, the code retrieves the address from the Web Service. This operation creates a local CompanyAddress instance with a copy of data from the server-side AddressImpl instance contained in the company. You can use this instance to see the contained data via the get methods on the CompanyAddress class.

Listing 6-4. Client-Side Access to the Company *Web Service*

```
CompanyImplService service =
    new CompanyImplServiceLocator();
CompanyImpl port = service.getCompany();
String name = port.getName();
System.out.println(name);
CompanyAddress address = port.getAddress();
System.out.println(address.getAddressLine1() + " "
    + address.getAddressLine2());
System.out.println(address.getCity()
    + ", " + address.getState() + ", " + address.getZipCode());
```

If you want to change the address on the company, you would first change some data in a CompanyAddress instance, then call the setAddress method on the CompanyImpl architecture adapter. The line that retrieves the address, port.getAddress(), is a remote operation on the Company Web Service. The Web Service calls the appropriate getAddress() method on the service implementation, then takes the results and serializes the data into a SOAP document with the address instance of the CompanyAddress complex type. The client side decodes the SOAP information and turns it into the CompanyAddress object instance for use on the client.

Understanding the SOAP Message Structure

Although the generated architecture adapters automate the entire communication path for us, it is still useful to look at the SOAP messages passed between the client and the Web Service. The SOAP message represents the address as nested XML response data, as shown in Listing 6-5.

Listing 6-5. Complex Object SOAP Contents

```
<?xml version="1.0" encoding="UTF-8"?>
<soapenv:Envelope xmlns:soapenv=http://schemas.xmlsoap.org/soap/envelope/
    xmlns:xsd="http://www.w3.org/2001/XMLSchema"
    xmlns:xsi="http://www.w3.org/2001/XMLSchema-instance">
<soapenv:Body>
<ns1:getAddressResponse
    soapenv:encodingStyle="http://schemas.xmlsoap.org/soap/encoding/"
    xmlns:ns1=
     "http://localhost:8080/axis/services/Company/axis/services/Company">
    <getAddressReturn href="#id0"/>
</ns1:getAddressResponse>
```

```
<multiRef id="id0" soapenc:root="0"
    soapenv:encodingStyle="http://schemas.xmlsoap.org/soap/encoding/"
    xsi:type="ns2:CompanyAddress"
    xmlns:soapenc="http://schemas.xmlsoap.org/soap/encoding/"
    xmlns:ns2="urn:Company">
    <state xsi:type="xsd:string">CO</state>
    <addressLine1 xsi:type="xsd:string">100</addressLine1>
    <city xsi:type="xsd:string">Broomfield</city>
    <zipCode xsi:type="xsd:string">80021</zipCode>
    <addressLine2 xsi:type="xsd:string">Eldorado Boulevard</addressLine2>
</multiRef>
</soapenv:Body>
</soapenv:Envelope>
```

Tracing through the SOAP response, you will see correlations between the WSDD file, the XML schema representing the complex type from the WSDL file, and the client-side and server-side JavaBeans. The SOAP message originates as a set of JavaBeans within the service implementation. The Apache Axis engine converts the response into the SOAP message in Listing 6-5. The client-side architecture adapter, generated by Apache Axis, deserializes the SOAP message back into JavaBeans, similar to those within the service implementation. These conversion processes substantially increase the path length of a typical operation call; therefore, the performance of your operations that use Web Services are sure to suffer. Chapter 16, "Implementing the Data Transfer Object Pattern," and Chapter 17, "Exploring the Partial Population Pattern," introduce additional patterns for minimizing the number of requests to the Web Service.

Understanding the Consequences of Using Business Objects with Web Services

The unfortunate side effect of moving toward Web Services is that your object design can suffer from the perspective of an object purist. You first stripped the complex logic from the object model (Chapter 8, "Exploring the Business Process Pattern" explains this detail in more depth), and now you are subtly flattening the object model itself. These are unfortunate side effects of dealing with an unknown set of client architectures and languages. The overall architecture of your system does not change as a result. The changes will be more subtle design and implementation changes in your business objects.

Interestingly, using Web Services is not the only influence on the structure of your business objects. Your choice of persistence mechanism will also lead you toward a flatter, more database-like object structure. Although Java Data Objects

(JDO) professes to be a pure object-oriented and natural mechanism for persisting objects, it does influence the object structure.

There are alternatives to allowing the object design to suffer. Leaving complex logic on the object does not mean you cannot leverage Web Services or other platforms; it only means that some of the new features of Web Services, such as business process metadata languages, will be less accessible. Further, complex logic types and their translation to Web Services and subsequent client complexity can always be mitigated using custom deployment components, though this last strategy typically depends on the platform you use to deploy the Web Services. The reality of Web Services is that they do not excel in rich object orientation; after all, Web Services is not an object-oriented paradigm. Many developers experienced the same paradigm shift moving from Java to Enterprise JavaBeans (EJBs) and Container Managed Persistence (CMP). EJB is a component model with rich heritage in relational persistence models, especially in the CMP type of EJB. The influences are similar to reduce the complexity of the object orientation and become highly cohesive, loosely coupled components.

A final strategy to mitigate the paradigm shift is to allow your business objects to naturally reflect the business domain at design and implementation time. Then, build a set of classes, adhering to the Adapter pattern, to translate between the flat object representation and the richer representation.

Identifying Important Classes and Files in the Case Study

Table 6-1 identifies the primary code discussed in this chapter, as well as related files of interest to you from the downloaded samples.

Table 6-1. Sample Location

FILE	LOCATION	DESCRIPTION
CompanyImpl.java	src\com\ servicefoundry\ books\webservices\ entities	This is the CompanyImpl service implementation described in Figure 6-3. This class takes an interesting approach to constructing its address information; it goes to the P.T. Monday Coffee Company representation in UDDI to gather address information.
TestCompany.java	src\com\ servicefoundry\ books\webservices\ tests	This is a client program that accesses the company Web Service.

Using Ant Targets to Run the Case Study

Table 6-2 gives the targets to run for the ant environment to see the programs and chapter samples in operation. Before running any samples, be sure you read and perform all of the install steps in Appendix A.

Table 6-2. Ant Targets

TARGET	DESCRIPTION
testcompany	Runs the client-side company access program

Summary

Business objects play a central role in modeling and implementing the behavior of an application. Java business objects that adhere to the JavaBeans specification enable an easy translation to Web Services through tools and also help to facilitate common Java object/relational techniques, such as JDO.

In this chapter, you saw a business object (the Company) that stands alone (is not collected) and illustrates the use of JavaBeans patterns to facilitate the Web Service architecture. The company contains an address that also uses the JavaBean patterns for data. The difference between the company and the address when translated into Web Services is that the methods on the company operate against a server instance, and the methods against the address operate against a local instance of the object stored in the client's workspace. To change an address, the client must request a copy through the company Web Service, change the copy, and then resubmit it to the company Web Service.

Single business objects, such as Company, are rare in terms of complete object domains represented in business applications, and, in fact, you do not have any stand-alone business objects in this application. Instead, business objects are collected and business processes operate against business objects retrieved from the collections; these patterns are used throughout the P.T. Monday Coffee Company application. The next two chapters address business object collections and business processes in more detail. This chapter is not in vain; the techniques shown in this chapter apply directly to the next two chapters.

Related Patterns

Business objects are rarely used as stand-alone objects in a Web Service environment; in pure object-oriented environments, stand-alone business objects are common. Instead, other patterns leverage the Business Object pattern to fulfill their own requirements. As a result, you will rarely see a business object as a service implementation; instead, you see them implemented purely in the service implementation's platform, with one of the two following patterns being the service implementation:

- **Business Object Collection:** More often than not, business objects are collected and require that the collection accessor surface as a Web Service rather than individual objects. Nonetheless, the same patterns of JavaBeans for complex types extend to the business object collection.

- **Business Process:** The business process leverages business objects, but more often business object collections. The same usage of JavaBeans and the associated JavaBean patterns apply to business processes when the processes use Java to implement them.

Additional Reading

- JavaBeans—Englander, *Developing Java Beans,* O'Reilly and Associates, 1997.

CHAPTER 7

Exploring the Business Object Collection Pattern

IN THE PREVIOUS CHAPTER, you learned about a generic pattern for representing business objects. The pattern assumed that the business object was a stand-alone object. This scenario is not realistic in business applications. Collections of business objects are far more common than stand-alone business objects. In fact, it is challenging to think of a simple business object that has value in a business application. Nonetheless, Chapter 6, "Exploring the Business Object Pattern" provided you with both a learning experience and a solid foundation for the Business Object Collection pattern.

Consider just about any scenario or common business concept, and it is very likely that you would use a collection to manage it. Sales orders, customers, and products are all business objects that you collect. In fact, the P.T. Monday Coffee Company application is full of collections; you will have collections of products for a product catalog, collections of products in your inventory, and collections of sales orders to keep track of your sales. Many of these collections will become Web Services to allow at least the querying of data by business partners. More often, applications place additional logic on top of the collection. For example, a browser-based interface would locate a particular order using the collection Web Service and then render the status of the order to the user.

Using the Business Object pattern as a foundation for collections of objects, you can easily establish a common pattern for building collections and subsequently representing the collections as Web Services. In addition to introducing business object collections, the sample content and code changes as well. Rather than spending time discussing Apache Axis and its deployment facilities and tools, I will assume you have enough knowledge and details about the environment and focus on the patterns.

Seeing Collections in Practice

Collections are a common construct in computer science, so much so that the Java platform contains several different types of collections. Most of the time, collections differentiate themselves based on how they sort (or do not sort) data stored within them. Some collections are simple queues with first-in first-out orders or last-in first-out orders. Other collections maintain objects in an order based on arbitrary data stored in the object. Collections common in enterprise applications often focus on persistent data and how to efficiently access the collections of persistent data.

To determine the common capabilities that collections offer, you can consider a simple business case of a collection of customers. In the context of customers, you need the collection to facilitate the following:

- Creating new customers

- Reading existing customer information

- Updating customer information

- Deleting customer information

These operations are the CRUD operations: create, read, update, delete. You will find these same operations on databases and any coherent collection implementation. The Java collections offer these operations in the form of the add operation, an Iterator that supports moving through the instances of objects in a collection and reading them, and the remove operation, which exists on the collection or iterator to delete elements from the collection.

You should note that there are no update operations on the base Collection interface in Java. Specific concrete collection types, such as the LinkedList, add set operations to update specific items in the collection, but in general, collections return references to objects and thus do not require specific update methods on the collection. For example, by getting an object out of a Vector, you can directly manipulate it and affect the "collected" object, as shown in Listing 7-1.

Listing 7-1. Simple Collection Example

```
Vector v = new Vector(1);
SimplePerson p1 = new SimplePerson();
p1.name = "Paul";
System.out.println("Putting Paul into the Hashtable");
v.add(p1);
```

```
SimplePerson p2 = (SimplePerson)v.get(0);
System.out.println("Getting the Person and Changing the Name");
p2.name = "Paul2";

SimplePerson p3 = (SimplePerson)v.get(0);
    // the following line prints "Paul2", showing the Vector
    // collects and returns references, not copies
System.out.println("Name from Vector was: "+p3.name);
```

The notion of having a reference to an object as opposed to a copy of the object is difficult to achieve with Web Services. Throughout this chapter, you will see the notion of object copying as opposed to object references inherent in the Java collections.

The Iterator class in Java is another difference between what is possible in Java and what a Web Service is capable of achieving. Java iterators are knowledgeable about changes that occur to a collection outside of your own thread. When the collection changes, an iterator throws an exception to let you know that your iterator is no longer valid. Web Services are stateless; maintaining references to individual iterators from the server-side object simply does not make sense. Further, translating iterators to the Web Service model could make for abysmal performance, especially considering the performance variability of Web Services and the need to continuously return to the server for each business object.

This chapter addresses the problem of the iterator by simply leaving it off your collection pattern. Instead, you will return to the original concept of a collection that contains the ability to create, read, update, and delete on the primary collection interface.

Understanding the Structure of Business Object Collections

Data stored in a collection consists of business objects, as defined in the previous chapter. The base structure of the Business Object Collection pattern simply adds an additional collection class to the business object structure built in the previous chapter (see Figure 7-1).

Of particular note in the generic collection pattern is the use of a BusinessObjectKey. Keys are a compromise between relational databases and the object world. Keys are useful in establishing the exact identity of an object and ensuring uniqueness across a set of attributes within a collection. Object purists often do not leverage keys, yet object/relational mapping tools typically require the use of keys, even if the keys are not directly exposed to the user. This pattern leverages keys because they are common in the business application usage of objects.

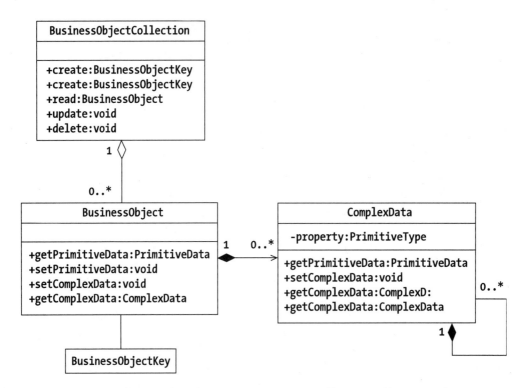

Figure 7-1. Generic class diagram representing collections of business objects

Understanding the Components of a Business Object Collection

There are four components of a business object; the fourth of which, the BusinessObjectKey, is optional in a pure object-oriented environment:

BusinessObjectCollection: The collection implementation surfaces lifecycle and query methods for the business objects in the collection. Typically, collections offer several flavors of the lifecycle methods, especially the read and creation methods, based on the domains that the collection serves. At this point, there is an interesting issue about the containment relationship between the BusinessObjectCollection and the BusinessObjects. Although it is true that there is containment, the mechanism for containment is at issue. Consider the case that you have collections with 1,000,000 objects. You really want a containment mechanism that allows you to efficiently select one or two objects that a client requests, without populating all 1,000,000 objects to find the one or two you want. In common solutions such as Java Data Objects (JDO) or Enterprise JavaBean (EJB) Container Managed Persistence (CMP), the collection interface does not populate all objects; rather, they retrieve only the necessary objects for use in a particular scenario. Using these types of managed persistence typically implies a direct relationship between the collection interface and an intermediate storage manager, rather than a primary collection type such as a LinkedList. This book is not about persistence mechanisms, but as you study the collection code, you will notice that you use JDO directly to retrieve the objects requested by a user.

BusinessObject: The business object represents the domain-specific concept collected by the collection implementation. Chapter 6, "Exploring the Business Object Pattern" discusses the concept of a single business object without getting into the details of creating or deleting a business object. Interestingly, by coupling the business object with the service implementation, you remove the ability to create or delete a single business object. It would cause a severe problem to delete the service implementation in terms of the Web Service. Collections address this problem.

ComplexData: As defined in Chapter 6, "Exploring the Business Object Pattern," the ComplexData is simply data that is not of a primitive type. The BusinessObject gates access to the object, although the data resides in a separate object.

BusinessObjectKey: The key is a unique identifier for each business object. Keys are important to business applications as a way to enforce uniqueness. Business object keys also help the transition of complex object data to a persistent relational model.

By surfacing the BusinessObject, it is implicit that there is complex data, as described in the previous chapter, contained within the BusinessObject. It is somewhat important to note that the business object is simply complex data itself in terms of the business object collection.

Understanding Collaborations with Business Object Collections

The primary client collaborations with the BusinessObjectCollection are via the create, read, update, or delete operations. Using a key on the operations helps to identify particular objects in a collection without having the complete object contents. Using a key reduces ambiguity. Often, if you use a complex key, a partially specified key returns a group of objects rather than a single object. Clients often persist keys to ease future lookups of the object. You could also store keys in cookies on a browser client so that when a client returns to a Web site, the last item they viewed could be brought up for them. Deletion operations receive a key or an array of keys for removal, and updates use the key to identify the exact object for updates.

Locating objects (reading them) occurs through one or more lookup operations. Lookup through a business object key returns a single object, though you should not have to know a key to locate an object. More often, a series of retrieval operations exists on the Web Service to return arrays of objects that contain attributes within a given set boundary. For example, retrieve all customers with a particular last name, such as Smith. Another operation may retrieve all customers with available credit ranging from $5,000 to $20,000 to make a special offer for bulk orders. Figure 7-2 shows a typical lookup scenario.

In the scenario, a client application creates an instance of a business object key. They then pass this key to a Business Object Collection pattern implementation to retrieve a business object. The collection stores objects in a mechanism that remains private to the collection. In the P.T. Monday Coffee Company application, you use JDO. With JDO, the collection exists in a database, and you use JDO Application Programming Interfaces (APIs) to return a type of collection known as an *extent*. An extent serves as an input to further filtering operations for JDO or for your own consumption. As a result, the extent may not hold fully populated business objects; the JDO implementation can optimize the content of the extent. From the extent, you retrieve one or more business objects, request that JDO fully populates it, and then return the business object to the

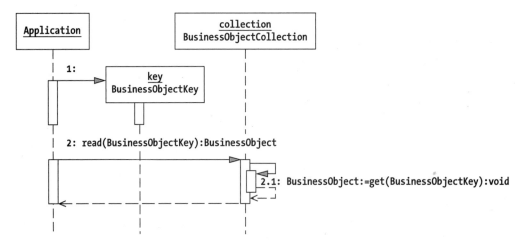

Figure 7-2. Retrieving an element from a business object collection

application. JDO does not get exposed outside of your Business Object Collection pattern implementation.

Many collections also contain a single location method that returns all objects. It is extremely important to remember that business applications rarely have small sets of business objects; rather, they contain thousands or millions of object instances. Surfacing a general operation that returns all objects can encourage performance and scalability problems from junior programmers who choose to ignore the better-suited query mechanisms. Unfortunately, these performance and scalability problems do not show up until well after system deployment because of the business object set being larger in an installed base.

Preparing to Implement Collections

Collections from an object-oriented paradigm combined with Web Services enable designers to get into trouble by accidentally exposing the underlying complexity of the service implementation platform and language. By leveraging the service implementation language too heavily, the types of clients that can easily access the Web Service will become limited. The following implementation tips show ways to ensure easy adoption of your collections by unexpected client platforms and types:

Do not expose open-ended query mechanisms tied to the underlying object implementation: Query mechanisms tie collections to the underlying representation of the data, objects use Object Query Language (OQL), and relational databases use SQL. This technique violates the ability to encapsulate the service implementation architecture and design.

Return arrays of data from operations that return more than one object rather than Java-specific collection types: There is no guarantee that a Web Service client has a mechanism to represent complex Java-specific types. For example, using a Vector on a service implementation may not translate easily to a type available for a COBOL programmer. Arrays are a more common programming construct and easily translate between most platform architectures.

Collections will exist on the client or on the server: A collection based on the pattern presented here does not span the client and the server. Always remember that the collection used by a client is a copy of the data on the server. Changes to the data on the client move back into the collection on the server through an explicit call to the collection interface.

Certain Web Service scenarios can avoid some of these rules by limiting the types of clients that can access your Web Service. For example, by ensuring that your clients are either .NET or Java clients, you can open up your interface to OQL and simple collection types that translate between platforms. Unfortunately, by putting a limitation such as this on your clients, you also limit the uses of the Web Service. For example, consider that a larger company may someday buy your company; object-oriented clients may restrict integration with their systems.

Implementing a Collection Sample

The theme of a collection of customers will continue for the sample implementation presented in this chapter. In the previous chapter, you went through a detailed scenario of business object deployment and the structure of the Simple Access Object Protocol (SOAP) messages that flow between the client and the server.

For this chapter, you will assume that deployment of the service implementation as a Web Service is less interesting than the structure of the service and how to access it from Java. This is a subtle change in tempo for the book, but it is necessary when you realize that Web Services are merely architecture adapters that tools generate for you. The real work becomes building implementations that are consumable by other languages yet allow you to leverage the mechanisms of an individual language for implementing and consuming the Web Service.

CustomerCollectionImpl is your service implementation class; it contains instances of CustomerImpl classes. The CustomerImpl class contains an AddressImpl, an instance of CustomerInformationImpl and some simple types, mostly strings. AddressImpl contains strings, and CustomerInformationImpl contains several more nested complex types. Figure 7-3 shows the entire class diagram.

From this hierarchy, an instance of CustomerCollectionImpl serves as the point object for the Web Service. A parallel hierarchy of serializable JavaBeans exists on the client after deployment of the Web Service and the creation of the client-side classes using WSDL2Java. These classes allow the client to create local data and call methods on the customer collection Web Service, as described in previous chapters.

For your implementation, there is an interesting side effect of your JDO usage. The association between the collection and the customer instances is an indirect relationship that works through the JDO persistence manager. The collection implementation queries extents that represent collections of customers. Figure 7-3 shows the logical structure rather than the actual physical implementation of the system.

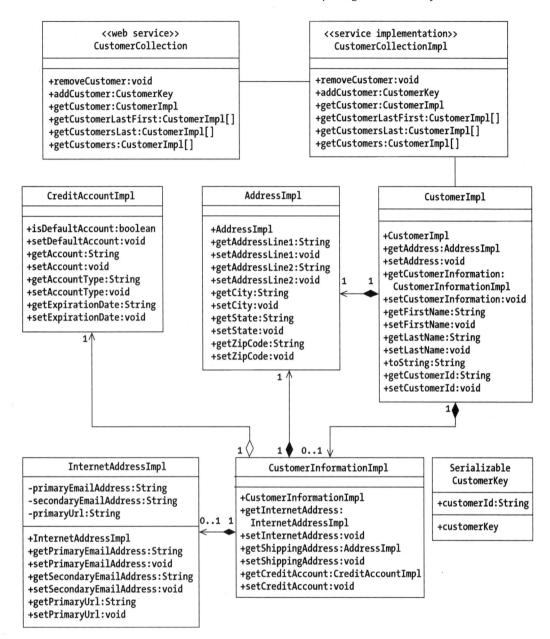

Figure 7-3. Customer collection implementation

Understanding Service Implementation Details

The CustomerCollectionImpl class contains several interesting characteristics. Listing 7-2 is not the complete source code for the class, but it is enough for you to get a feel for the implementation. Of particular interest is the series of query methods: getCustomer, getCustomers, getCustomersLastFirst, and getCustomersLast.

The difference between the getCustomer method and the getCustomers method lies in the expected set of objects returned from the method. The getCustomer method must return zero or one instance because of the unique key on the parameter list. The other methods do not guarantee a single instance and, therefore, return arrays.

A second point to note with the retrieval methods is the lack of method overloading. Overloading methods works well in object-oriented languages, but you cannot guarantee that only object-oriented languages will access your application. Rather than place a burden on the user of the Web Service, this code limits the use of overloading to ease usage of the Web Service.

Listing 7-2. Customer Collection Implementation

```
public class CustomerCollectionImpl {
 public void removeCustomer(CustomerKey key) {
    // see implementation in sample code
 }

 public CustomerKey addCustomer(CustomerImpl customer) {
  CustomerKey key = null;
  if (customer.getCustomerId() == null) {
   customer.setCustomerId(
      KeyGenerator.generateKey(KeyGenerator.CUSTOMER));
  }
  key = new CustomerKey();
  key.customerId = customer.getCustomerId();
  PersistenceManager pm = getPersistenceManager();
  Transaction t = pm.currentTransaction();
  t.begin();
  pm.makePersistent(customer);
  t.commit();
  return key;
 }

 public CustomerImpl getCustomer(CustomerKey key) {
    // see implementation in sample code
 }
```

```
public CustomerImpl[] getCustomersLastFirst(
    String lastName, String firstName) {
    // see implementation in sample code
}


public CustomerImpl[] getCustomersLast(String lastName) {
  PersistenceManager pm = getPersistenceManager();
  Transaction t = pm.currentTransaction();
  t.begin();
  Extent ext = pm.getExtent(CustomerImpl.class, false);
  String filter = "lastName==last";
  String parameter = "String last";
  Query q = pm.newQuery(ext, filter);
  q.declareParameters(parameter);
  Collection c = (Collection)q.execute(lastName);
  pm.retrieveAll(c);

  CustomerImpl returnCustomers[] = new CustomerImpl[c.size()];
  Iterator i = c.iterator();
  int j=0;
  while(i.hasNext()){
   returnCustomers[j] = (CustomerImpl)i.next();
   j++;
  }
  q.closeAll();
  t.commit();
  return returnCustomers;
}


public CustomerImpl[] getCustomers() {
    // see implementation in sample code
  }
}
```

The addCustomer method from Listing 7-2 is straightforward. The client cannot necessarily guarantee a unique key; therefore, the collection code will generate a unique key for each new customer and return this key to the client. In theory, you could use a social security number or other identifier, but there is no guarantee your customer has a social security number or other state-issued identifier.

The getCustomersLast is a more interesting method. Consider that JDO returns a Collection from the query of the customer extent. This method could return this collection directly to the client. On the other hand, by returning the collection you leave some ambiguity about how your architecture adapters will handle the collection interface along with the data contained in the collection. Rather than leave ambiguity in the interface, the method returns a type-safe array of classes that leaves no ambiguity about their type. This flattening of the data requires you to create a copy of the information contained in the collection and return it to the Web Service that invoked the method.

Querying a Collection

Several client-side scenarios are available to you; you will see a simple one using the getCustomers method. This code actually retrieves the customer collection from the Web Service and removes every customer using the removeCustomer method on the Web Service.

In this method, it is crucial to remember that the customer query returns copies of the collection to you rather than giving you an iterator to the collection that resides on the server. Generic queries that return large numbers of instances cause a heavy load to the network, server, and client in terms of memory and bandwidth. Looking at Listing 7-3, you can see that you use only a single field from each customer, the id field. The amount of data serializing and deserializing to retrieve the customer ID for each customer in the database is enormous.

Listing 7-3. Querying the Customer Collection

```
CustomerCollectionImplService service =
        new CustomerCollectionImplServiceLocator();
CustomerCollectionImpl port =
        service.getCustomerCollection();
Customer[] ci3 = port.getCustomers();
if(ci3!=null) {
        for(int i=0 ; i<ci3.length ; i++){
    CustomerKey ck = new CustomerKey();
    ck.setCustomerId(ci3[i].getCustomerId());
    port.removeCustomer(ck);
  }
}
```

A second point to note in Listing 7-3 is the use of the array structure. Arrays are not very dynamic; on the other hand, it did not use collection instances on methods. The client code points out another interesting reason to avoid collections as parameters and return types. Consider that you received a collection of objects in a dynamic collection that you could easily expand through an add method call. Changes to the collection *only* occur on the client side. Modification of the server-side collection *must* occur through the CustomerCollectionImpl interface. Using the static array structure on the return of the query methods may help you avoid programming errors when clients modify the locally held collection without submitting new data to the Web Service.

Leveraging Collections in the Case Study

The case study application uses collections modeled after the pattern identified in this chapter throughout the application design. Collections hold virtually all of the data in the application, from the products offered by the application to the inventory, customers, and sales orders. These collections all become first-class Web Services in your application. Interestingly, the use of collections as identified with this pattern brings some limitations to the scenario:

Collections that hold additional collections do not have a mechanism to return references to Web Services rather than an array of data: This mechanism would be useful to allow lazy retrieval of information rather than a forced copy of the entire class containment tree.

There is no mechanism in place to ensure that the client is aware of changes to the server-side collection: This guarantee is natural to the Java Iterator class as it throws an exception when another thread modifies the collection while you iterate across it. Loss of this mechanism could cause problems in the event that your application expects to have the current copy of data at all times.

Despite these limitations, you will heavily leverage collections in the application. An important part of creating collections and encouraging pragmatic usage of them is to identify simple query methods that will return the minimal amount of data required for the client to achieve their task with the data.

You will not see a list of all of the requirements that the combination of the Business Object and Business Object Collection patterns fulfill, but Table 7-1 lists some of them.

Table 7-1. Requirements Fulfilled by the Business Object and Business Object Collection Patterns

ID	DESCRIPTION
U1	The application shall have Web-based access to the customer profile for update directly by customers.
U2	The application shall allow customers to access the current order status through a programmatic mechanism and through a user interface.
U3	The application shall enable a customer to access product catalog and sales information through a user interface and programmatically.

The requirements in Table 7-1 show an interesting mix of business objects and collections. For example, U1 shows a user interested in a single customer profile. The customer profile is contained in a business object collection, whereas the profile itself is a business object. On the other hand, a product catalog could be considered a business object containing a business object collection, the latter being a collection of products with their associated prices.

The two concepts of a business object and a business object collection go hand in hand. There are cases where the business object lives without the business object collection, but those cases are few and far between.

Identifying Important Classes and Files in the Case Study

Table 7-2 shows the primary code discussed in this chapter that you should browse in the downloaded source code.

Table 7-2. Sample Location

FILE	LOCATION	DESCRIPTION
TestCustomerCollection WebService.java	src\com\servicefoundry\ books\webservices\tests	A client-side program that uses the deployed Web Service interface to the customer collection.
CustomerCollection Impl.java	src\com\servicefoundry\ books\webservices\entities	The service implementation for the CustomerCollectionImpl class presented in Listing 7-1. This class relies heavily on JDO for storing and retrieving data.

Using Ant Targets to Run the Case Study

Table 7-3 describes the targets to run for the ant environment to see the programs and chapter samples in operation. Before running any samples, be sure you read and perform all of the install steps in Appendix A.

Table 7-3. Ant Targets

TARGET	DESCRIPTION
testcustomercollection	Runs the example code from Listing 7-3

Summary

This chapter extended your knowledge of how Web Services represent objects and object collections as well as some practices for efficiently using Web Services to surface your data. Using object collections is pervasive in business applications, and creating a common interface will make the collections more predictable and, therefore, usable. In designing your collections with upfront knowledge that they would become Web Services, you are able to get your collections ready for client consumption by eliminating some programming practices that are extremely specific to object-oriented computing, such as method overloading and using the Java-specific collection interfaces as parameters and return types on your methods.

With a practical example of a collection of customers, you should also understand that there are inherent limitations and inefficiencies related to exposing large collections of data via Web Services. Multiple copies of the collection exist in different forms, clients can quickly become out-of-sync with the actual data in the collection, and you lose some of your ability to fully leverage the Java platform in your application.

The next chapter identifies the final "primitive" data and service structure that you expose using Web Services, the Business Process. Business Process computing is, in many ways, the holy grail of business application programming, and Web Services give a convenient mechanism for enabling this goal.

Related Patterns

Several patterns relate to the business object collection, mostly because of a use or used by relationship. For example, a business object collection uses the Business Object pattern. The following are common relationships:

Business Object: Collections contain business objects. The primary difference between the business object in Chapter 6, "Exploring the Business Object Pattern," and the business object considered in this chapter is the change in the business object from being the service implementation in Chapter 6 to being merely a complex type with a specific structure in this chapter.

Business Process: The Business Process pattern leverages collections throughout common processes, such as sales order entry and customer contact processes. In fact, many methods on business object collections represent business processes, such as creation of a sales order and a customer.

Partial Population: As demonstrated in the chapter example, there are cases where you only need simple pieces of data yet you receive complex data. This practice burdens the network, client, and server memory, and it strains the performance and scalability of your system. Using partial population can relieve these problems.

Additional Reading

- "Hands on Java Data Objects" by Paul Monday on IBM developerWorks Java Zone: http://www-106.ibm.com/developerworks/java/

CHAPTER 8

Exploring the Business Process (Composition) Pattern

THROUGH THE BUSINESS OBJECT and Business Object Collection patterns, you enable capabilities that are already available in today's programming languages. Specifically, you have a type of proxy model to connect data representations across a network. To access the data, the client of the Web Service must re-create the object model on the server in its own language. There are many limitations to the Web Service model when you attempt to use them to fulfill an object-oriented architectural style (Chapter 6, "Exploring the Business Object Pattern," and Chapter 7, "Exploring the Business Object Collection Pattern," document these points more fully):

There is a mismatch in the component-style model of Web Services with the capabilities of object-based languages: For example, Web Services (which are a variation on a component-style architecture) do not have a rich inheritance model or use polymorphism. You are also missing the concept of object references vs. object copies in Web Services. The data you retrieve from a collection are always copies of data.

The unpredictable nature of the architecture of a client program that accesses your Web Service limits the richness of the object structure that you can usably expose to the client: Beyond Java, languages such as Perl, Python, C, and even a language such as COBOL could access Web Services. The more complex your structure, the more difficult it will be for users of these languages to access your Web Service.

Despite the weaknesses of business objects combined with Web Services, they will always have a place in an application. In many cases, the Business Object and Business Object Collection patterns remain pure-Java implementations, and you will use either an adapter or a business process that hides the use of the Business Object and Business Object Collection patterns.

Businesses gamble on Web Services because of the evolving and growing use of business processes as formal building blocks for applications. The EbXML glossary (available at `http://www.ebxml.org/`), defines a *business process* as the following:

The means by which one or more activities are accomplished in operating business practices.

Essentially, business processes address how to model business, whereas business objects address how to model the physical representation of entities within a business. Using business processes as a model for one or more activities in a business does not preclude the use of business objects, and it does not imply the use of business objects. Instead, you look at a business purely from the aspect of the activities that business conducts. These business activities compose into larger business processes defined by common process interfaces. A business process in Web Services is a *composition* of business activities that may or may not be other Web Services. A business activity may or may not be a first-class business process.

It is important to realize that there are two facets to discussing business processes; one facet addresses the structure of a business process, and the other facet addresses how to standardize interfaces to business processes. This pattern describes a general pattern for the structure of a business process implementation, not the deeper discussion of the standardization of business process interfaces. For more information on the standardization of business process interfaces, you should refer to the e-business Extensible Markup Language (XML) effort and the specifications produced by the ebXML standards body or the Organization for the Advancement of Structured Information Standards (OASIS) group (`http://www.oasis-open.org/`). Each of these groups has processes for standardizing business processes and committees that you can join to develop the standards. Beyond the formal standards bodies, you will likely find contacts in your industry trying to make *de facto* standards for Web Service interfaces or larger groups focused just on your own industry. Perhaps the most interesting part of viewing the work of the larger bodies, such as ebXML and OASIS, is the document templates and standards they have produced. These documents can serve as a starting point for designing your own business processes.

Seeing Business Processes in Practice

The business process as a formal unit of computing is an extremely difficult concept to understand and fully utilize for many reasons:

- **Business process concepts overlap with common computing architectures and styles:** This overlap makes it difficult to legitimize the business process over existing computing techniques.

- **Business process implementations differ dramatically between companies:** In fact, in many companies the way a business process gets implemented gives a competitive edge to the company.

- **Large business processes often span multiple companies:** Usually there are steps or input in the business process that involve coordination from outside processes and activities.

The concept of a business process is less a computing concept than a business concept. Only recently have people attempted to model the business process as a tangible computing step. Business process computing equates to a set of business objects representing a physical domain, such as a warehouse and its inventory. Instead of using classes to represent a physical structure, you can use business processes to model and deconstruct how a business functions, such as the process a business uses to count stock in a warehouse.

Before business processes were a formal unit of a model, business processes tended to be part of the object-oriented representation of a business or part of the custom logic that lived outside of the business object model. Unfortunately, business processes are extremely fluid in nature, with each company having its own approach to implementing a particular business process. Often, a company's implementation of a particular business process gives the company a competitive advantage over another company. Because of this fluidity, it is difficult to create a single object model that represents all businesses, and, in fact, your application will be at a competitive disadvantage in the marketplace if it imposes a particular business process on the purchaser of an application. Further, businesses that compete in a space based on their business processes need to be able to treat the process itself as a selling point for an application, the object model behind the business process becomes merely a way of accessing data to feed the business process.

A good example of the fluidity of business processes is in the P.T. Monday Coffee Company shipping process. The company works on a model of personal service within a radius of the distribution point, maintaining a "retro" feeling about the company that the customers enjoy; in the morning, a customer can wake up and get fresh roasted coffee at their doorstep along with their milk delivery from another company. This personal service is a competitive advantage to the P.T. Monday Coffee Company and an unexpected twist to most application builders. Not only does the shipping process have to consider traditional shippers, the process must also consider the P.T. Monday Coffee Company itself as a potential shipper of the coffee. By considering an application as a collection of business processes that contains a set of activities that the process carries out, you should be able to quickly locate the activities that need adjustment in the process.

Using Business Process Model Languages

Just as there are standards for modeling object-oriented classes, there are standards for modeling and representing business processes. XML documents represent a model of a business process. At this time, there are two primary standards:

- **Business Process Execution Language (BPEL):** Proposed by BEA Systems, IBM, and Microsoft.

- **Business Process Modeling Language (BPML):** Proposed by just about everyone except the BPEL team. The backers of BPEL include webMethods, SeeBeyond, Adobe Systems, and more.

The structure defined in this chapter mirrors the structure of BPEL relatively closely. BPEL is a structured XML representation of a business process. The XML data generated through modeling also runs as a first-class Web Service in a business process engine. The XML data does not have to serve a dual role as modeling and execution language; many business processes could simply exist in a programming language, such as Java, or could even be generated into a programming language from the XML model.

At the time of writing, the primary way of modeling business processes with BPEL is through an enhanced XML editor that represents business processes in a tree-like structure. The long-term goal of business process modeling includes modeling languages that are derivations of workflow modeling and, essentially, advanced flow models.

Understanding the Marginalization of the Object Model

For an object-oriented programmer, the marginalization of the object model is disconcerting at first. Instead, the business process is more of a pure, flat, component model with an interface definition and an implementation. An interface defines a particular business process. In the case of Web Services, this interface is a Web Service Description Language (WSDL) file identified by a particular technical model (tModel) residing in a Universal Description, Data, and Discovery (UDDI) directory. Each business implements the interface as the composition of one or more Web Services or service implementations, thus the alternate labeling of this pattern as a composition rather than a business process.

A business process can also contain other business processes. Implementing a unit of work breaks down into an atomic business activity that may or may not be a method on an object that is a service implementation.

BPEL even further marginalizes the object model by moving flow logic, such as branch statements and the ability to repeat actions, into XML. Implementing a complex business process with BPEL requires little, if any, complex logic in a particular programming language such as Java. Figure 8-1 illustrates, from a high level, the capabilities of BPEL to create complex business logic. With BPEL, a BPEL container runs a business process definition that is in the form of a BPEL XML document. The business process is a Web Service through the creation and registration of the WSDL document. Clients simply call the Web Service that forwards requests to the BPEL container. The service implementation is the BPEL container and its interpretation of the BPEL definition document related to the BusinessProcess definition.

The business process leverages a variety of metadata constructs that resemble common programming language constructs. The operations include sequencing, basic logic constructs such as looping, and switch statements. Also, operations included simplify the construction of a business process such as the ability to invoke other Web Services and store data in locations within the BPEL container.

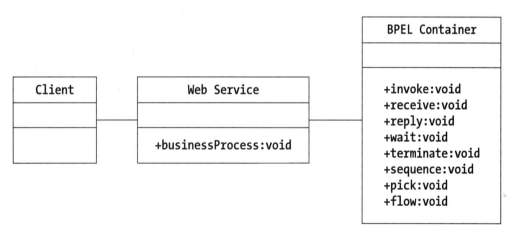

Figure 8-1. Business process logic implemented using BPEL

Even with the movement of logic into metadata, there is substantial room for languages such as Java. It will likely be many years, and possibly never, before metadata replaces languages such as Java. Java provides good performance, rich syntax and semantics, and abilities that are not reasonable to implement in metadata. For example, nowhere in the BPEL specification does it talk about persistence or database semantics; instead, Java handles all of the interactions between logic, data, and persistence.

> **NOTE** *Despite the advanced state of BPEL, I build the business processes in this chapter using the Java language. As long as you maintain a good structure and separation in the Java implementation, the process should be translatable into BPEL. Interestingly, a consumer of a business process does not know whether you use BPEL because the Web Service that surfaces a particular business process abstracts away the implementation details.*

Understanding the Motivation for the Business Process Pattern

Overall, the intent of the Business Process (Composition) pattern is to illustrate and provide guidance for combining business activities into a single, consumable Web Service with a well-defined interface.

This pattern is also an attempt to change your mindset from a Java-language, object-oriented perspective to a business process perspective. Rather than envisioning a Web Service as a reflection of an object model, you start to consider the business process as the primary construct in the application. Eventually, particular business activities within the business process are business object methods or business object collections, but the bulk of the thought goes into design and implementation of the coarser business process.

There is quite a bit of overlap between the concept of the business process and the concept of composition, thus their inclusion in this book as a single pattern. The only time the terms are not interchangeable is when you forgo using business processes altogether and leverage Web Services as an object proxy model. Nonetheless, the general structure easily translates between the two paradigms.

Implementing a Simple Business Process Structure

This chapter does not cover all of the features of BPEL or other metadata models; instead, it focuses on the core constructs involved in creating business activities to build a business process. With these constructs, you can create business processes in Java or any other language. Figure 8-2 shows the structure of the Business Process (Composition) pattern.

In Figure 8-2, it is important to treat the diagram as a set of relationships rather than a series of classes and objects. In the case of BPEL, the BusinessProcessImpl is actually a BPEL file with XML-based metadata. A BPEL container receives the file and exposes it via the `BusinessProcess`, a WSDL interface definition. The metadata defines a sequence of business activities, other business processes, and data relationships between the activities and processes that are necessary to fulfill the complete sequence. A business activity may or may not be another business process.

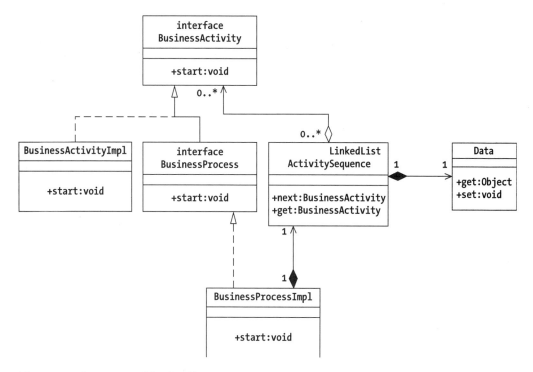

Figure 8-2. Structure of the Business Process (Composition) pattern

The business process could also be a set of Java class relationships with the `BusinessProcess` being a Java interface exposing the `BusinessProcessImpl` concrete class. The sequence itself becomes an ordered collection of steps to complete a particular business process, and the business activities are other Java classes or Web Services.

Understanding the Components of a Business Process (Composition)

Figure 8-2 is a basic Business Process (Composition) pattern. Depending on the mechanisms you use to construct a business process, the method of processing a sequence of business activities can be extremely complex. Further, the way the data flows between business activities can become complex as well. The primary components of a business process are the following:

BusinessProcess: This is the interface to the business process. In reality, there are multiple interfaces to the business process that all represent the same process but are built for different consumers. One registered with UDDI represents a common interface to the business process for any architecture to use or implement a Web Service adhering to the interface guidelines. This interface does not contain binding information. Instead, it is like an interface with no concrete implementation behind it—simply a specification to the Web Service that others could build. Other interfaces in UDDI are associated with specific instances of the business process that clients bind to for usage. Finally, the interface in UDDI is translated to a language-specific interface that clients write the business process implementation to in a specific programming language such as Java. Web Service users call the final interface and implementation through the interfaces registered with UDDI. Businesses look up the WSDL version of the interface via the UDDI query mechanisms and use it as a means of determining the contract for a business process for client usage or for implementation of the business process.

BusinessProcessImpl: The business process is the service implementation of the business process interface. As Web Services mature, there will be fewer complex business processes in Java and more residing in generic metadata languages processed by business process engines. BPEL is one of these metadata languages. Before metadata implementations of business processes are ubiquitous, metadata languages must address security, transactional mechanisms, and performance. The implementation class, combined with the business activities themselves, contains the logic to form a complex state machine. In the case that the process is simply a set of steps with no complex logic, the process implementation can simply execute each activity in the `ActivitySequence` in order.

ActivitySequence: The sequence is the list of business activities that must occur before the business process completes. This sequence does not have to be synchronous in nature, and it is not required to follow a single path. Several steps in the business process may execute asynchronously, with synchronization points built into the process. Further, complex branching implemented in a business process implementation may select the proper business activity based on data collected as the sequence progresses. For example, if a customer resides within five miles, you would want to schedule one of your trucks to deliver coffee rather than submit the order to a shipper for pickup and delivery.

Data: Each business activity may have side effects in the form of new data that other business activities require. For example, when creating an order, you want to retrieve the credit card number for a customer and use the customer identity as a key to an order. In both cases, the business activity simply retrieves the customer identifier from a common pool of data. Like the sequence itself, different data may route to a particular business activity based on the results of some of the data or on the results of a business activity. For example, a pound of coffee that a customer purchases as a gift would not ship to the customer's address; instead, it would ship to an alternate address. In this case, you must ensure that the business activity used for shipping obtains the alternate shipping address rather than the primary shipping address.

BusinessActivity: Each business activity is a unit of work that is a prerequisite to completing a business process. A business activity may itself be a business process but is not required to be one. Instead, the designer that breaks down the system for implementation is responsible for choosing the correct coarseness for a particular business activity. A business activity could even be a single method call on an object.

Throughout the previous definitions, I have purposely stayed away from tying one of the components to a particular implementation. There is no reason that each of the above units must be a class in Java. Instead, look at the business process as a composition of completed steps that affect the business; you can worry about the concrete mechanisms to implement the business process later in the chapter.

Understanding Collaborations Between Business Process Components

Clients access a Web Service defined by the `BusinessProcess`. The `BusinessProcessImpl` implements the `BusinessProcess` and processes the client request after invocation. Typically there will be a `start()` operation or similar operation (the `Command` pattern forms a simple business process structure and can have a similar interface).

The business process implementation processes the sequence of business activities based on data the activities may have stored as side effects of their execution. There are varieties of logical conditions that may be applicable between sequential steps of a business process, depending on how expressive the business process language is. The mechanism used to represent a sequence of business activities must be rich enough to embody all of the business processes in a particular domain. The sequence itself is merely an ordered collection of business activities with enough contextual information to allow the business process to call the activities in the appropriate order.

The business process implementation and business process activities are responsible for maintaining data and moving it to individual business activities, whereas the business activities use the data to determine how to process an individual step in the business process. Figure 8-3 shows a sequence diagram illustrating the base interactions that fulfill a business process.

Business activities are not typically self-contained; rather, they rely on individual business objects, business object collections, or other business processes to achieve a particular task within the business process. For example, creating a sales order in your own application requires constructing an order object (a collected business object) and associating a set of order lines (a collection of business objects). Each of these steps to create and insert data into collections is a business activity that interacts with additional business constructs.

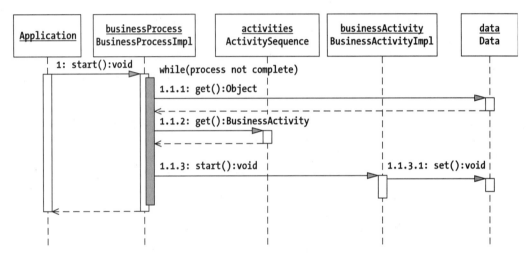

Figure 8-3. Business process execution sequence

Preparing to Implement a Business Process (Composition)

Determining how to implement a business process is one of the keys to successful application programming. The primary concerns during the implementation phase of business processes revolve around performance, flexibility, and granularity of the business process:

Keep the business process implementation flexible: Business processes are a competitive advantage to businesses, and they often change as economic and competitive forces change. The application a business uses can either facilitate the business or hinder it. Using a business process modeling technique along with a metadata language is the goal of business processes. Implemented the right way, modeling can become the tool of the business rather than a tool of a programmer, allowing the business analyst to alter the flow of a business process at a moment's notice. Until standards are settled and modeling and metadata are as versatile as programming languages, this paradigm will be a tough sell to application implementers.

Different parts of a business process may have different performance requirements, so make sure you understand performance to a relatively granular level: An example of a business process with different performance characteristics is an order-to-fulfillment scenario. Consider a Web-based application: The user wants to determine if their order processed, but determining when the order ships is of less concern to the user. In effect, only the first portion of the business process needs to be performance sensitive, though the entire business process must scale.

Use standardized business process definitions and interfaces as often as possible: Over time, standard business process definitions will govern a large percentage of business application implementations. This change will occur in specific industries and ripple into others. Using an existing tModel containing a WSDL file to jump start your own business process will significantly reduce your effort in analysis and design, leaving only the internal system design and implementation.

Isolate business activities that span computer systems, architectures, and companies: The business activity is a convenient location to place logic that must leverage other Web Services to reach out of the application implementation. For example, the order-to-fulfillment scenario must communicate with a shipping process. Treating this unit of work as a business activity, you can isolate how you communicate with the shipper and the logic used to deal with the shipping. Later, you can replace the business activity with a few lines of code in the primary business process implementation.

Avoid exposing the internal object model to the business process interface: There are two primary reasons for avoiding the exposure of your internal object model. The first is to protect potential clients of your Web Service from complexity. The second is to protect you from limiting the application's capabilities by exposing too much of your implementation outside of the core tasks for your process. The business process can be a place where you isolate the underlying implementation from the client experience. By exposing too much of the underlying application model, you lose your ability to change the underlying model because of the effects the change would have on your external interface. Finally, remember that your client may not be using an object-oriented language. If you expose a robust object-model to your client, there is no guarantee that they will be able to consume it from an architecture that does not support objects. Further, the potential client of your Web Service may not understand the object-semantics that you attempt to force onto them.

Implementing a Business Process (Composition)

To illustrate how to construct a simple business process and how to compose business activities, you will look at a simple business process from the P.T. Monday Coffee Company domain. Specifically, a user will place an order for a particular product. This example is simplified; it does not have credit checking or the ability to search for additional product if it is not contained within your warehouse, but it will suffice to show the basics of composition and a business process.

From a user's perspective, the business process inputs include the following:

- A customer key that identifies the customer making the order

- An order structure that contains the key to the ordered products and the quantity of each product to order

The output from placing the order is a key to the order used by the customer or the application for tracking the progress of the order.

The sequence of steps that occurs within the business process is as follows:

1. An application starts the business process by submitting a `customerId`, an array of `productSkus`, and a matching array of `quantities`. The arrays of `productSkus` and `quantities` must match in size.

2. The business process puts the input data into the common pool of data for all of the business activities to access.

3. The business process determines that the first step is to determine if the products exist in the warehouse and reserve them.

4. The warehouse reservation business activity uses the common data structure for the product data and reserves the products in the warehouse. Assuming the activity completes successfully, the activity places a success record into the data structure and returns to the main business process.

5. The business process checks the state of the data structure and then launches the business activity to create the order.

6. After successful order creation, the business process launches an activity to notify the warehouse staff to send out the order.

7. After the process notifies the warehouse staff, the process finally returns an order identifier to the user.

All kinds of permutations of the previous sequence and potential locations can modify the process. For example, you could do additional validation along the way to ensure that a customer has enough credit for the order (you have customer credit card numbers stored in the customer information profile). You could also create the order identifier before going through the remainder of the steps, allowing the rest of the business process to execute asynchronously. This latter permutation requires some additional mechanics that Chapter 9, "Exploring the Asynchronous Business Process Pattern," discusses.

You can represent the previous business process in a variety of ways. You could use simple workflow diagrams for documentation, or you could explore the current generation of business modeling tools. High-end modeling tools generate the appropriate business process from the modeled diagram, much as Unified Modeling Language (UML) editors generate code from the diagram. Instead of using this approach, the next sections go into the construction of the business process based on the simple specifications mentioned previously.

Defining the Interface to a Business Process

Rather than starting with a service implementation, you will work from the interface to the service implementation this time. In theory, the future has a large set of standardized business process interfaces already available and accessible via a tModel in UDDI. Even now, there are working groups that help to define these standards and make them available.

> **NOTE** *See ebXML's Web site (*`http://www.ebxml.org/`*) or OASIS's Web site (*`http://www.oasis-open.org/`*) for more information on business process standards.*

The interface is a WSDL file with everything required to define a service, but without the location information for a particular service implementation. This file is similar to one you would retrieve from a tModel residing in UDDI for a generic service interface. Within the WSDL file are the following:

- Definitions of `Array_of_int` and `Array_of_String` types are in the first portion of the WSDL file. Both are complex types and therefore must be defined within the WSDL file.

- There are two message types defined in the WSDL file: `createProductOrderReceive` and `createProductOrderResponse`. The former defines the message for invoking the `ProductOrder` Web Service, the latter defines the expected return message.

- A single port type, product order, exists in the WSDL file. The port contains a single operation, `createProductOrder`.

- The file also contains a binding for the product order port, `ProductOrderSoapBinding`, but this binding goes ignored when you create your own service that adheres to the WSDL interface.

Using a tool provided with Apache Axis (WSDL2Java), you generate a Java interface for a service that adheres to the WSDL specification. This interface serves as the basis for the Java business process implementation. Other users of the WSDL file can implement the same business process interface in other languages. WSDL2Java generated the interface definition shown in Listing 8-1.

Listing 8-1. Interface Definition Generated from WSDL for a Business Process

```
package com.servicefoundry.books.webservices.processes;

public interface ProductOrder extends java.rmi.Remote {
  public java.lang.String
    createProductOrder(
        java.lang.String customer,
        java.lang.String[] productSkus,
        int[] quantity)
    throws java.rmi.RemoteException;
}
```

From the Java interface, you can see a reversal in techniques as to the complexity of the data passed to and from the process. In the previous chapters, you built up the complexity of the interface because you were essentially creating proxies to an object model. In this chapter, I have reversed that trend, even to the point of passing keys to the order, products, and customers as strings rather than key classes.

This change from a rich object model back to basic, flat data is an important trend for the application. As mentioned in the previous chapters, the richer the object model, the more difficult to translate the object model to the other architectures involved in the network. You will use the business process as a buffer to the object model. Users of the business process need only a small set of data types; you will manipulate the richer data structures from within the process.

Implementing the Business Process

Implementing the business process is similar to the pattern shown in Figure 8-2, but because you are using Java to implement the business process, you can add additional information to the generic pattern. Figure 8-4 illustrates the concrete example of the business process implementation for creating a new order. In the class structure, you keep the abstract definition of a business activity to provide flexibility and a generic sequence processing. The association between the ProductOrderImpl and the BusinessActivity is fulfilled by a LinkedList of business activities that need to complete to finish the business process itself. Recall that the previous section generated the ProductOrder interface from the WSDL file defining the business process interface. You modified some of the inheritance structure to facilitate the more generic BusinessProcess framework. Nonetheless, the data passed into the ProductOrderImpl on the createProductOrder operation (with the same signature as Listing 8-2) will be inserted to the common Hashtable data structure. All of the business activities access this data structure as a common data pool.

The logic for processing the individual business activities is in the createProductOrder method on the ProductOrderImpl class. After each business activity, the createProductOrder method places the result data into the Hashtable using a predefined key. This Hashtable contains all data accessible to a business activity; the only catch is that you should determine the keys to the data before creating the business process. Listing 8-2 illustrates a simple example of implementing a business process using this technique. The code is overly lightweight with respect to exception handling, but I wanted to keep the focus on the business process itself.

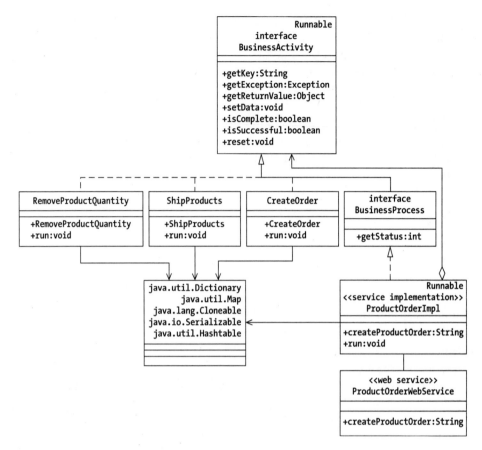

Figure 8-4. Product order business process

Listing 8-2. Implementing the Product Order Business Process

```java
public class ProductOrderImpl implements ProductOrder {
  LinkedList sequence = null;
  Hashtable data = null;

  public String createProductOrder(
    String customer,
    String[] productSkus,
    int[] quantity) throws java.rmi.RemoteException {

    setup();
    data.put("PRODUCT_ORDER.CUSTOMER.ID", customer);
    data.put("PRODUCT_ORDER.SKUS", productSkus);
    data.put("PRODUCT_ORDER.QUANTITIES", quantity);
```

```
  PersistenceManager pm = getPersistenceManager();
  Transaction t = pm.currentTransaction();
  t.begin();

  String orderId = null;
  boolean successful = true;

  Iterator i = sequence.iterator();
  while(i.hasNext() && successful) {
    BusinessActivity activity = i.next();
    activity.setData(data);
    activity.run();
    successful = activity.isSuccessful();
    data.put(activity.getKey(),
        activity.getReturnValue());
  }

  if(t.isActive() && successful){
    t.commit();
  } else {
    if(t.isActive() && !successful) {
      t.rollback();
    }
  }

  return orderId;
}

protected void setup() {
  sequence = new LinkedList();
  data = new Hashtable(5);

  BusinessActivity removeProducts = new
      RemoveProductQuantity();
  sequence.add(removeProducts);
  BusinessActivity createOrderLines =
      new CreateOrderLines();
  sequence.add(createOrderLines);
  BusinessActivity createOrder =
      new CreateOrder();
  sequence.add(createOrder);
}
```

```
protected PersistenceManager getPersistenceManager() {
  return JDOUtilities.getPersistenceManager();
}
protected PersistenceManager pm = null;

}
```

There are a couple of interesting points to note in Listing 8-2. First, by implementing the entire business process and all business activities in Java, the Java Data Objects (JDO) transactional capabilities help make the business process robust and keep the data within the application coherent. This ability becomes more difficult to implement as the business process and business activities remove themselves from the context of a particular language and start to span multiple companies and active systems. There are evolving transaction semantics for Web Services, but go into application planning assuming you will have to spend considerable time getting transaction scopes and fault tolerance correct.

A second interesting point to note about Listing 8-2 is the fine line between a business process, a business activity, and simple methods on objects. Simply put, a business activity can very well be another business process, but not all business activities will be formal business processes. Often, business activities will be more fine-grained than a business process. Object methods can represent a business process or a business activity. Most often, a series of object methods achieve a particular business process or activity.

After implementing the `ProductOrderImpl`, you create the appropriate WSDD file for Apache Axis and deploy it to the Axis engine. After that, clients can access your implementation of the `ProductOrder` interface, as defined by the WSDL structure you originally retrieved from UDDI.

Leveraging Business Processes in the Case Study

The case study leverages the business process as the primary interface to the outside world. The Business Object/Business Object Collection patterns, with respect to Web Services, are used internally and, in some cases, exposed but not expected to be consumed by clients other than yourself.

In some cases, a business process may consist of a single business activity. When this occurs, the business process constructs represent points of flexibility in the system. Without the business process abstraction, your application would become inflexible in certain business processes and, in theory, be less maintainable in the future. Further, without the business process abstraction, you will have a more difficult time interacting with applications that choose to standardize on a business process interface (assuming you use a standardized WSDL file for your business process interface). Simplifying the standardized interface would undermine the fundamental value of Web Services: interoperability.

The business processes in the application are not standards based. Depending on when you build your own application and what domain it is in, you may find existing business process standards and behavior guidelines. Be sure to allocate a proper amount of time to research and leverage standards early in development, preferably before creating your internal object model. The earlier you can reuse another person's (or group's) analysis, the more benefits you will derive from that analysis. Reusing a business process definition will shape the internal object model and its implementation of business activities.

Identifying Important Classes and Files in the Case Study

Table 8-1 shows the primary code discussed in this chapter that you should browse in the downloaded source code. This source code evolves over the next few chapters, so you will see some slight modifications in the source code. For this chapter, look primarily at the structure of the `ProductOrderImpl` class and the business activities on which it relies.

Table 8-1. Sample Location

FILE	LOCATION	DESCRIPTION
ProductOrderImpl. java	src\com\ servicefoundry\ books\webservices\ processes	The product order business process from which Listing 8-2 originated
ProductOrderTest. java	src\com\ servicefoundry\ books\webservices\ tests	A main program that uses the product order business process from a client program

Using Ant Targets to Run the Case Study

Table 8-2 describes the targets to run for the ant environment to see the programs and chapter samples in operation. Before running any samples, be sure you read and perform all of the install steps in Appendix A. Like the programs themselves, this sample evolves over the next few chapters, so there are some remaining concepts before you understand the whole test program and Web Service implementation.

Table 8-2. Ant Targets

TARGET	DESCRIPTION
testproductorder	Runs the product order sample business process

Summary

This chapter covered the third, and final, primary Web Service construct used in the case study. The business process is an abstraction of complex business logic that consists of one or more business activities, the logic and path in which the activities run, and the path that data takes through the business process. UDDI hosts the business process interface as a tModel. Clients and application builders who want to implement the business process retrieve the WSDL interface definition from UDDI and build language-specific interfaces to use for implementing the business process or accessing an existing implementation of the business process.

This chapter also discussed the ability to represent business processes in metadata through languages such as BPEL. This technique has advantages over specific programming languages because of its innate ability to prevent users from leveraging constructs available in a particular language and the metadata language's ability to limit the programming environment to only those constructs that are useful to a business process programmer. You can use BPEL in three ways: The first is as a representation of a business process model, the second is as a directly executable business process language in a container that interprets and runs the business process, the third is as a metadata representation from which you generate a business process implementation in a specific language, such as Java.

Additionally, the chapter introduced a simple example of a business process implementation and how to construct it from an existing WSDL file, located in UDDI. The business process in this chapter is synchronous, and no logic is required to determine the order or processing of the business activities. As business processes become more complex, several business activities execute at the same time, and some business activities may not execute at all. Further, the data that feeds a particular business activity may follow its own path and decisions within the business process.

With the business process pattern under your belt, you have completed the three primary constructs used in the case study. From here, you will enhance the constructs with some well-known and some not-so-well-known design patterns. For example, client applications often leverage event mechanisms to determine when a particular business process completes, especially when the business process is a long-running business process that you execute asynchronously. The next chapter explores a pattern to create an asynchronous business process, and after that you spend time discussing event patterns.

Related Patterns

Business processes are an important step in building your pattern catalog, but like the Business Object pattern, there is an additional pattern into which the business process fits. The business process is a necessary building block to the Asynchronous Business Process pattern, yet both have enough details that they can stand on their own. Other patterns help the Business Process pattern fulfill the tasks it is required to complete:

Business Object/Business Object Collection: These constructs embody many of the business activities called within the context of a business process. Further, in some models, the business object and business object collections may house the business processes themselves. I discourage the blending of the business object and business object collection with the business process and instead recommend keeping the business process as its own first-class construct.

Asynchronous Business Process: This is an evolution of the Business Process pattern. Business processes tend to be long-lived, and executing them synchronously frustrates clients. On the other hand, running a business process entirely asynchronously would be just as frustrating because there would be no accurate feedback on the submission of the order and a returned order identifier. The key is in fulfilling the expectations of the user while also allowing the bulk of the business process to run asynchronously.

Service Factory: As mentioned in the chapter, individual business activities are often first-class business processes themselves. Some of these nested business processes may not exist within your own business. The Service Factory pattern is a pattern similar to a class factory where the most applicable business process is located at runtime rather than statically bound at design time.

Additional Reading

- ebXML Web site: http://www.ebxml.org/

- OASIS Web site: http://www.oasis-open.org/

- Gamma, Erich et. al. *Design Patterns: Elements of Reusable Object-Oriented Software*. Addison-Wesley, 1995.

Exploring the Asynchronous Business Process Pattern

CALLS TO A BUSINESS PROCESS can take between a few milliseconds and a few days to complete. The variability lies in the coarseness of the business process as well as the dependent business activities. For example, from the time that a client submits an order to the time it becomes available for pickup by a shipping company may be a few minutes or a few days. In fact, the most interesting business processes will have this variability associated with them, whereas the length of business activities tend to be much more predictable. On the other hand, the aggregation of business activities to fulfill a business process complicates predictability.

Several application requirements come into play when determining what to do with unpredictable and long-running business processes. First, consider that clients usually use browser-based mechanisms for accessing applications based on Web Services and business processes. Users of browser-based interfaces do not expect a long wait for a business process to complete. To facilitate a 10-second response time in a browser-based interface (the generally agreed upon upper limit of a client's patience with browser-based interfaces), the core of the application logic must execute relatively quickly. Consider the number of layers of application above the business logic before you calculate the amount of time your business process has to respond:

- A browser-based user interface rendering mechanism must translate the user's action into actionable steps and then translate the results of the action(s) back to a graphical interface.

- If the business process leverages Web Services, the request must flow through the requesting language into the Web Services paradigm and then back into the language of the service implementation.

- Each step of the previous process is separated by an interprocess communication mechanism and, possibly, physical distance. These variables make the amount of time spent on communication between business activities the most unpredictable variable, eating up anywhere from a small percentage of your 10 seconds to more than 10 seconds.

The second influence on your asynchronous business process, from a requirement point of view, is the increase in browser-based interactivity and the acceptance of mail-based notification mechanisms for business process completion. Clients tend to accept that server-side business processes are complex, but they do not accept situations where no quick response occurs on the progress of a business process. In the event that the client has a session available, a Web application can deliver asynchronous notifications to the client when the business process makes progress. More often, the client's session is closed and Web applications should use email notification. In fact, the simplicity of email notification for delivering information on the progress of a business process quickly drives you toward this latter solution.

The notion of asynchronous behavior helps mitigate the unpredictable nature of business processes. This chapter examines asynchronous business processes in the Web Service environment. This chapter does not address how to provide notifications to a client that uses an asynchronous business process.

Seeing Asynchronous Business Processes in Practice

There is substantial precedent for asynchronous business processes. Consider virtually any browser-based storefront, payroll application, or calculation-intensive process. Clients take responsibility for launching business processes, and Web applications take responsibility for notifying the client of progress.

Figure 9-1 illustrates a high-level view of an asynchronous business process that a storefront may use, presented from the perspective of a client using the business process. In the flow diagram, a client selects a book to purchase and have delivered. After entering their account information, the client submits the order and information to the server for processing. The entire business process lasts until the client receives the book from the shipping company.

In reality, a client neither expects, nor do they want, to have to wait for control of their computer to return when they receive the book. Instead, a client detaches from the business process when there is sufficient information to fulfill the client's needs. The point at which the client separates from the business process tends to vary depending on the responses that a client expects immediately or the responses that a client expects from an alternate notification mechanism. For example, a client expects an order number and confirmation (even if they do not want to maintain their order number themselves) within 10 seconds. The client does not expect the application to block until the order reaches the shipping dock or arrives at their doorstep.

On the other hand, a business process that represents payroll processing starts from a scheduler acting as a client. The scheduler does not expect any response from the business process. Instead, the business process uses notification frameworks throughout the process to keep managers apprised of the progress of payroll processing. The two processes discussed have different points of detachment from the client. In general, there is no rule for detachment, only guidelines for client information and immediacy.

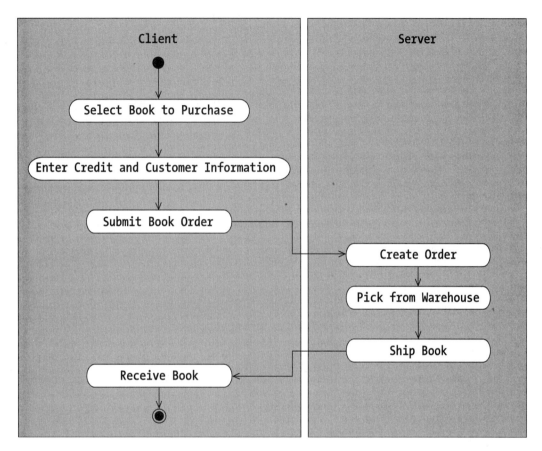

Figure 9-1. Task flow illustrating a book order process

Understanding the Asynchronous Business Process Structure

An asynchronous business process structure is different from an asynchronous thread of execution in a programming language. A thread is a transient structure that a platform introduces. The thread is bound to the length and boundaries of an application. A business process is a long-running process that can span applications and the length of an application.

Within a platform's representation of a thread of execution, there is typically a mechanism for the programmer to identify a particular thread and, subsequently, manipulate the thread via an identifier. With the Java platform, this mechanism is an object reference that an application holds to the thread. This reference is good only for the life of the application. The challenge in a Web Service environment, or even in a Java platform environment, is to create a mechanism for identifying a process that spans the life of an application. Web Services further this challenge to give a mechanism for identifying a process that also spans platforms and languages.

Figure 9-2 illustrates the basic structure of an asynchronous business process. The asynchronous business process representation assumes more of a job management structure than a single process structure. Internally, the service launches jobs and maintains their state. The interface to the BusinessProcessManager contains both methods to create business processes, as well as methods to determine the status of a particular business process. The BusinessProcess is a similar structure to that described in the previous chapter. An additional persistent object, ProcessState, is necessary to maintain information pertaining to a particular process. The process information often duplicates the data held by a particular business process. Considering that a thread running a business process will eventually terminate and disappear, the process state information remains available after the active process terminated. You can use this process information either to recover a process after a system crashes or to obtain process information after the entire process finishes.

The complexity of the asynchronous business process exists because of the need to track multiple processes. Consider that a client has no way of maintaining state in most Web-based application architectures and therefore cannot maintain a connection with a business process spawned by their request. Instead, clients require a unique identifier returned by the business process to identify the business process to the server. After process creation, clients make

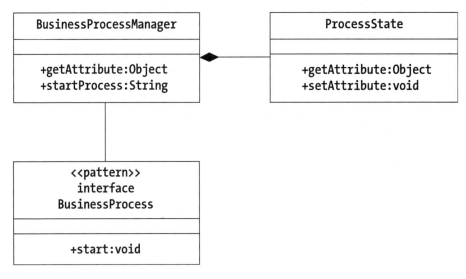

Figure 9-2. Structure of the Asynchronous Business Process pattern

requests relative to particular business processes by passing in the unique identifier that the service uses to locate the particular thread or results or status.

Understanding the Components of an Asynchronous Business Process

In addition to the business process components identified in the previous chapter that form the structure of the Business Process pattern, two additional classes form the structure of the Asynchronous Business Process pattern:

> **BusinessProcessManager:** The BusinessProcessManager is responsible for surfacing a way to start a business process and operate against an individual business process. A manager returns a unique identifier on creation of a new instance of a business process, or it uses that unique identifier for identifying a particular instance of the business process. The BusinessProcessManager facilitates the ability of clients to look up attributes of a particular business process that they may be interested in, such as the progress of an order. The BusinessProcessManager conceptually contains zero or more BusinessProcess instances as well as a ProcessState object instance.

> **ProcessState:** Instances of the business processes are transient in nature because the process has a well-defined start and termination point. However, the transience crosses application invocations instead of the normal definition of a thread of execution in a program. The ProcessState instance retains information about the specific business processes and any information that a client or server may need after a process completes. This information may also be valuable in the event that the process manager crashes or goes down for system maintenance.

Not illustrated in Figure 9-2 are the mechanisms that act between the business process manager, business processes, and the process state object instance. The BusinessProcessManager will likely have a thread pool at its disposal in which to start business processes. Upon termination, the threads return to the pool and the final process state information remains in the process state object instance. The process state may leverage a database for persistence, and thus the process manager uses an object/relational mechanism for gathering information about the final process state.

In a Web Service environment, it is highly unlikely that the interface to the business process manager is a generic, object-oriented, highly dynamic job manager. Although a particular process manager may use a generic job manager under the covers, Web Services users expect a self-contained component interface without a web of dependencies.

Understanding Asynchronous Business Process Collaborations

Figure 9-3 illustrates a simple design sequence using the asynchronous business process structure described previously. In the sequence, a client calls an instance of the BusinessProcessManager to create a new instance of a business process. The client then returns to the BusinessProcessManager to check an attribute of the business process, such as the status.

An interesting disconnect through this structure and sequence diagram is . the connection between a business process, the business process manager, and the process state. You have a few options for maintaining the connection between the two design components. One option is to allow each business process to retain its own process state information. In this case, retrieval of process attributes goes to the business process rather than a separate process state object.

A second option puts the burden of coordination of the process and attributes on the BusinessProcessManager instance. In this second case, the BusinessProcess may have event interfaces on it so that the manager can keep it in sync with the process state information in the database. In the end, there is likely a compromise. Much of the state for a business process will reside within the business process itself, and there will probably be a process state object for tracking active processes.

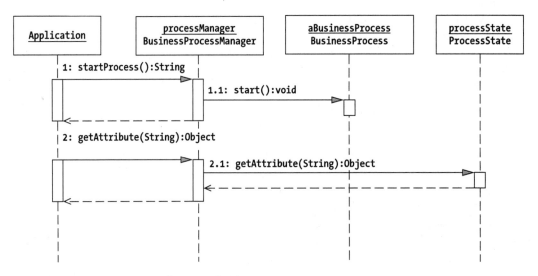

Figure 9-3. Asynchronous business process sequence

Preparing to Implement an Asynchronous Business Process

The guidelines for implementing a `BusinessProcessManager` and the Asynchronous Business Process pattern are similar to those for implementing any asynchronous processes. These guidelines center on performance and reusability of the infrastructure:

Build a generic job manager and reuse it for all business processes: Job management is a difficult and complex task for programmers. Funneling all business processes through a single job manager allows you to centralize policies for process priorities and simplify the management of the asynchronous behavior of your system.

Evaluate your clients carefully: If your business process can guarantee execution time under the client's threshold of pain, keep the process synchronous. Simply put, the burden of job management for a short process can double or triple the amount of time it takes to fulfill the process. Further, clients enjoy immediate responses from a system whenever possible. The corollary to this rule takes into account processes that sometimes or always exceed a client's threshold of pain. An application should create a consistent and usable interface. If an asynchronous job is needed some of the time, you may as well submit it to the job manager all of the time. Not only will the interface be consistent for the end user, but the programming environment is simpler and easier to manipulate.

Build job recovery into your job manager: Some of the business processes you implement can take days and weeks to complete. To ensure you do not lose important processes, the state must remain consistent and available in persistent storage. When an application restarts, the job manager needs to restart any partially completed business processes when the system went down.

Spend time understanding how external Business Process pattern implementations called from your own business activities fit into your own asynchronous business process implementation: Specifically, what are the identifiers and data returned that you have to retain and track, how does this data affect the status and progress of your own business process as reflected to the user, and is the asynchronous or synchronous behavior of a business process and the identifying data standardized? Each of these decisions can increase the complexity of your underlying Business Process pattern implementation as well as affect your asynchronous business process logic.

Use a thread pool for executing business processes: Business processes are the most active part of an application. Creation and completion of threads creates a heavy burden on the Java Virtual Machine's garbage collector. Using thread pooling helps alleviate some of this burden.

Implementing an Asynchronous Business Process

The implementation for the asynchronous business process is a modification of the simple business process presented in Chapter 8, "Exploring the Business Process Pattern." The interface to the BusinessProcess now includes the following:

- The return of a unique identifier when a client starts a business process

- The addition of interfaces to monitor attributes of the business process, including the status, given the unique identifier

Figure 9-4 illustrates the modifications to the business process. In addition to the updated interface, there is a new class, ProductOrderManager, which serves as the interface to the Web Service. The business process class, ProductOrderImpl, implements the java.lang.Runnable interface as it runs in its own thread in the Java platform.

Rather than having a client block until the process is complete, the client application returns from the Web Service call quickly, but it must maintain a durable unique identifier for later use. Because of this requirement, the business process invocation cannot be a completely asynchronous call because the service implementation generates the unique identifier, not the Web Service environment. Future client-invoked operations use the unique identifier to query the business process for a specific attribute—in this case, the status of the business process.

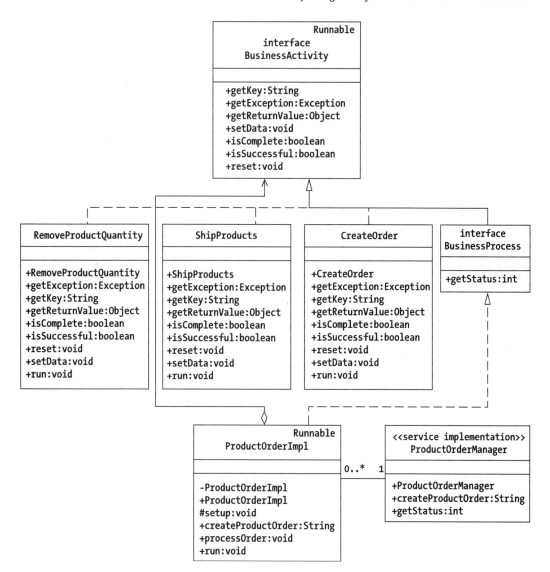

Figure 9-4. Asynchronous product ordering business process

Starting a Business Process

In the case of the business process for ordering products, the unique identifier to the business process is the key to an OrderImpl business object. The CreateOrder business activity creates the order instance that, in turn, returns a unique key to the ProductOrder business process. The ProductOrder business process passes this key on to the ProductOrderManager instance that, in turn, returns the key to the client. For this particular asynchronous business process, the OrderImpl business object serves as the location to retrieve process state; thus, the OrderImpl represents the ProcessState design component. Figure 9-5 shows this sequence of collaborations.

The primary difference between the invocation of the business process in this chapter and the one in the previous chapter is that this implementation returns to the client before the entire business process completes. The client then needs to save the unique identifier to the business process to check on the business process later. You are also calling the new Web Service interface, the ProcessOrderManager, though it is simply an evolution of the ProcessOrder Web Service from the previous chapter. The ProcessOrder business process itself still plays an important role as an internal implementation class.

Listing 9-1 shows the invocation of the business process through the architecture adapter representing the ProcessOrderManager to the Java client. The unique identifier returned from the start of the business process gets stored in a local instance variable for use later in the client application.

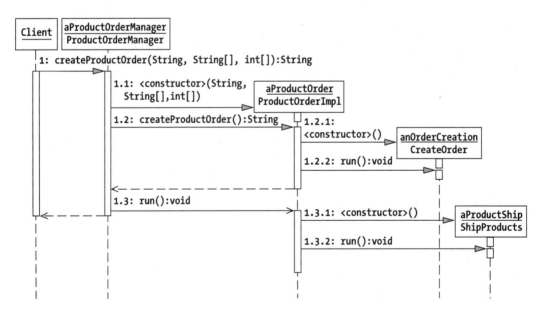

Figure 9-5. Sequence diagram for the product order asynchronous business process

Listing 9-1. Invocation of an Asynchronous Business Process

```
ProductOrderManagerService service =
  new ProductOrderManagerServiceLocator();
ProductOrderManager port = service.getProductOrderManager();
String customer = "1035664203330"; // id of paul monday
String productSkus[] = {"1035664206840"}; // id of French roast
int quantity[] = {2}
String jobIdentifier = port.createProductOrder(
  customer,
  productSkus,
  quantity);
```

Interestingly, the client's usage of a local instance variable for the process identifier storage creates a problem. Once the client exits, it will be difficult to locate any business processes that the client kicked off. There are several ways to deal with this situation. In the event that the client is a browser-based client, a cookie should be stored on the client that a server-side process can recover when the client reconnects. A specific mechanism for retaining process identifiers is outside of the scope of this book.

Querying Business Process Attributes

Once the client starts the business process, the client uses the unique identifier, saved as part of the creation process, to query various attributes of the business process. Figure 9-6 illustrates an application retrieving the status of the product order placed in the previous section, "Starting a Business Process."

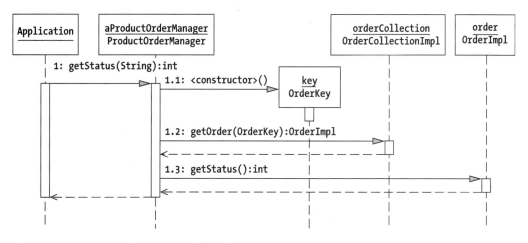

Figure 9-6. Querying the status of a product order

The Java client simply uses an architecture adapter to the ProcessOrderManager Web Service. The code reuses the jobIdentifier variable from Listing 9-1, as well as the port instance variable referring to the Web Service:

```
int jobStatus = port.getStatus(jobIdentifier);
```

There is one major loose end in the previous code—interpreting the status returned by the operation. There are varieties of ways to solve this problem, but they are all variations on the same theme: provide a robust enough contract for potential clients to interpret the return codes.

Leveraging Asynchronous Business Processes in the Case Study

The application makes heavy use of asynchronous business processes, one of which was demonstrated in the previous section, "Implementing an Asynchronous Business Process." No Business Process pattern implementations are first-class service implementations in the application. Instead, the Business Process pattern turns into a pure-Java implementation with the Asynchronous Business Process pattern fulfilling the role of the service implementation.

Table 9-1 shows the types of requirements that the asynchronous business process fulfills. In these requirements you see potentially long-running business process with clients being able to monitor the business process in multiple ways, through a Web Service (the programmatic access route) and through user interfaces.

Table 9-1. Requirements Facilitated by the Asynchronous Business Process

ID	REQUIREMENT
U2	The application shall allow customers to have access to current order status through a programmatic mechanism and through a user interface.
F3	The application shall provide programmatic access to submit orders, observe the fulfillment process, and pay invoices.

Identifying Important Classes and Files in the Case Study

Table 9-2 shows the primary code discussed in this chapter that you should browse in the downloaded source code. This source code undergoes a final evolution in Chapter 11, "Implementing the Observer Pattern," so you will see some slight modifications in the source code. For this chapter, you should look, primarily, at the structure of the ProductOrderManager class and the business process on which it relies. Also, examine the interaction between the business process, the business process manager, and the Order business object for the linkage between the business process and the process state.

Table 9-2. Sample Location

FILE	LOCATION	DESCRIPTION
ProductOrderManager.java	src\com\ servicefoundry\ books\webservices\ processes	The product order business process discussed throughout the chapter.
OrderCollectionImpl.java	src\com\ servicefoundry\ books\webservices\ entities	The point object for order collections. Each order within the collection serves as the persistent location to obtain information about a particular product order's state.
ProductOrderTest.java	src\com\ servicefoundry\ books\webservices\ tests	A main program that runs the sample.

Using Ant Targets to Run the Case Study

Table 9-3 describes the targets to run for the Ant environment to see the programs and chapter samples in operation. Before running any samples, be sure you read and perform all of the install steps in the appendix.

Table 9-3. Ant Targets

TARGET	DESCRIPTION
testproductorder	Runs the product order sample business process

Summary

This chapter introduced the asynchronous business process, a critical pattern that allows processes to run separately from the client thread that calls the business process. Virtually all complex or variable-length processes run asynchronously in the case study and in others. Business processes are unpredictable by nature, as discussed in this chapter, and it can become difficult to fulfill a user's need for a 10-second response time. Further, even the best programmers cannot affect the ability of a manual shipping process to take less time than 10 seconds. To achieve a complete order-to-fulfillment scenario for most direct sale customers, you would have to use *Star Trek*–like Transporter technology. Even then, it is doubtful that Scotty could get all of the books beamed to customers within 10 seconds during the holiday season.

There are many variations for how best to implement an asynchronous business process. The example in this chapter created the purchase order and used the order identifier as the unique identifier for the business process. This is convenient and easy to implement, but it drives you to creating custom implementations instead of using a simple submission straight to a job manager. On the other hand, there are more often than not business processes that need at least some processing done before decoupling from the client. A client will usually want to know that the company will immediately fulfill an order or that the purchase becomes a back order.

Realizing that each business process is unique yet has portions that are similar is an important step in deciding how to arrange the infrastructure that aids your service implementations. For example, splitting a business process into two parts and having a custom implementation coupled with a portion of the process that a job manager handles is the most likely implementation for your business process.

With the Asynchronous Business Process pattern under your belt, you have completed the primary constructs used in the case study. From here, you will enhance the constructs with some well-known and some not-so-well-known design patterns. For example, client applications often leverage event mechanisms to determine when an asynchronous business process completes, an obvious gap in this chapter.

Related Patterns

This section contains the patterns directly related to the Asynchronous Business Process pattern. Other patterns, such as the Business Object and Business Object Collection patterns, are indirectly related, often through the implementation of particular business activities within a process:

> **Business Process:** The Business Process pattern is the synchronous brother of the Asynchronous Business Process pattern. In most cases, the Asynchronous Business Process pattern subsumes this synchronous version simply to protect the client from variability in the length of time it takes to complete a business process.

Event Monitor: The Asynchronous Business Process pattern leaves a problem for clients—how to determine the progress of the business process. There is no way to determine when a business process completes, fails, or makes any progress with the initial structure of the Asynchronous Business Process pattern. An Event Monitor pattern is an inefficient, but effective, mechanism to track the progress of a business process.

Observer: Event monitors are inefficient mechanisms for tracking the progress of asynchronous business processes. A client may poll hundreds or thousands of times before the status changes when using an event monitor. An Observer, a classic GoF pattern, gives control back to the server for notifying a client when a change in a business process, or business object, takes place.

CHAPTER 10

Exploring the Event Monitor Pattern

THE PREVIOUS SEVEN PATTERNS were studies in the Web Service architecture and the basic patterns of components that leverage the Web Service architecture. The remainder of the book, starting with this chapter, focuses on patterns for using Web Services and for enhancing the basic patterns to fulfill broader needs. The first pattern in the usage category, the Event Monitor pattern, has broader application than Web Services. As companies integrate systems, it is commonplace to use monitoring as a mechanism to determine whether a data- or process-centric event occurred in a system.

An event monitor is, essentially, an event mechanism that relies on client implementation without server-side component participation. This makes the Event Monitor pattern an effective way to integrate applications without interfering with existing components. The Event Monitor pattern is one of the most basic patterns in this book. It is a client-side pattern designed to leverage existing server-side components rather than a pattern for designing new server-side components.

Seeing Event Monitors in Practice

Programmers often construct applications that contain business information but give no efficient way for a client to monitor changes in the information. Further, in cases where you implement the Publish/Subscribe design pattern (discussed in Chapter 12, "Implementing the Publish/Subscribe Pattern") or a related event mechanism, it is frequently the case that the following is true:

- The architecture of a client interested in the changes is a different architecture than the publish/subscribe mechanism supports.

- The granularity of the published events relating to the business information does not meet the client's needs.

169

An event monitor is a client-side design pattern that programmers implement outside of the scope of the server-side component. The event monitor polls the information in a business object, collection, or process for particular state changes and then notifies any components that registered with the event monitor.

Integrating Enterprise Applications

The most common scenario illustrating the usefulness of an event monitor is an Enterprise Application Integration (EAI) scenario. In EAI scenarios, heterogeneous applications get integrated to appear as seamless as possible. For example, if a user enters data for a customer using one application, that data should appear in other applications that the company uses. Even better, a user should be able to access all applications and data with a single user experience. Basically, integrating heterogeneous applications involves making more than one application work together as a single, cohesive implementation.

Often, the first task in making applications appear seamless is to integrate their databases. For example, two applications contain customer information that should be coordinated between the integrated systems. After the integration process, users will be able to enter customer information in one application and have the data in the second application automatically update. In a system that is not integrated, users must enter customer information in two separate applications.

Databases rarely have effective publish/subscribe mechanisms attached to them. Using the Event Monitor pattern, you can produce a mechanism that moves data from one database to the other as changes occur; this is termed *near-real-time* data transfer, as shown in Figure 10-1. The event monitor watches both databases, and when a change occurs in one, the event monitor inserts a similar change into the second database.

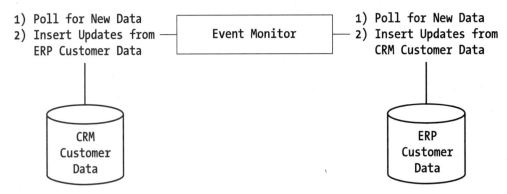

Figure 10-1. Polling databases for change

Scenarios like those in Figure 10-1 occur frequently in complex integration strategies. Often, rather than using a single component, the event monitor posts the change onto an event bus that, in turn, allows any number of listeners to receive the change and convert it to the format necessary for their own components.

Using Web Services and Event Monitors

Clients of Web Services have many opportunities to leverage an event monitor. Event monitors are popular in Web Services for several reasons:

Standardization (or lack thereof): Because there is no standardized event mechanism in Web Services, clients of Web Services must construct their own way to determine when data changes. An event monitor is a simple mechanism that a client controls for detecting events.

Appropriate level of granularity: Client architectures, the data that clients expect to monitor, and the level of event granularity for Web Services are extremely unpredictable when deployed for general usage on the Internet. As a result, the server component creator cannot easily predict what type of events clients require. For these reasons, a client will often have to construct their own mechanism for detecting the appropriate events.

Easy integration: Businesses often deploy Web Services into EAI scenarios as mechanisms to access data and processes in an existing application. In these cases, the Web Service serves as a conduit to one or more database table or process. Despite the Web Service interface, clients still require a mechanism to determine when particular events occur in the data residing in the application. Event monitors are easy to add without intruding on code already deployed into a client environment.

In a Web Service environment, a client is the most likely user of an event monitor. You will likely find many scenarios where a partner gives you a Web Service interface or you find an available Web Service with data or processes that you require, and you build a client around that Web Service. Consider the case of a bank that wants to provide partners with a mechanism for checking home mortgage rates. Rather than architecting a full-blown event strategy, the bank's first version of the Web Service will likely contain an interface for entering the term and type of mortgage and capabilities for returning a rate for the mortgage. It would be difficult for you to tell the bank to modify its Web Service. As a result, you would poll the mortgage service on a regular interval so that you can track the rate changes.

With Web Services, you would write the client-side event monitor in the native client architecture, such as the object-oriented Java environment, and continuously poll and retrieve updates from the target Web Service, as shown in Figure 10-2. In the figure, the event monitor implements a client-side notification mechanism so that multiple clients can use the same event monitor.

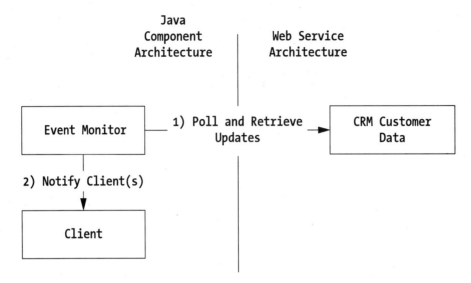

Figure 10-2. Web Service polling structure

This pattern applies to just about any Web Service domain. For example, you could use the event monitor to determine when changes occur to customer data in a Customer Relationship Management (CRM) application. The application with the event monitor could then synchronize its own data with the external CRM application's data.

Understanding the Event Monitor Structure

An event monitor can take on a variety of structures. The one discussed in this section assumes that the event monitor is a component within a larger architecture. The event monitor serves other components within the architecture through the Observer pattern implemented in the Java language. The Observer pattern, as implemented in Java, gives a mechanism for allowing clients to register with a target object and thereafter receive events from the target when data changes. Chapter 11, "Implementing the Observer Pattern" discusses the Observer pattern and how it relates to Web Services in greater depth. For this chapter, you will look at the Observer pattern merely as a mechanism for allowing a client to have multiple interested components use a single instance of the event monitor.

Figure 10-3 illustrates the structure of the Event Monitor pattern. Event monitors are rarely generic enough to service any business object, business object collection, or business process. Instead, you create as much isolation as possible by creating an information snapshot that is replaceable at compile time. By doing so you can change quickly to service other targets or facilitate more rapid change if you become interested in different data.

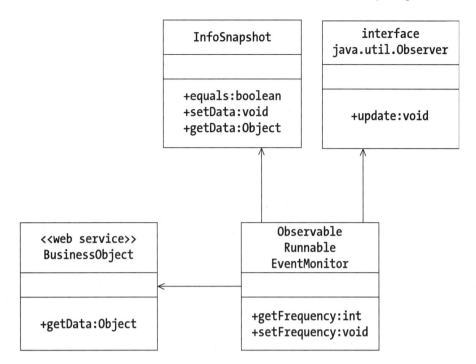

Figure 10-3. Event monitor structure

Unfortunately, without the participation of the component designer for the target object—in this case, the target Web Service (the business object, collection, or process)—a high amount of customization goes into creating each event monitor. Companies that eliminate and ease the burden of creating customized event monitors make substantial profit from their tools. Typically, the event monitor is part of an end-to-end solution for integrating two applications, but event monitoring certainly is useful beyond this relatively limited tool domain. An example is a monitoring framework that scrutinizes device status. It is highly unlikely that hardware devices expose events for the exact needs of your software, especially in the event that the hardware device goes offline. For this scenario, an event monitor fits your needs to determine when a particular device goes offline.

Understanding the Components of an Event Monitor

The Event Monitor pattern employs several components spread across processes and physical computer systems. On one system, the target of the event monitor makes important information available that clients must monitor. The event monitor, residing in another process space, uses a proxy (in this case, an architecture adapter) to the target for contacting and retrieving information. The following interfaces and classes are typical in an event monitoring scenario:

EventMonitor: The EventMonitor class contains logic that interacts with one or more business objects to determine when an event of interest occurred in the business objects. This logic is typically custom built for each type of event that can occur in the target business objects. A copy of the latest data must be stored internally to the event monitor, in the InfoSnapshot, to determine what data, if any, changed from the last query of the target object. The EventMonitor class typically runs within its own thread, freeing it up to look for changes in the target object independent of the primary application thread. The EventMonitor class implements the Runnable interface required by Java to run in its own thread. The EventMonitor can facilitate multiple listeners to the events that it is watching for from the target business object. The Observable interface that the EventMonitor class extends is merely the Java language–supplied interface for the Observer pattern.

Observer: Components interested in changes to the target object implement the Observer interface. A class implementing the Observer interface can register with the event monitor through the observable interface that it implements.

InfoSnapshot: The InfoSnapshot class encapsulates the exact changes that a particular event monitor is looking for in a data set made available from the business object. An information snapshot is highly dependent and tightly coupled to the event monitor; however, it does slightly partition responsibilities to allow easier modification of the application. Because of this separation of code, the author of an EventMonitor class can just worry about interacting with and gathering data, and the logic for determining interesting changes can be programmed and changed separately.

BusinessObject: The BusinessObject is entirely out of the sphere of control for the event monitor. The target of the event monitor does not have to be a business object; it could just as well be a business object collection or a business process. In this book, the business object is a Web Service, but this pattern applies generically with the business object being a class or service in a different architecture.

Many of these classes are optional. For example, an event monitor used by a single component may not implement the observer/observable relationship and instead implement a proprietary interface between the event monitor and the interested component in the event monitor's architecture.

Understanding Event Monitor Collaborations

Collaborations between the involved components are relatively straight-forward. The EventMonitor class uses custom logic to interact with the BusinessObject Web Service or another basic object or process pattern. This interaction connects to the target business object and retrieves all of the necessary information to determine if a useful event occurred in the business object. The EventMonitor class takes the new information and gives it to the information snapshot that encapsulates the actual comparison logic. This separation of responsibility simplifies the coding of the event monitor and can help extend the event monitor to allow different policies for determining when an event occurred.

Clients in the EventMonitor class's architecture register with the event monitor through the event monitor's Observable interface. When significant events occur, the event monitor is responsible for delivering the events to the interested parties. Figure 10-4 shows the entire sequence.

The application responsible for instantiating the event monitor uses the Runnable interface to dispatch the event monitor into its own thread. An event monitor does not have to have its own thread of control, but it typically does, allowing the application programmer independence from the wide performance variance that the target business objects may have. Figure 10-4 does not show this startup portion of the sequence diagram.

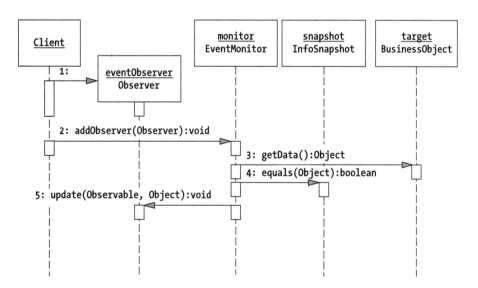

Figure 10-4. Collaborations between design components

Preparing to Implement Event Monitors

Implementations of the event monitor vary widely. The following are a few guidelines for building an effective event monitor:

Apply the Observer pattern to the event monitor so that more than one observer can use a single event monitor: This is perhaps the biggest performance boost you can achieve in terms of network bandwidth and processor performance. Often, many parts of an application will be interested in changes to a set of data from the original business entity. Allowing a single event monitor to query the business entity will substantially reduce the amount of overhead on both the system with the event monitor as well as the system in which the business entity resides.

Allow control of polling frequency: It is difficult to predict how a component programmer may use a component such as an EventMonitor class beyond its original conceived purpose. Further, it is difficult to predict an application's requirements in terms of desired event frequency balanced with performance. For these reasons, you will want to allow configuration of the EventMonitor class's polling frequency. Consider the case where a piece of data changes once every second. Over the course of a day, observer-based systems would process 86,400 data transactions in each system. This is useful if the client requires the data immediately upon change. However, clients require only periodic updates in many scenarios. For example, rather than getting individual event notifications for stock that is depleted, why not receive out-of-stock events once per day before the application places the daily replenishment order? In this case, 86,399 more event notifications took place than were necessary. Changing the monitoring frequency to once every 24 hours avoids overhead.

Minimize the amount of data transferred: Creating a minimal set of data to be queried and returned during a polling operation can save network bandwidth and create better performance for the event monitor. For example, rather than requesting the entire state of an object, the application should simply request the properties on which you rely. Consider the example of an order with several line items. In some cases, each line item ships to a customer separately, in which case the customer wants notification on each shipped line item. This is a fine-grained mechanism that says that each time an order line switches to *Shipped*, you send a notification. On the other hand, clients also want a final ship notice when all order lines have shipped. For this second event, you need a custom granularity that waits to fire until all lines are marked *Shipped*. This second mechanism could also be used to mark the overall order as *Shipped* and do any additional processing that must occur to close the order and put it in the books.

It is worth talking about some of the dangers of using an event monitor as well. There are many cases where clients must use an event monitor but they do not consider all of the potential consequences of using an event monitor. The following are some of the dangers:

Potential for missed changes: There is a real danger of "missing" changes that occur in the BusinessObject class that is being observed by the EventMonitor class. No matter what frequency an event monitor uses to poll a process or object, multiple changes can occur to the data within the BusinessObject during the given polling period. The creator of an event monitor needs to consider this possibility. If missing a data change is catastrophic to the observer, an event monitor is not a good option. The only exception is if the event monitor can guarantee that the frequency of the polling is higher than the frequency with which updates can occur to the data.

Near-real-time mode is not real-time mode: A system implemented using event monitoring can appear to perform and operate quickly and in near-real-time mode. It is important to remember that this near-real-time operation is not the same as real-time operation. Event monitoring is simply not useful for systems that require real-time operation and reaction, such as medical devices. Fortunately, near-real-time event detection is more than adequate for most business systems.

Processor consumption: Architects and designers often overlook the topic of performance and processor consumption with respect to event monitoring. The practice of deferring these topics can be catastrophic when you consider the impact of deploying event monitors. Consider the case of a single event monitor polling each second and consuming a processor for five milliseconds. Consider a system where you deploy 200 of these event monitors and you will quickly learn what it means to have a system halt from overutilization. Further, this simple analysis only took into account the processor where the event monitors reside. To be complete, you would have to consider the processor utilization on the target system to fulfill the requests. A good strategy to mitigate the processor impact would be to consolidate event monitors using observer mechanisms for events that occur over the same data. This way a single event monitor could facilitate more than one client component, easing the burden of polling and comparing data. There is simply no substitute for thinking about performance up front.

Bandwidth consumption: Just as event monitors consume processor and cause performance bottlenecks, event monitors also chew up network bandwidth as they move state changes around a network. To consider the ramifications on network bandwidth, consider data requests that pass 1 kilobyte (KB) of data in an Extensible Markup Language (XML) document back and forth on each request. Now consider 200 of these requests occurring in a second, passing 200KB of data each second. This does not completely swamp today's 1 Megabyte (MB) or 10MB connections, but it certainly puts a dent in them, especially a 1MB network. In other words, attempt to minimize the amount of data transferred across the network on each polling cycle.

Implementing an Event Monitor

Generally, new applications with only inward facing dependencies do not require event monitors. Event monitors are often necessary when there are external dependencies to an application where the new application's design cannot influence the interface to the external dependency. This scenario is common in enterprise application integration scenarios, as well as scenarios where there is a wide variance between architectures, such as device management where a component architecture must interact with a storage appliance.

For this chapter's sample implementation, you will start with the business process built in Chapter 8, "Exploring the Business Process Pattern," and wrapped with a business process management interface in Chapter 9, "Exploring the Asynchronous Business Process." Business processes and the manager allow clients to query the status of a particular business process while the business process works in a separate thread (and entirely separate computer).

As a Java-based client application, you can use the generic event monitor structure virtually off the shelf. Figure 10-5 illustrates the class diagram for the event monitor portion of the application. The ProductOrderImpl class is your architecture adapter that translates Java-based method requests to the Web Service implementing the order creation process (actually, this is more of a logical abstraction of the monitoring process; you must actually monitor the order creation process through the business process manager).

ProductOrderEventMonitor is the primary class that drives contact with the Web Service, retrieves relevant information, and funnels that information to the snapshot class for comparison of data between time slices. The information snapshot, now OrderStatusInfoSnapshot, encapsulates equality tests between the previous status and the status retrieved by the order monitor. If the status changes between monitoring cycles, the order monitor will use the Java Observable implementation class provided by the Java class libraries. The order monitor itself runs in a thread created by the application program consuming the monitor.

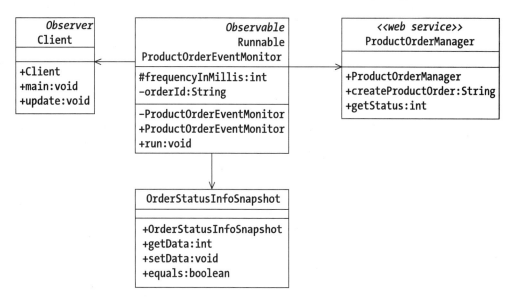

Figure 10-5. Event monitor implementation class diagram

In terms of pattern implementation, the event monitor is relatively straightforward. Two pieces of code expose the bulk of the event monitor functionality: the invocation of the order monitor and the interaction with the order business process.

Invoking the Event Monitor

You will first tackle how to invoke the order event monitor. The next section, "Monitoring the Web Service for Status Changes," explains what occurs within the event monitor after the application spawns the event monitor thread and registers an interest in changes detected by the event monitor.

Invoking the order event monitor, in this scenario, is a simple constructor call. Once the new object instance is in hand, two interfaces on the class drive your next actions. First, the event monitor implements the Runnable interface, making the event monitor easy to dispatch into a thread that allows the event monitor to process changes independent of the primary application thread. Second, because the thread is separate from your own thread, you use the Observable interface to register an interest in any detected changes. Listing 10-1 illustrates this scenario.

Listing 10-1. Application Invocation of an Event Monitor

```
ProductOrderEventMonitor em =
    new ProductOrderEventMonitor(orderId, 5000);
em.addObserver(c);
Thread t = new Thread(em);
t.start();
```

All of the interactions between the client of the event monitor and the event monitor itself take place within the Java language and, in fact, in the same Java Virtual Machine. You first create an instance of the event monitor passing in an order identifier. The order identifier originated outside of the piece of code, likely saved when you created the product order.

You then add your own instance, c, as an observer of changes that the event monitor detects. You register through the interfaces exposed by the Observable implementation that the event monitor subclasses. Next, you create a new thread and start it, allowing the event monitor to poll the product order status every five seconds independent of your own thread of control.

Upon receiving an event of interest, the event monitor calls back to your own object instance, c, through the Observer interface method that the class implements. Listing 10-2 shows a simple implementation of a callback method that fulfills the Observer contract.

Listing 10-2. Callback Method on the Observer Interface and Client to the Event Monitor

```
public void update(java.util.Observable observable, Object obj) {
    System.out.println("Received update");
    OrderStatusInfoSnapshot info = (OrderStatusInfoSnapshot)obj;
    System.out.println("Status changed to: "+info.getData());
}
```

Listing 10-2 simply prints the data that the event monitor flagged as changed and returned to you through the second parameter on the update method. In practice, the contents of the second parameter are fixed by contract by the event monitor. Clients have to understand the contents of the second parameter and whether it contains a structured document or a specific Java class type.

Monitoring the Web Service for Status Changes

Once the application created the event monitor and started the thread that the event monitor runs within, it starts monitoring the target Web Service. Using the architecture adapters generated by Axis makes implementing the event monitor straightforward. In fact, ignoring the setup code, the event monitor appears to be a simple loop that queries a Java class for information. Listing 10-3 illustrates the setup and a simple algorithm for polling the target business process for the latest status of the process.

Listing 10-3. Setting Up and Monitoring a Business Process

```
public void run() {
    try {
        ProductOrderImplService service =
            new ProductOrderImplServiceLocator();
        ProductOrderImpl port = service.getProductOrder();

        OrderStatusInfoSnapshot snapshot = new OrderStatusInfoSnapshot();
        OrderStatusInfoSnapshot currentData =
            new OrderStatusInfoSnapshot();

        while(true){
            int status = port.getStatus(orderId);
            currentData.setData(status);
            if(!snapshot.equals(currentData)){
                snapshot.setData(status);
                setChanged();
                notifyObservers(snapshot);
            }
            try {
                Thread.sleep(frequencyInMillis);
            } catch (InterruptedException ie) {

            }
        }
    } catch(Exception e){
        e.printStackTrace();
    }
}
```

Listing 10-3 first sets up the architecture adapter, sets up an object instance of the ProductOrderImpl class generated by Axis, and then creates a baseline OrderStatusInfoSnapshot to compare new and old values. Once these object instances are set up, you go into a loop to check the target business process identified by orderId that you passed in the order identifier when you created the event monitor.

Each check of the status then determines if the current data is different from the last version of the data with the `equals` method on the information snapshot. If the data changed, `equals` returns false and you notify the observers of the change. Notice that you send a copy of the snapshot to the observers so that they will have a copy of the new data and not have to call back to the event monitor to retrieve the data. At the end of the loop, the code puts the thread to sleep for the allotted amount of time before polling the target business process again.

Leveraging Event Monitors in the Case Study

The P.T. Monday Coffee Company application is interesting in that you are defining the end-to-end interfaces and implementations for all parties involved. With this type of leverage, it is unlikely that you will use an event monitor in the application. The primary location for the event monitor will come either when outside applications attempt to use your services or when you attempt to integrate your business with a company over which you do not have leverage.

In the first case, it is difficult to predict all of the places where explicit registration and notification are necessary for every potential customer. For example, a future customer may be interested every time your company updates the product catalog or individual prices for products. Rather than trying to overdesign your Web Service for these infrequent uses, you have to rely on exposing enough information to allow clients to locate their own interesting data and data changes. It is safe to say that if you build a popular set of Web Services, you will not be able to predict every way that someone wants to leverage your information. One way to determine locations that client may use event monitors on your services is to look at your requirements, as shown in Table 10-1. Any time there is information that changes, a customer may poll this information regularly, perhaps several times in a day.

Table 10-1. Requirements Identifying Places That Clients May Use Event Monitors

ID	REQUIREMENT
B1	The application shall have the ability to integrate into the reseller's value chain.
U2	The application shall allow customers to access the current order status through a programmatic mechanism and through a user interface.
U3	The application shall enable a customer to access product catalog and sale information through a user interface and programmatically.
F3	The application shall provide programmatic access to submit orders, observe the fulfillment process, and pay invoices.

The second case when you may use the event monitor in your own application is to monitor the Web Services from another company. It is highly likely that you will eventually integrate with a company that does not adhere to your own technical model definitions and that does not surface all of the interfaces you need. When you reach this point, you will have to employ an event monitor to look for changes in the Web Services you leverage. Again, you can look at your own requirements to determine locations in your applications that you may have to employ an event monitor. Table 10-2 identifies a few of these requirements that should raise a red flag. For example, for requirement B2, you may want to have an event monitor that watches for changes in prices of your bean suppliers' catalogs, thus always maintaining a low price for your supply.

Table 10-2. Requirements Identifying Places That You May Use Event Monitors on External Services

ID	REQUIREMENT
B2	The application shall have the ability to integrate bean suppliers into the company's value chain.
F9	The inventory management system shall automatically request additional beans from suppliers based on management-configured parameters for the definition of low supplies and grower preferences.

Just as all of the requirements in Table 10-2 identify places where you may employ an event monitor in your application; they also identify places where you may create or use more robust, server-side event mechanisms. The next two chapters—Chapter 11, "Implementing the Observer Pattern," and Chapter 12, "Implementing the Publish/Subscribe Pattern"—go into more details on planned event mechanisms.

Identifying Important Classes and Files in the Case Study

Table 10-3 identifies the primary code discussed in this chapter, as well as related files of interest to you from the downloaded samples.

Table 10-3. Sample Location

FILE	LOCATION	DESCRIPTION
ProductOrderEventMonitor.java	src\com\servicefoundry\books\webservices\patterns\eventmonitor	The code from Listing 10-3 that monitors a remote Web Service from within a thread.
OrderStatusInfoSnapshot.java	src\com\servicefoundry\books\webservices\patterns\eventmonitor	Code to compare data between two snapshots of order information. The ProductOrderEvent Monitor class uses this class to determine if any significant data changed between order snapshots.

Using Ant Targets to Run the Case Study

Table 10-4 gives the targets to run for the Ant environment to see the programs and chapter samples in operation. Before running any samples, be sure you read and perform all of the install steps in the appendix.

Table 10-4. Ant Targets

TARGET	DESCRIPTION
testeventmonitor	Runs the client-side event monitor code.
changeorderstatus	A mechanism to change the order status. The event monitor that started using the testeventmonitor Ant target will react appropriately to the changed status.

Summary

This chapter explored the first simple pattern that leverages and works around some of the Web Service details. Clients create event monitors when they have little or no control over a server-side component, such as an independently created

Web Service, and need to be aware of state changes in the server-side component. The event monitor has many limitations, detailed in this chapter, with its primary strength being a client's ability to build the event monitor after the fact.

The sample code for the event monitor builds on top of the business process created in the previous two chapters. Business processes are often good targets for event monitors because they are long running and must run asynchronously.

Although event monitors may be necessary in programming, a better strategy is to build up adequate event interfaces before you deploy Web Services for client usage. Imagine having 100 independent clients polling your Web Service every second, or, worse, imagine 10,000 clients polling your Web Service every second. By providing appropriate event mechanisms, you control when and how often event delivery should occur.

Related Patterns

The two other patterns presented in this text that relate to events are the Observer and the Publish/Subscribe patterns. You can apply all of the event patterns on top of the existing Business Object, Business Object Collection, Business Process, or Asynchronous Business Process patterns:

Observer: Observers are a more natural representation of a notification model than the reliance on a client to mine your interfaces for state changes. Further, implementing the Observer pattern helps you regulate usage of your objects. In the case where you do not have many state changes, clients could poll your service too much. In the event that you change state quickly, a direct notification mechanism serves clients well so that they do not miss state changes. Whenever you can predict client interest in a particular state change, the Observer pattern is a worthwhile extension to your Web Service.

Publish/Subscribe: The Publish/Subscribe pattern is another event pattern variation that centralizes event publication and subscription responsibilities. The Publish/Subscribe pattern can facilitate observer-like event notifications, but it can also go beyond the observer to allow publication of events that do not correlate to a specific Web Service. The Publish/Subscribe pattern is common in applications that have dynamic aspects to them, such as the ability to add and remove services at runtime. Finally, the Publish/Subscribe pattern is valuable in scalable applications where registration with all of the objects that publish events becomes prohibitive.

Additional Reading

- Gamma, Erich et. al. *Design Patterns: Elements of Reusable Object-Oriented Software.* Addison-Wesley, 1995.

- Schmidt, Douglas C. *Pattern-Oriented Software Architecture, Volume 2: Patterns for Concurrent and Networked Objects.* Jon Wiley & Sons, 2000.

CHAPTER 11

Implementing the Observer Pattern

THE EVENT MONITOR PATTERN fulfills many needs, but it falls short in many other ways, as documented in Chapter 10, "Exploring the Event Monitor Pattern." Some of the shortcomings in the Event Monitor pattern include the following:

- **Client usage of the event monitor introduces an unpredictable variable to the Web Service that the monitor targets:** The more clients who need updates on data at regular intervals, the more impact your Web Service will have to facilitate.

- **Clients may miss important changes to an object state:** Because clients are not aware of changes between polling cycles, a client may miss important data and behave incorrectly. The result of enough misses will be a decrease in time between polling cycles as the client tries to catch all of the changes. This results in an increase in processor cycles that the Web Service consumes, an increase in bandwidth consumption, and an overall decrease in customer satisfaction.

The Observer pattern corrects many of the shortcomings of the Event Monitor pattern. The Observer pattern has many variations, each with subtle distinctions that are not necessarily "standardized." For the purpose of this book, the Observer pattern allows clients to register for event notifications with some object or service that contains an interesting state that may change. When a change in state occurs to the target object, the target object notifies the interested observers of the change.

One variation of the Observer pattern, the Publish/Subscribe pattern, uses an intermediate object or service for event registration and delivery rather than the primary object containing state. Chapter 12, "Implementing the Publish/Subscribe Pattern," covers the Publish/Subscribe pattern in more detail.

The event monitor has a distinct shortcoming when addressing the liveliness inherent in a system. One aspect of a system's overall liveliness is how quickly it reacts to user input or to underlying changes in data. The event monitor puts an artificial bound on the liveliness of the application, coupling the ability to react to a change to the polling cycle of the event monitor. By implementing the

Observer pattern, the target Web Service takes responsibility for delivering events to clients rather than forcing the clients to determine when events occur. Now, a client receives an event notification as soon as it possibly can, outside of a polling cycle, thus increasing the overall liveliness of the application.

This change in implementation also turns the responsibility of detecting a change from the observer of an object to the object itself. This responsibility lies naturally with the object because it already knows the change as it modifies the data. It also solves several problems created by forcing the client to determine when an event occurs in a server component. For example, a client does not have to worry about missing an important event. On the application hosting side, a Web Service does not have to be concerned with servicing hundreds or thousands of queries when no changes have occurred to the Web Service.

The Observer pattern is so important in practice that the Java language contains classes to help you implement the pattern. The book *Design Patterns: Elements of Reusable Object-Oriented Software* (Addison-Wesley, 1995) contains the original documentation for the Observer pattern. This chapter goes over the fundamentals of the Observer pattern and its implementation in a Web Service paradigm.

Seeing the Observer Pattern in Practice

There are many examples of the Observer pattern in practice. Java programs rely heavily on the pattern and Web Service implementations are beginning to use it to create more dynamic and timely interactions between services.

In Java, data objects are frequently implemented with the Observer pattern to facilitate user interfaces. As data changes, the data objects fire events to interested listeners, the observers. The observer then refreshes client user interfaces to stay in sync with the underlying data. Without the Observer pattern, or a similar event mechanism, a user must manually refresh a data view, much as an event monitor polls a data object looking for changes.

The Universal Description, Data, and Discovery (UDDI) version 3 specification recognizes the usefulness of the Observer pattern as well. In the specification, clients register to receive event notifications based on changes to particular business entities, services, templates, or models. Without the event pattern, users of UDDI data must occasionally check the UDDI registry for changes to elements on which they rely.

In the case study, the P.T. Monday Coffee Company application, you want to do everything you can to ensure customers have the latest information. Consider a restaurant that uses two separate coffee bean suppliers. In the case that both suppliers can fulfill a large order, the restaurant may purchase coffee beans based on price. You may have harvested this price from your Web Service earlier in the week, depending on the polling cycle of the event monitor. By allowing your partners to use an observer rather than an event monitor, they could possess the latest price data, an invaluable tool to a dynamic business. Further, managers at the restaurant can be constantly apprised of the progress of their order if the restaurant application programmers choose to use your Observer pattern implementation.

Understanding Data Models in Java and the Observer Pattern

The Java class libraries contain an implementation of the Observer pattern used as the basis for simple event models in Java classes and components often associated with data objects. This pattern implementation is useful in single-process Java programs. Objects that want to implement a mechanism for delivering notifications to observers extend the java.util.Observable class. Clients who want to register for events from the Observable class implement the java.util.Observer interface. The addObserver method on the Observable class, inherited by the concrete observable implementation, takes registrations for notifications using a reference to an Observer implementation as a target to call when an update occurs. Figure 11-1 shows the Java classes that implement the Observer pattern: the Observer and the Observable classes. Also in the diagram are examples of extensions; ConcreteObserver implements the Observer interface, and ConcreteObservable extends the Observable class.

In the Java implementation, the Observable class handles maintenance of observers that register with the Observable class. Further, the Observable class handles notification of the observers when a subclass changes the class and properly uses the setChanged method to indicate that a change occurred in the concrete implementation class.

An observer that wants to receive event notifications from a subclass of an Observable must implement the Observer interface. This implementation must provide a concrete update method that the observable calls when an update occurs to the target object.

Note that the ConcreteObservable class implements the Runnable interface, as the class must run in its own thread to deliver notifications. The implementation of the class pauses for a second and then delivers a notification to all registered observers. The ObserverDemo class is a simple driver program that registers the observer, an instance of ConcreteObserver, with the observable, an instance of ConcreteObservable. Listing 11-1 shows the ObserverDemo driver program.

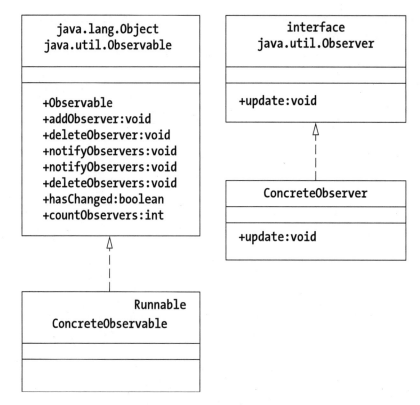

Figure 11-1. Java observer implementation class diagram

Listing 11-1. Java-Based Observer Pattern Driver Program

```
public class ObserverDemo {
    public static void main(String args[]) {
        ConcreteObservable observable = new ConcreteObservable();
        ConcreteObserver    observer  = new ConcreteObserver();
        observable.addObserver(observer);
        Thread t1 = new Thread(observable);
        t1.start();

        Object o = new Object();
        try {
            synchronized(o) {
                o.wait();
            }
        } catch(Exception e) {
            e.printStackTrace();
        }
    }
}
```

You will see similar code to Listing 11-1 in the "Implementing the Observer Pattern Using Web Services" section. Listing 11-1 simply instantiates the ConcreteObserver and ConcreteObservable classes and creates and starts a thread with the observable object instance running in it. The program registers the observer with the observable and then waits for notifications to arrive.

The Java Observer pattern implementation has a few limitations. One is that the pattern is strictly a single-process implementation. Another problem is that the Observable implementation is a class, not an interface. With the Java single-inheritance model, this implementation is extremely limiting. Often, programmers end up implementing their own Observable interface rather than tying their class to the Observable class at the root.

Using UDDI Version 3

Version 3 of the UDDI specification introduces the Observer pattern to UDDI directory implementations. The pattern supports the ability to notify interested parties of changes that occur to various directory entries. This feature allows clients to easily track a variety of registry activities, such as the following:

- **Periodic updates of technical models (tModels) that represent service interfaces:** The effect of a change to a tModel may be a required change to a program owned by your company.

- **Information updates about contacts at a company:** This type of notification is for helping maintain current contact information for individuals at a company or up-to-date mailing information.

- **The availability of registered companies for particular industries:** In this case, your application could monitor a UDDI registry to find growers and roasters that automate their supply chain.

Before the introduction of the pattern to UDDI, you had to locate changes to directory entries through a manual process or through—you guessed it—an implementation of the Event Monitor pattern.

Several pieces of the UDDI observer implementation make it particularly interesting. One such trait is its ability to send change notifications to an email address rather than an HTTP location. For many entities, UDDI entries will not change frequently, so email is a reasonable solution for change notification. With this mechanism, clients can monitor interface changes or business information changes without having to leave a Hypertext Transfer Protocol (HTTP) port open.

Another interesting trait of the UDDI subscription is the registration mechanism itself. A subscriber gives UDDI a binding key that can identify either Web

Service binding information or an email address for notifications. Although Web Services Description Language (WSDL) and Simple Object Access Protocol (SOAP) inherently support multiple transport protocols, the UDDI event specification is an interesting application of the binding information to allow single subscription methods to service both HTTP interfaces and the Simple Mail Transport Protocol (SMTP) interfaces.

At the time of writing, no version 3 UDDI implementations were available. The versatility of the approach may prove to be an exceptional model for implementing state-based notifications. Reading the UDDI version 3 specification and understanding the new notification mechanism is well worth your time because it is one of the first Web Services–based, standardized event notification mechanisms.

Understanding the Observer Structure

The Observer pattern implementation structure from the Java language, diagrammed in Figure 11-1, is richer than you need for the pattern definition. Further, the Observable class implementation needs to be an interface definition for use in the Web Service paradigm. You will use a structure that is more akin to the original Observer structure presented in the Gang of Four (GoF) design pattern book. These changes are enough to redraw Figure 11-1 with the updated structure, shown in Figure 11-2.

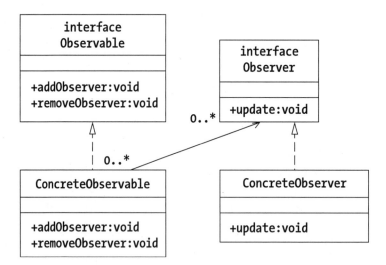

Figure 11-2. Observer pattern class diagram

Using the interface for the Observable implementation gives you more flexibility for the ConcreteObservable itself. Figure 11-2 also shows a better representation of the relationship between ConcreteObservable and Observer. This relationship is 0 or more on both the client and the supplier cardinality. An Observer can service multiple Observable relationships, as long as the logic in the Observer can tell the difference between the targets with which it registers.

Understanding Components of the Observer Pattern

The Observer pattern contains two critical interface definitions: Observer and Observable. In addition, two concrete Web Service implementations perform the collaborations. The components are as follows:

Observable: This is the interface to a Web Service that contains data of interest to others. For example, business processes typically have the process status associated with them. As processes change state, perhaps from packaging to shipping, clients will want notification to update their own data and, perhaps, a user of the receiving application. There are two primary operations, an addObserver and a removeObserver operation. The addObserver method, which takes a single parameter of the location of the particular Observer implementation, adds a particular concrete observer to the list of observers to notify when a state change occurs. The removeObserver operation removes a particular Observer from the list of observers to notify. Identification of an observer's location can occur in a variety of ways. You can use a string with the binding information or a more robust identifier such as a tModel or a WSDL file that contains binding information.

ConcreteObservable: The concrete implementation of the Observable interface bears the responsibility for maintaining a list of Observers interested in state changes. The service implementation maintains a list of the target clients and delivers the notifications to the target Observer.

Observer: The Observer is the definition of the interface that the concrete observable implementation calls to notify a client of a change to a business entity, collection, or process. There is only a single important operation on this method: the update operation. The Observable implementation calls this operation for change notification.

ConcreteObserver: The concrete observer adheres to the Observer interface. Upon changing state, the concrete observable delivers a message to each concrete observer registered in its list of interested parties. ConcreteObservable requires the address of ConcreteObserver, typically a Uniform Resource Locator (URL), in order to bind to ConcreteObserver. The ConcreteObserver implementation then acts on the update.

Understanding Observer Collaborations

The collaborations in the Observer pattern occur between the concrete implementations, the ConcreteObservable and the ConcreteObserver. The collaborations
between Observer and Observable are relatively straightforward and follow those
collaborations of the original Observer pattern (see Figure 11-3).

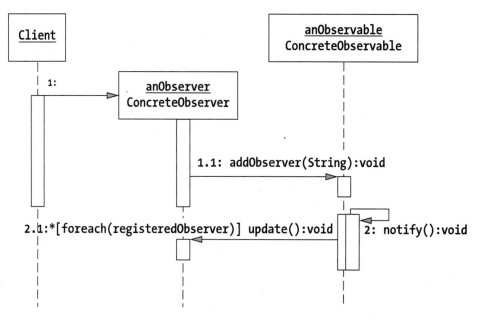

Figure 11-3. Collaborations in the Observer pattern

A client creates a concrete observer. Upon creation, the concrete observer
registers with the concrete observable via the addObserver method, or a separate
client could register the concrete observable. Recall that the parameter of the
addObserver method identifies the location that the observable uses to communicate with the observer. When an observable determines it is time to notify
observers of changes, it calls the update operation on each registered observer.

Preparing to Implement an Observer

Implementation details for the Observer pattern seek to constrain the environment and ensure that clients have the latest data:

The Observer pattern typically applies to coarse change events:
Examples of these are "a change occurred in this object" or "the state of
this business process changed." Extensions to the Observer pattern
often apply to the attribute level of an Observable object, though the
base pattern does not cover this level of granularity. For example, Java
extends the Observer pattern within the language with the JavaBean
Property Change patterns.

**When notifying a client of a change through the update method,
include a reference to the object that changed:** This allows clients to
use the same Observer implementation for multiple Observable objects.

**Include data from the changed object in the update method that you
think the Observer will use:** Without the data, the Observer is highly likely
to call back to your Web Service for more information about changes.

**You need to register an Observer with every object that has interesting
state changes:** The implications of this are profound if you consider
a massive application. Each component may be registered with dozens
or hundreds of components, with each having its own event delivery
mechanism. Further, the burden on the client for maintaining these
relationships can be daunting. Consider the case where an application
goes down; upon restart, the observers must be registered again with
every interesting target.

**The Observer pattern only works with target objects that *already
exist*:** It is difficult to target an object for changes when the object does
not exist. There are interesting webs of objects to address this issue. As
an application programmer, you may add an Observer interface to
a business object collection *and* to the business objects within the collection. With this mechanism, clients can observe both object creation
and deletion operations as well as observe changes to individual business objects.

Implementing the Observer Pattern Using Web Services

Object-oriented computing uses observers heavily, and Web Services promise to
use them just as heavily. There are some interesting twists to a Web Service
implementation of the Observer pattern.

The first consideration is what the implication of the Web Services is on the
base interfaces and concrete implementations of the Observer pattern.
Essentially, each interface becomes a WSDL interface definition published in
UDDI. Clients are then able to retrieve the WSDL file and build their own
Observer implementation and, subsequently, register it with an Observable Web
Service. Because neither the Observer nor the Observable knows each other's

underlying service implementation architectures, both concrete implementations must be Web Services and adhere to the WSDL interface published by the Web Service owner. Further, registering the Observer with the Observable uses binding information rather than object references. This is a critical difference because binding information is not tied to an underlying service implementation architecture so you can safely pass it between Web Services.

Perhaps the most interesting corollary to the previous information is that the *client* must implement a Web Service interface. This requirement brings considerable weight to the client application deployment. You look at this requirement in more depth and learn ways to lighten your burden in Chapter 13, "Exploring the Physical Tiers Pattern" and Chapter 14, "Exploring the Faux Implementation Pattern." Figure 11-4 shows a sample deployment diagram for the scenario just discussed.

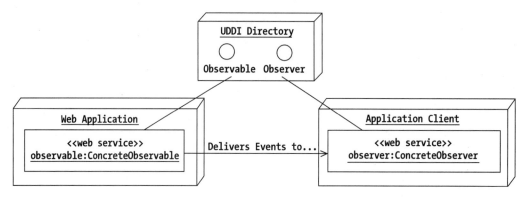

Figure 11-4. Deployment scenario for the Observer pattern in Web Services

The Observer pattern can apply to any one of your four base types (business object, business object collection, business process, or asynchronous business process). For the sample implementation, you will enhance the ProductOrderManager from the case study one last time. By using the Observer pattern, you will end up publishing an Observer interface to UDDI in addition to the process interface. Clients will use the Observer interface, a ProductOrderObserver, to implement their own Web Service to receive change notifications for your processes and collections, including the ProductOrderManager Web Service.

Building an Observer

The observer for this sample is a simple Java class that prints a message upon having its update method called. You deploy the class, shown in Listing 11-2, with Apache Axis to make a stand-alone Web Service that is ready to receive update messages from an outside Web Service, which is a modified `ProductOrderManager` Web Service. You also want to take the WSDL interface from this class and publish it to UDDI to ensure that outside applications could build their own Web Service that receives messages from the `ProductOrderManager` Web Service.

Listing 11-2. `ProductOrderObserver` *Implementation*

```
public class ProductOrderObserver {

    public ProductOrderObserver() {
    }

    public void update(String orderId){
        System.out.println(
            "Received an order change event for order: "+orderId);
    }
}
```

The `update` method in `ProductOrderObserver` receives an order identifier from the `ProductOrderManager` Web Service. With this simple mechanism, you can reuse the single observer instance to listen for changes to multiple processes. In the next section, you will notice that there is a similar mechanism for adding an observer to a particular business process because the `ProcessOrderManager` handles all product order business processes.

Enhancing a Business Process to Facilitate Observer Registration and Notification

There are two parts to enhancing `ProcessOrderManager` to be an observable Web Service. The first is to enhance the service interface and implementation, and the second is to adjust the interactions between the business processes and the manager. This book discusses only the first task. The second task, adjusting the inner workings of the business process manager, is actually an effort in applying the Observer pattern within a Java environment.

Adhering to the pattern description, you will add three new operations to the `ProductOrderManager` service implementation—addObserver, removeObserver, and notify—with only the first two being exposed through the Web Service interface. The addObserver and removeObserver operations keep track of observers, and notify centralizes the logic for delivering messages to the observers. Listing 11-3 contains the implementations of the addObserver and removeObserver operations, and Listing 11-4 contains the notify implementation.

Observer maintenance in this example is an exercise in Hashtable and Vector maintenance. You would likely use a more robust mechanism, such as persistent objects, because of the inability of clients to realize when they need to reregister with the Web Service if the service implementation goes down and loses its registrations. In Listing 11-3, a Hashtable (listeners) maintains a set of vectors keyed on orderId. Each vector contains URLs identifying the location of the observers interested in the change of state for a particular business process.

Listing 11-3. Observer Maintenance

```
public void addObserver(String orderId, String subscriptionUrl){
        Vector orderListeners = null;
        orderListeners = (Vector)listeners.get(orderId);
        if(orderListeners==null){
            orderListeners = new Vector(2);
            listeners.put(orderId, orderListeners);
        }
        if(!orderListeners.contains(subscriptionUrl)){
            try {
                URL url = new URL(subscriptionUrl);
                orderListeners.add(url);
            } catch (MalformedURLException mue){
                mue.printStackTrace();
            }
        }
    }

    public void removeObserver(String orderId, String subscriptionUrl) {
        Vector orderListeners = null;
        orderListeners = (Vector)listeners.get(orderId);
        if(orderListeners!=null){
            orderListeners.remove(subscriptionUrl);
        }
    }
```

Upon discovery of a change to the state of one of the business processes managed by the ProductOrderManager, the Web Service calls the update method on any registered Web Services. For each URL registered as an observer through the addObserver operation, the observable builds an architecture adapter with the appropriate URL from the registration list. After building the architecture adapter, the observable calls the update method on the target Web Service with the order identifier of the order that changed state. You isolate all of the notification code in a notify method that is local to the ProductOrderManager class, as shown in Listing 11-4.

Listing 11-4. Notification Process Observers of Changes

```
protected void notify(String orderId){
        Vector orderListeners = null;
        orderListeners = (Vector)listeners.get(orderId);
        if(orderListeners!=null){
            for(int i=0 ; i<>orderListeners.size() ; i++){
                try {
                    ProductOrderObserverService service =
                        new ProductOrderObserverServiceLocator();
                    ProductOrderObserver port =
                        service.getProductOrderObserver(
                            (URL)orderListeners.elementAt(i)
                        );
                    port.update(orderId);
                } catch (Exception e){
                    e.printStackTrace();
                }
            }
        }
    }
```

> **NOTE** *The link between changes to a business process and the notification process from Listing 11-4 is available in the source code accompanying this book.*

Running the New Web Services

With the registration mechanism and deployed observer, you can order products and register the observer with one or more of the business processes built to support the product order. Listing 11-5 illustrates the creation of the product order (the same code from the last two chapters) and adds the observer in the last line of code, which is the call to addObserver.

Listing 11-5. Registering an Observer from a Client Program

```
ProductOrderManagerService service =
      new ProductOrderManagerServiceLocator();
ProductOrderManager port = service.getProductOrderManager();
String customer = "1035664203330";
String productSkus[] = {"1035664206840"};
int quantity[] = {2};
String jobIdentifier = port.createProductOrder(
      customer,
      productSkus,
      quantity);
port.addObserver(
      jobIdentifier,
      "http://localhost:8080/axis/services/ProductOrderObserver");
```

Listing 11-5 presents several interesting problems that are not initially obvious. First, the code is not a part of the Observer Web Service, but it takes responsibility for registering the Observer Web Service with the Observable Web Service. This implies that the client code knows the address of the observer. Keeping the WSDL file nearby the client with the binding information addresses this problem. Second, there is no route between the Web Service running within the Apache Tomcat process and a client program running within its own process. Consequently, notifications delivered to the observer go unacknowledged by a client program. The Physical Tiers pattern addresses the second problem. Chapter 13, "Exploring the Physical Tiers Pattern" and Chapter 14, "Exploring the Faux Implementation Pattern," elaborate on this problem.

Leveraging Observers in the Case Study

The Observer pattern is a critical pattern to the success of Web Services and to the usefulness of your application. Making clients rely on the event monitor to determine when important changes of state occur is a recipe for disaster. First, clients will be unable to build applications that have timely, lossless notifications of state changes. Second, as clients start to build applications that rely heavily on timely data, the polling of event monitors increases, forcing your own application to require more resources. You do not want to wait for clients to complain about a lack of functionality or for clients to drive your servers into the ground. Instead, you should use observers on any Web Services that may be interesting to clients.

Like the previous chapter, you can use the application requirements to help determine where to use the Observer pattern. Table 11-1 illustrates a few of the requirements that can lead you to decide to use the Observer pattern.

Table 11-1. Sample Requirements Leading to the Observer Pattern

ID	REQUIREMENT
U2	The application shall allow customers to have access to current order status through a programmatic mechanism and through a user interface.
U3	The application shall enable a customer to access product catalog and sale information through a user interface and programmatically.

In both of these requirements, you could easily imagine clients using an event monitor to determine when their order ships or when your company has a sale on roasted beans. Supplying an Observer interface to the clients may allow you to push current information to them rather than simply acknowledging that your client will have out-of-date information. The previous user requirements are on an asynchronous business process and a business object collection, the two primary types of Web Services in your application (remember that the other types, business object and business process are heavily used from within the Web Services).

The Observer pattern primarily affects the interface to your Web Services. Physical tiers, presented in Chapter 13, "Exploring the Physical Tiers Pattern" affects how efficiently clients can use the Observer pattern. If clients do not get creative with how to leverage the Observer pattern, they may be unhappy with the results. Clients may not like the need to deploy a full Web Service to leverage your notification mechanism, and they may not think you have the right level of granularity of messages. Clients may also find that the complexity of your service environment is gradually increasing.

In addition to the Observer pattern, it is important you also supply an email-based notification mechanism and a usable Web interface that does not require sophisticated application writing styles. It may be some time before clients deploy Web Services or are sophisticated enough to take advantage of Observer pattern implementations.

Identifying Important Classes and Files in the Case Study

Table 11-2 contains the source files for the code listings in this chapter, as well as some of the related code.

Table 11-2. Sample Location

FILE	LOCATION	DESCRIPTION
ConcreteObservable.java	src\com\servicefoundry\ books\webservices\ simpleexample\observable	Java-based Observable subclass that sends an event notification every second
ConcreteObserver.java	src\com\servicefoundry\ books\webservices\ simpleexample\observable	Java-based Observer implementation that plugs into ConcreteObservable
ObserverDemo.java	src\com\servicefoundry\ books\webservices\ simpleexample\observable	Driver program for simple Java Observer pattern implementation
ProductOrderManager.java	src\com\servicefoundry\books \webservices\processes	Concrete observable implementation in the Web Service paradigm
ProductOrderObserver.java	src\com\servicefoundry\ books\webservices\patterns\ observer	Client-side observer implementation used by ProductOrderManager to deliver event notifications
ProductOrderTest.java	src\com\servicefoundry\books \webservices\tests	Test program that connects ProductOrderObserver to ProductOrderManager

Using Ant Targets to Run the Case Study

Table 11-3 describes the targets to run for the Ant environment to see the programs and chapter samples in operation. Before running any samples, be sure you read and perform all of the install steps in the appendix.

Table 11-3. Ant Targets

TARGET	DESCRIPTION
testjavaobserver	Runs the Java observer program from Listing 11-1.
testwebserviceobserver	Registers the Observer Web Service to the Observable Web Service, as in Listing 11-5. The results display to the Apache Axis console window because the Observer implementation from Listing 11-2 simply uses the System.out facilities.

Summary

This chapter reviewed the Observer pattern and its usefulness and implementation in a Web Service environment. The chapter started by looking at how the Java language implements the Observer pattern in its core class libraries through the java.util.Observer interface and the java.util.Observable class. It also discussed the increasing usage of the Observer pattern and derivations of it in the UDDI version 3 specification.

The Observer pattern implementation does not change much from the Java language implementation to a Web Service derivation of the pattern. In fact, many of the interfaces and sequences remain the same. The core difference between the object-oriented paradigm and the Web Service paradigm is in the pattern implementation. The Java language relies on a single-process Observer pattern implementation. The Web Services paradigm is inherently multiprocess, driving the need for both the Observer and Observable to be interfaces rather than having one or both be concrete implementations.

A major limitation of the pattern is its dependency on the client implementing a Web Service with the Observer interface. This dependency brings substantial bulk to the client, at least with Apache Axis as a Web Service host. (I address this limitation in later patterns, but for now it certainly appears to be a limiting factor in this pattern's usefulness.)

Related Patterns

The Observer pattern relates to the other two event patterns documented within this book: the Event Monitor pattern and the Publish/Subscribe pattern. There are also mechanisms to ease some of the problems identified in this chapter, such as the need for a client to deploy a full Web Service environment. The following patterns relate to the Observer pattern:

Event Monitor: Clients use the Event Monitor pattern when there is no discernable event notification mechanism available on a target Web Service or when the available mechanism does not adequately fit the needs of the client.

Publish/Subscribe: The Publish/Subscribe pattern is an evolution of the Observer pattern. Whereas the Observer pattern relies on registration directly with a particular Web Service, the Publish/Subscribe pattern decouples the service that delivers notifications from the service that receives notification. This allows multiple services to send the same notification; it also abstracts the responsibility for event delivery and subscriber registration to a common class.

Faux Implementation: The Observer and Publish/Subscribe patterns are predicated on having a Web Service implemented by the client set up to receive event notifications. This is a heavy burden to place on potentially resource-constrained application environments. Fortunately, there are other lightweight mechanisms for registering and receiving event notifications that make it appear as if you have deployed a full Web Service environment.

Physical Tiers: The Observer pattern and the Publish/Subscribe pattern, as presented, do not plug into a stand-alone application. This is obviously a problem because the usefulness of the pattern implementations is limited. The Faux Implementation pattern indirectly addresses the problem because the listener becomes a part of the primary program. On the other hand, there are environments where self-encapsulated Web Services are best for observing event notifications. For these environments, physical tiers show how to connect the Web Service to one or more outside applications.

Additional Reading

- UDDI version 3 specification: `http://www.oasis-open.org/committees/uddi-spec/tcspecs.shtml#uddiv3`

- Gamma, Erich et. al. *Design Patterns: Elements of Reusable Object-Oriented Software*. Addison-Wesley, 1995.

- Schmidt, Douglas C. *Pattern-Oriented Software Architecture, Volume 2: Patterns for Concurrent and Networked Objects*. John Wiley & Sons, 2000.

CHAPTER 12

Implementing the Publish/Subscribe Pattern

THE OBSERVER PATTERN IS pervasive in object-oriented computing and continues to make inroads with Web Services. In some schools of thought, the Publish/Subscribe pattern is synonymous with the Observer pattern, being essentially different terms for the same pattern. Other schools of thought treat the Publish/Subscribe pattern as slightly different in nature and more in line with some more robust event patterns, such as the Event Channel pattern that is a part of the Common Object Request Broker Architecture (CORBA). CORBA's Event Channel pattern is a distributed computing pattern using proxies on both sides of a single event service. The service receives events from proxies and delivers events to proxies that register an interest for particular events. In this book, the Publish/Subscribe pattern is a subtle, but important, extension of the Observer pattern and a subset of the more robust Event Channel pattern. This book does not discuss the Event Channel pattern further. If you would like to learn more about the Event Channel pattern, you can locate the specification at the Object Management Group (OMG) Web site (http://www.omg.org).

The Publish/Subscribe pattern illustrates some interesting aspects of Web Services:

- The ability to offer generic, utility-based Web Services that any client and service implementation can leverage

- The ability to use a third-party Web Service to enhance the communication between two other Web Services

- The ability to facilitate notifications between Web Services without adding a mechanism and interface to the Web Service that is implementing the business behavior

Primarily, using a Publish/Subscribe pattern implies the usage of a dedicated Web Service for receiving and distributing events. One Web Service receives events from an application and distributes those events to interested

parties. Web Services, by definition, are small, self-contained application components with low cohesion to other Web Services. By abstracting out the event
handling to another Web Service, you start creating a whole network of related
Web Services, which is contrary to the direction of Web Services as self-
contained applications.

On the other hand, there are distinct possibilities for generalized, stand-
alone event services that follow the Publish/Subscribe pattern. For example,
a simple, generic, event service can sit on a network and service an arbitrary
number of customers. The event service implemented in this chapter does not
require any modification to facilitate Web Services using it as an intermediary.
The service allows registration and posting of any event topic.

You could use the Publish/Subscribe pattern as an alternative mechanism
to the Observer pattern for notifying clients of changes to Web Services throughout the P.T. Monday Coffee Company application. The Publish/Subscribe pattern
offers several strengths over the Observer pattern in addition to its ability to simply replace the Observer pattern. One strength of publish/subscribe is its ability
to send events that are not related to a particular Web Service. This opens up
your event strategy to additional event types, such as the ability to publish an
event relating to an internal system state without having it associated with a special System Web Service with which observers would have to register. Consider
the differences between the Event Monitor pattern, the Observer pattern, and the
Publish/Subscribe pattern implemented in this book. In most cases, one of these
will fit any type of event that your Web Services may be interested in or interested in communicating.

Seeing Publish/Subscribe in Practice

Component-based systems heavily use the Publish/Subscribe pattern. Developers
use the pattern in single-process applications and applications that are distributed across systems. In many embodiments, the Publish/Subscribe pattern
eases application development through centralizing event distribution and
allowing a single event mechanism to service all events. Thus, developers write
and debug a single event mechanism instead of many. Further, this event mechanism becomes one person's expertise area rather than a requirement on all
developers.

Publish/subscribe is also useful in systems built without prior awareness of
all instances of objects that can surface a particular event. Systems that show
this behavior are becoming more common as applications attempt to federate
systems together into a single, logical application. The Seti@Home project is one
of the most visible attempts to create ad-hoc federations of computers to extend
application resources. This application uses computer screen savers and idle
processing time to work on complex equations. There is little chance that the
span of the entire application and working processors will ever look the same

from moment to moment. In this way, it is difficult to predict and register with each node to receive and send events as the Observer pattern would have you do. Instead, you can centralize the event mechanism in an event service using the Publish/Subscribe pattern, thus easing the burden of event registration and disbursing.

The Jini platform from Sun Microsystems and the Federated Services Project (FSP) from the Jini community service a similar application space. Federations of devices are difficult to predict. Consider an application written for a data center to service all of the disk arrays that have server components on them. Further, consider that the application may have plug-in components and policies that determine how to deal with faults that occur in the arrays. System components are assembled at runtime and throughout the day. (Remember that the system can change even after it is deployed because of the dynamic nature of a set of data center devices.) It is impossible to predict ahead of time what components will have requirements on events from other components. The FSP has a nice solution to this problem built around the Publish/Subscribe pattern.

> **NOTE** *For more information on the Jini platform, see the Jini.org Web site at* `http://www.jini.org`. *For more information on the FSP, see* `http://fsp.jini.org`.

Understanding the FSP Event Service Design

The FSP introduces a centralized event service design based on the Publish/Subscribe pattern. The centralized design helps address the dynamic nature of the expected domain that FSP services, the hardware management domain. Distributed components register their interest in events by connecting to a centralized event service and registering a proxy to their own class that handles the event when it is received. The event service has no prior knowledge of the events that flow through it and therefore must use a generic interface for all types of events. This technique loses the semantic exactness of the Observer pattern but leverages object-oriented techniques for creating a robust and dynamic service.

Figure 12-1 shows the two major structures that make up FSP's event service. Keep in mind that more classes make up the entire solution structure. The EventService interface and an underlying implementation that uses a variant of Java's Remote Method Invocation (RMI) make up the centralized event service. Clients register a RemoteEventListenerImpl with the event service to receive events. The registration methods themselves take a topic string, discussed in the next section, to identify what events to deliver to the listener.

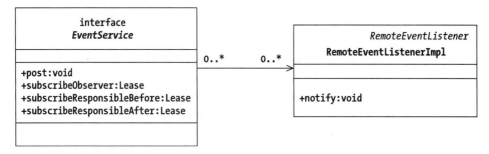

Figure 12-1. FSP event service interface

There are four interesting methods in the event service implementation and one in the event listener:

EventService.post: This method allows clients to publish events to the event service. The event service receives the event and forwards it to subscribers.

EventService.subscribeObserver: This method gives subscribers a mechanism for registering for events they want to observe. Observation in this case implies a listener that will not take action on the event that would affect the event itself or other components in the federated application.

EventService.subscribeResponsibleBefore and EventService.subscribeResponsibleAfter: These methods allow event listeners to subscribe for events they may be able to affect. The result is an event handling chain where each listener has the opportunity to affect the event. For example, if a file system runs out of space on a host, there could be various recourses, such as expanding the file system. Once the event is altered, there may be no reason for the remaining listeners to be concerned with the event.

RemoteEventListenerImpl.notify: This is the event service callback method. All subscribers receive event notification through this method; thus, the data associated with the method is generic in nature.

The responsible listener methods are not a part of the Publish/Subscribe pattern; however, they are useful additions for particular domains. The remaining methods appear similar in nature to the Observer pattern with the addition of the post method. This method allows clients to publish methods and decouples the responsibility of recognizing a useful event from the event service and into external classes.

Using Topic-Based Registration Mechanisms

An interesting part of FSP's implementation of the Publish/Subscribe pattern is its use of topic-based event registration, a technique you will use throughout the rest of the chapter. Topics are character-based mechanisms for identifying an event that does not require adherence to a particular interface or knowledge of the event originator. For example, to identify a problem with a storage network, one could use the topic `storage.network.problem`. More often, the company, followed by details about the event itself, scopes topics. For example, `com.ptmonday.productcatalog.updated` identifies a change to your company product catalog. In most cases, the event topics form a hierarchy; Figure 12-2 shows an example event hierarchy.

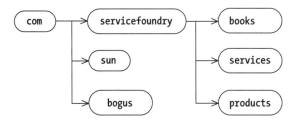

Figure 12-2. Topic hierarchy

   The embodiment of event topics as a hierarchy is a useful expression as subscribers can often register for whole branches of the hierarchy with wildcards or partial hierarchy specification. Registration for the topic `com.servicefoundry` in the FSP event service results in subscriber notification for the `com.servicefoundry.books`, `com.servicefoundry.services`, and `com.servicefoundry.products` events, as well as any events that may be branches below the third level of the topic hierarchy. The event hierarchy itself does not have to be static in nature; publishers can originate any topic at any point in the application's lifecycle.

   Topic-based mechanisms increase the ability of the event service to ignore the details of the events flowing through it by not forcing the event service to load classes for each event that passes through it; this is a Java Virtual Machine artifact. This technique adapts well to Web Services for several reasons:

> **Topic hierarchies give an element of object orientation without the complexities of class inheritance:** By using dot-delimited topics, you can have an arbitrary level of topic nesting. Traditional object-orientation would use event subclasses to achieve a similar technique, and you are trying to discourage such liberal use of pure inheritance in an environment where the clients are unpredictable as to their architecture.

You can pass arbitrary data types with the event service as long as both the client and the Web Service that originated the event have an informal contract in place: Using this technique, the Web Service can serialize Extensible Markup Language (XML) to the client as a means of creating an architecture-independent data transfer.

The Publish/Subscribe pattern is a good technique for unpredictable networks of objects. It is also a good technique for unpredictable subscriber architectures. Both add up to a good tool for Web Services.

Understanding the Publish/Subscribe Structure

The Publish/Subscribe pattern structure is similar to the Observer pattern structure, but it has several important differences. Recall that the Observable portion of the observer structure is actually a part of a service that contains some state about which the Observer wants to receive notifications. This is not the case with the Publish/Subscribe pattern. With publish/subscribe, subscribers register with an intermediate service responsible for delivering events. Publishers *also* use the service to deliver events. There are many implications of this structure, including the following:

- Subscribers can subscribe a single time, yet they can receive events from many publishers. This technique, called *anonymous publishing*, is useful for systems that do not have a static set of objects responsible for events in the system.

- Publishers do not have to re-create event publishing and subscriber tracking mechanisms for each class that delivers events.

- The application and system can change around an event service without a change to the event service itself.

The pattern structure, shown in Figure 12-3, illustrates the constituent parts of a publish/subscribe implementation. As before, the interfaces indicate an interface available as a Web Services Description Language (WSDL) file and through a Universal Description, Data, and Discovery (UDDI) directory. The PublisherImpl does not have an associated interface simply because the publisher is not required to be available to others. Implementations often allow subscribers to contact a publisher directly to request additional information, in which case an interface representing the publisher makes more sense.

Because EventService does not have any interesting state and is not observable itself, a publisher, PublisherImpl, is likely the originator of an event. The publisher could also be a proxy to an object that has an interesting state. The Publish/Subscribe pattern allows a wide variation of implementation techniques.

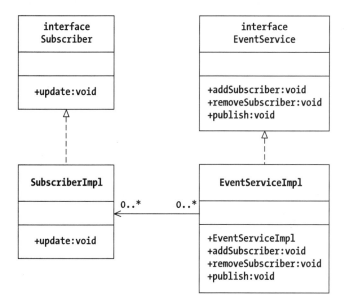

Figure 12-3. Class diagram for the Publish/Subscribe pattern

Understanding the Components of the Publish/Subscribe Pattern

The components in the Publish/Subscribe pattern are similar to those in the Observer pattern, with the responsibility of publishing an event split out from the EventService class to an external publisher. In addition, EventService contains an additional operation that allows external publishers to publish an event through the event service. These are the components in the Publish/Subscribe pattern:

Subscriber: The Subscriber component is the definition of the interface that an event service implementation calls to notify a client when a publisher delivers a message to the event service. There is only one important operation on this interface: the update operation. The update operation usually receives an event identifier to ensure that the subscriber is aware of the event that prompted the event service to call the subscriber. A single subscriber may service multiple event registrations. The operation also receives data that fits an informal contract between the subscriber and the publisher.

SubscriberImpl: The concrete subscriber is a Web Service that adheres to the Subscriber interface, or it is a Java component that can send and receive SOAP messages and has a distinct address that the EventService can use to communicate with the subscriber. Upon receiving a message, the event service locates the subscribers registered for the message, and then the event service delivers the message to each concrete subscriber registered in its list of interested parties. The event service requires the address of a subscriber, typically a Uniform Resource Locator (URL) for binding to the subscriber's port. The subscriber then acts on the update message from the event service.

EventService: The EventService interface contains similar operations as the previous chapter's Observable interface, with the addition of an operation used to publish messages. The additional operation, publish, is necessary because of the separation of responsibility for recognizing and publishing events to an external component—in your case, the PublisherImpl. The publish operation receives an event identifier and data that is forwarded to any subscribers. The other operations, addSubscriber and removeSubscriber, receive an event identifier that the subscriber wants to receive notifications for, as well as a reference for use by the event service to call back to the subscriber.

EventServiceImpl: The implementation of the event service maintains subscriber lists and the event types for which a subscriber registers via the addSubscriber and removeSubscriber operations. Publishers publish an event to the event service with an associated event type via the publish operation. The event service determines what subscribers registered for the event and delivers the event to them. Event services existing outside of the processes that use the event service should use a persistence mechanism to preserve the subscriber list when the event service shuts down.

PublisherImpl (not pictured): A publisher does not have a specific contract to fulfill unless the publisher expects callbacks from subscribers for more information. A publisher assembles the information that a subscriber expects to see, which is an implicit contract between the subscribers and the publishers, and delivers the event data along with a planned event identifier to the event service. Publishers could simply reflect events from business entities, collections, and processes. On the other hand, publishers may surface events that are more complex than a single object instance or that are not associated with a concrete service. For example, a publisher may surface events when parts of a system crash or go down for maintenance. In this sense, there is no business representation of a service that is lost to the user and therefore no concrete service to which users can attach themselves. Instead, if the user just registers with the event service for event types that relate to system events, they do not have to care what form the publisher takes to deliver those events.

Like the Observer pattern, the potential deployment scenarios are interesting. Figure 12-4 illustrates a likely scenario. Consider that for an application like the P.T. Monday Coffee Company application, a single Web server and the Apache Axis environment houses the event service and any publishers within the same physical deployment node.

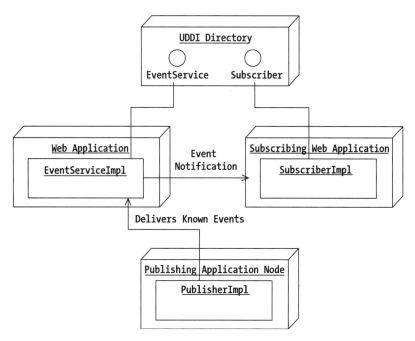

Figure 12-4. Possible deployment scenario for the Publish/Subscribe pattern

Understanding Publish/Subscribe Collaborations

The collaborations between the components in the Publish/Subscribe pattern are similar to the collaborations in the Observer pattern. A client registers a subscriber with an event service. As part of the registration through the addSubscriber operation on the event service, the client identifies the events that they want to receive through a string-based identifier as well as the port information for the subscriber Web Service. Once registered, the subscriber receives events with a topic that matches the identifier.

Publishers create the data surrounding an event and publish the event through the publish operation on the event service. The publisher itself uses an architecture adapter to connect to the Web Service and deliver the message. Once delivered, the event service searches through the subscribers to locate all of those interested in the event and delivers the event to the subscribers. Figure 12-5 illustrates the entire sequence.

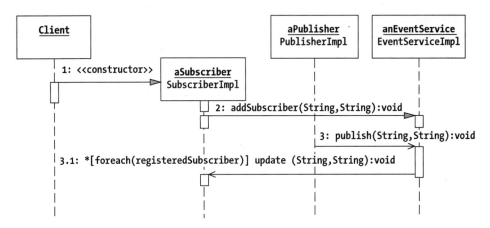

Figure 12-5. Publish/Subscribe sequence diagram

The operations identified as 2 and 3.1 in Figure 12-5 occur across architecture adapters for a Web Service implementation. In the first case, the addSubscriber method registers the client-side subscriber with the EventService Web Service. Apache Axis forwards this registration request to the EventSerice Java implementation. In the latter case, the Java-based EventService calls the update method on client-based Subscriber Web Services through an architecture adapter. The Apache Axis environment on the client receives the update operation and forwards it to the appropriate Java Subscriber service implementation.

Preparing to Implement Publish/Subscribe

The implementation details that surround the Observer pattern are also applicable to the Publish/Subscribe pattern. By moving the responsibilities for publishing events out of the entity that originates the events, you need to understand some additional implementation details that are not as intuitive as when the business entity holds the event information and the subscriber lists:

The subscription lists should be persistent: With Web Services, it is unlikely that publishers, subscribers, and the event service itself reside in a single process. This creates an issue if the event service crashes or goes down for maintenance while the subscribers and publishers do not. The expectation of publishers and subscribers will be that they do not have to register again with the event service. This is even truer if the publisher and subscriber do not notice that the event service went offline. Assuming the event service is a Java implementation, simple object-relational mapping mechanisms or even XML binding techniques may be sufficient to provide the persistence across restarts of the event service.

The event service can quickly become a bottleneck between publishers and subscribers: Unlike the observer, all events in a system end up funneling through a couple of methods using a few subscription tables that could become hard pressed to keep up with requests. Some ways to alleviate this problem are to have multiple event services, use multiple threads within the event service, or build in some complex load balancing techniques. On the other hand, if you treat the event service as near-real-time data transfer and not real-time data transfer, your clients should be fine as long as you do not actually lose events or their subscriptions.

Consider the event data structure and topic as part of the interface: Unlike the Observer pattern, the event service in a Publish/Subscribe pattern serves more than one type of event. In fact, in extreme cases, developers can build the event service separately from the applications that use the event service to publish events. Therefore, there are no semantically rich operations on the event service. You should consider the event identifiers and the event data as part of the publisher's interface and contract to ensure that a subscriber has a stable definition from which to program.

Implementing Publish/Subscribe

To implement the sample, you will build an event service with the proper operations to subscribe for events and publish events. The implementation matches the structure described in the previous section. Next, you will build a subscriber and see how to register for events with the event service. Finally, you will build a simple program to publish events that the event service will forward on to the subscribers.

Implementing the Event Service

The event service implemented in this section is an extremely simple example that lacks many of the features desired for a robust, enterprise application. The subscriptions are stored in `java.util.Vector` instances within a `java.util.Hashtable` instance keyed on event topic. Subscribers register the URL that the event service can use for binding. The `publish` operation iterates through subscribers registered for a particular topic and delivers the event to each subscriber. Listing 12-1 is the code that implements the event service.

Listing 12-1. Event Service Implementation

```java
public class EventService {

    public EventService() {
    }

    public void addSubscriber(String topic, String subscriptionUrl){
        Vector subscribers = null;
        subscribers = (Vector)topics.get(topic);
        if(subscribers==null){
            subscribers = new Vector(2);
            topics.put(topic, subscribers);
        }
        if(!subscribers.contains(subscriptionUrl)){
            try {
                URL url = new URL(subscriptionUrl);
                subscribers.add(url);
            } catch (MalformedURLException mue){
                mue.printStackTrace();
            }
        }
    }

    public void removeSubscriber(String topic, String subscriptionUrl) {
        Vector subscribers = null;
        subscribers = (Vector)topics.get(topic);
        if(subscribers!=null){
            subscribers.remove(subscriptionUrl);
        }
    }

    public void publish(String topic, String data){
        Vector subscribers = null;
        subscribers = (Vector)topics.get(topic);
        if(subscribers!=null){
            for(int i=0 ; i<>subscribers.size() ; i++){
                try {
                    SubscriberService service =
                        new SubscriberServiceLocator();
com.servicefoundry.books.webservices.eventservice.stubs.Subscriber
                    port = service.getSubscriber(
                        (URL)subscribers.elementAt(i)
                    );
```

```
                port.update(topic, data);
            } catch (Exception e){
                e.printStackTrace();
            }
        }
    }
}


    protected Hashtable topics = new Hashtable(2);
}
```

The only part of particular interest in the event service code is the publication method. For each registered subscriber, you construct a new service locator for the subscriber, retrieve the URL from the vector of subscribers registered for a particular event, and call the update method on the subscriber. Of course, by now you realize that the port instance variable is actually an architecture adapter representing the subscriber's Web Service.

Once created, you deploy the Java implementation of the event service through Apache Axis. At this point, subscribers and publishers have access to the event service. The service is entirely generic in nature and can therefore represent any event and pass it on to the proper subscribers.

A Simple Subscriber and Its Registration with the Event Service

The event service in the previous section assumed a subscriber interface that contains an update method, as described earlier in the chapter. Listing 12-2 illustrates a simple subscriber implementation that contains the update method that the event service calls when a publisher publishes an event that matches your topic. In this case, it includes a simple main method that registers the subscriber, after it is deployed as a Web Service, with the event service.

Listing 12-2. A Simple Subscriber

```
public class SubscriberTest implements Subscriber {

    private static String topic =
        "com.servicefoundry.books.events.ProductOrderUpdate";

    private SubscriberTest() {
    }
```

```
    public void update(String eventId, String data) {
        System.out.println("Received an event: "+eventId);
        System.out.println("Data: "+data);
    }

    public static void main(java.lang.String[] args) {
        try {
            EventServiceService service =
                new EventServiceServiceLocator();
            EventService port = service.getEventService();
            port.addSubscriber(topic,
                "http://localhost:8080/axis/services/Subscriber");
        } catch(Exception e){
            e.printStackTrace();
        }
    }
}
```

You saw in Listing 12-1 how the event service calls the update method. The main method in the subscriber is relatively interesting. In it, you use an architecture adapter to register the URL of a deployed subscriber Web Service and an event topic with the EventService Web Service. You could also register a single subscriber for multiple topics with the event service. This one-to-many relationship is important to remember for EventService implementations because including the topic identifier with a specific event helps to enable the one-to-many relationship. With the event identifier contained in the event itself, the client can create custom logic based on the event identifier.

This example code does not put any assumptions on the data passed to the subscriber. The most likely scenario is that the subscriber receives an XML data stream from the publisher. Also, remember that the contract between the publisher and subscriber for the formatted data is implicit and even somewhat fragile. One of the downsides of using an event service is the inability to generate type-safe notification mechanisms tailored to a particular event type.

Once deployed using Apache Axis, all of the necessary Web Services are available and waiting for a publisher to deliver events. Logically, you consider the subscriber Web Service as part of a client program, along with the Apache Tomcat service that Apache Axis runs in and the Apache Axis container itself. This is a heavy weight to bear simply to register for an event or two from a publisher.

Publishing an Event to the Event Service

The publisher is the only one of the three concrete implementations that does not have to be a Web Service. The simple publisher example for this chapter, shown in Listing 12-3, is a `main` program that creates an architecture adapter to the event service and calls the `publish` operation on the event service Web Service.

Listing 12-3. Publishing an Event to the Event Service

```
public class Publisher {

    private static String topic =
        "com.servicefoundry.books.events.ProductOrderUpdate";
    private static String data = "orderId:updated";

    public static void main(String args[]) {
        try {
            EventServiceService service =
                new EventServiceServiceLocator();
            EventService port = service.getEventService();
            port.publish(topic, data);
        } catch(Exception e){
            e.printStackTrace();
        }
    }
}
```

The `data` static instance variable contains the information that the subscriber expects upon receiving the event. There is little information passed here—just an identifier and information about what occurred. Again, some publishers may have much more data to pass to their subscribers, and there may be cases where there is less. For example, if the publisher had information about a Web Service that changed state, the publisher could send binding information to clients who identify the changed Web Service. In this case, subscribers could then attach directly to the changed Web Service to request more information.

Leveraging Publish/Subscribe in the Case Study

The P.T. Monday Coffee Company application now has three different event patterns to choose from for helping clients access current and timely data: the Event Monitor pattern, the Observer pattern, and the Publish/Subscribe pattern. Each has advantages and disadvantages. Over the years, I have grown to appreciate the loose coupling and flexibility inherent in a publish/subscribe mechanism. The ability to separate concerns for optimal delivery of events to clients is also a heavy advantage to the publish/subscribe technique of using a generic event service.

On the other hand, the Observer pattern creates better semantics for clients and helps to compartmentalize the application. Basically, someone browsing products and desiring notifications when the product catalog gets updated has to understand only a single Web Service, instead of two plus a set of topics.

Also, keep in mind that you are not limited to a single event pattern for your application. The P.T. Monday Coffee Company will use a combination of the Publish/Subscribe pattern and the Observer pattern throughout the application. The former sends events that are not associated with a particular Web Service, and the latter allows clients to access events on a particular Web Service or business object used by a Web Service.

In your own applications, it is worth weighing the benefits of one pattern against another. In the end, both patterns achieve similar goals but have different advantages and disadvantages. One, the Publish/Subscribe pattern requires a client to know about multiple Web Services; the other, the Observer pattern, is not as flexible with the event originator and requires more code. Both techniques fit well into a Web Service paradigm.

Identifying Important Classes and Files in the Case Study

Table 12-1 shows the primary code discussed in this chapter that you should browse in the downloaded source code.

Table 12-1. Sample Location

FILE	LOCATION	DESCRIPTION
SubscriberTest.java	src\com\ servicefoundry\ books\webservices\ tests	This is the subscriber service implementation as shown in Listing 12-2. This service implementation gets deployed using Apache Axis and lies dormant. A second registration step must take place to register it after the Web Service is active; this subscription registration is contained in the static main program of this listing.
Publisher.java	src\com\ servicefoundry\ books\webservices\ tests	The program that publishes events to the event service, as shown in Listing 12-3.
EventService.java	src\com\ servicefoundry\ books\webservices\ eventservice	The event service implementation as shown in Listing 12-1.

Using Ant Targets to Run the Case Study

Table 12-2 describes the targets to run for the Ant environment to see the programs and chapter samples in operation. Before running any samples, be sure you read and perform all of the install steps in the appendix. Like the programs themselves, this sample evolves over the next few chapters, so there are some remaining concepts before you understand the whole test program and Web Service implementation.

Table 12-2. Ant Targets

TARGET	DESCRIPTION
`registerwitheventservice`	This registers the subscribing Web Service, deployed via Apache Axis, with the `EventService` Web Service. You saw the registration code in Listing 12-2.
`publishtoeventservice`	This publishes an event to the `EventService` Web Service. Assuming that a client is running and registered for the proper event topic (hard-coded in the programs), the event will appear in all registered clients.

Summary

In this chapter, you looked at the Publish/Subscribe pattern. There are many interpretations of the Publish/Subscribe pattern. Some interpretations simply mirror the Observer pattern. Other interpretations completely separate publisher and subscriber and have an intermediate service that acts as a conduit from publishers to subscribers. In this chapter, I chose the latter interpretation and used the FSP (formerly the Jiro platform) event service as an example outside the scope of Web Services.

The structure of the Publish/Subscribe pattern includes three concrete implementations. An event service, derived from a WSDL interface, is a conduit between publishers and subscribers. A subscriber, derived from a WSDL interface, receives messages from the event service. A publisher publishes messages to the event service. The publisher is the only structure that does not have an associated interface. The primary difference between publish and subscribe is the separation of the state or events that a subscriber is interested in away from the structure responsible for delivering events to the subscribers.

You have now seen three different mechanisms for using events from the Web Service paradigm. The first, the event monitor, placed the burden of event recognition on the client of a Web Service. The second and third required the subscriber, or observer, to be Web Services themselves. In implementing the latter two patterns, there are two major disadvantages exposed. The first disadvantage is that the subscriber Web Services had no way to converse with a more robust main program, such as a servlet or Java Server Page (JSP). The subscribers were simply stand-alone Web Services that received messages and printed information. The second disadvantage is the weight that the subscribers bring to the client programs. To implement a subscriber, you used Apache Tomcat (a servlet engine), Apache Axis (the Web Service container), and the subscriber service itself. This makes the footprint of a client program huge and the installation relatively complex. In the next two chapters, you will look at patterns to help mitigate these problems.

Related Patterns

The following patterns from this text relate to the Publish/Subscribe pattern:

Event Monitor: Clients use the Event Monitor pattern when there is no discernable event notification mechanism available on a target Web Service or when the available mechanism does not adequately fit the needs of the client.

Observer: The Observer pattern is a simple version of the Publish/Subscribe pattern. The primary distinction between the Publish/Subscribe pattern and the Observer pattern is in the partitioning of the responsibility for event ownership out of the event service and into a separate publishing entity. The Observer pattern keeps responsibility for event ownership in the Observable object.

Faux Implementation: The Observer and Publish/Subscribe patterns are predicated on having a Web Service implemented by the client set up to receive event notifications. This is a heavy burden to place on potentially resource-constrained application environments. Fortunately, there are other lightweight mechanisms for registering and receiving event notifications, and the Faux Implementation pattern discusses these.

Physical Tiers: The Observer pattern and the Publish/Subscribe pattern, as presented, do not plug into a stand-alone application. This is obviously a problem as the usefulness of the pattern implementations is limited. The Faux Implementation pattern indirectly addresses the problem because the listener becomes a part of the primary program. On the other hand, there are environments where self-encapsulated Web Services are best for observing event notifications. For these environments, the Physical Tiers pattern helps better structure your application for logic reuse.

Additional Reading

- Event Service specification:
  http://www.omg.org/technology/documents/formal/event_service.htm

- Monday, Paul; Connor, William. *The Jiro Technology Programmer's Guide and Federated Management Architecture.* Addison-Wesley, 2001.

CHAPTER 13

Exploring the Physical Tiers Pattern

CHAPTER 2, "INTRODUCING THE P.T. Monday Case Study," discussed the n-tier application architecture used to implement the P.T. Monday Coffee Company application. Within the architecture, the logic tier separates the business-specific logic from the Web tier's logic. The Web tier is responsible for facilitating interaction with users outside of the system through one or more different types of Web clients, such as a Web Service or a Web browser.

The P.T. Monday Coffee Company application's evolution has encouraged a logical separation of the Web tier and the logic tier, but that separation has *not* been enforced at deployment time. At this point, the separation between the Web tier and the logic tier is at development time only. At deployment time in the current services, the business logic embodied in the service implementation runs within a thread under the control of the Web Service container, Apache Axis, and indirectly through the Apache Tomcat process. This makes the logic tier *physically* deployed with the Web tier, not an independent logic tier.

You have not pursued physical separation of the tiers until this stage of the book for a couple of reasons. The first reason is simplicity. Apache Axis and most Web tier environments are easy to demonstrate and learn when you do not pursue physical tier separation. The second reason you did not pursue tier separation is necessity. Only in the previous three chapters did you start to see compelling reasons, though they were only subtly implied, to create physical separation between the Web tier and the logic tier.

The event patterns in the previous three chapters introduced the first real problems with not pursuing physical tier separation. Typically, event subscribers are not self-contained application components; rather, they are gateways into larger applications that must react to events occurring within other application components. For example, when the Web Service that subscribes to a change in a remote Web Service receives an event, it is the beginning of a larger chain of events that occurs within your own application.

On the other hand, in an enterprise application, a change to a remote Web Service often ripples further than a single business object. The result of a change in a remote Web Service may change the state of running applications or there may be a whole chain of services affected by the change. Rather than have each event subscriber manage related business objects within its own process, it is often easier to delegate handling of events to a physically separate logic tier. This separate logic tier has the advantage of being separately deployed and configurable, and it has the ability to coordinate groups of threads without ceding control to an unknown environment, your acquired Web Services environment.

In this chapter, you will spend time looking more closely at the Web Service environment you used in the previous chapters. Specifically, you will look at how Apache Axis executes the Web Service and the service implementation as well as how the current application comes together in this highly componentized environment. You will then look deeper at a desired *physical* process state that adheres to your n-tier architecture and enforces the architecture at deployment time. This physical separation is the Physical Tiers architecture pattern. It is subtly different from the N-Tier Architecture pattern in that it enforces physical separation and goes beyond the logical concept of tiers and layers. You will enable the Physical Tiers architecture pattern with the Connector design pattern. The Connector pattern gives you a simple design to connect tiers that span physical boundaries.

Looking Deeper at the Need for Physical Tiers

The previous several chapters have implied that there are shortcomings in the event patterns; however, the chapters have not been explicit about the reasons or about the techniques to mitigate the shortcomings. In fact, the environment was sufficient to illustrate the structure of patterns (Event Monitor, Observer, and Publish/Subscribe) and led to simple deployment and programming examples.

Two scenarios illustrate the boundary you run into by allowing yourself to have logical tiers without physical tier separation. The first scenario, described in "Using Web Service Events" illustrates how you trap yourself within the Apache Axis process when you build event subscribers with Web Services. The second scenario, described in "Avoiding Service Implementation Bloat," shows how you drag your persistence mechanisms into the Web tier along with the entire logic tier at deployment time. This second scenario creates bloat in your Web tier in terms of the deployment packages and the footprint of your Web tier and runs the danger that the persistence mechanism does not perform as expected. Finally, you will look at how you solve both problems with the Remote Method Invocation (RMI) capability of Java 2 Standard Edition (J2SE) or similar interprocess protocol by using the Connector pattern.

Using Web Service Events

The subscriber from the previous chapter illustrates the most obvious problem with your use of Web Services—the inability of your Web Services to interact with an application or component running in a separate process. Consider the scenario where you have a stand-alone Java-based client that wants to receive notifications from one of the event mechanisms constructed in the previous two chapters. The Java-based client runs in one process, and the Web Service subscriber runs in a separate process. For this reason, you need a mechanism that connects the Java application to the Web Service.

Figure 13-1 illustrates a containment scenario using Apache Tomcat and the Apache Axis Web Service engine. The diagram also illustrates the concept of a separate Java client process. As you can see, the event subscriber used in the previous two chapters is in a physically separate process from the application classes that need to be notified of the event. The subscriber that receives messages from the event service exists within the Apache Tomcat process, and the application is in its own Java client process.

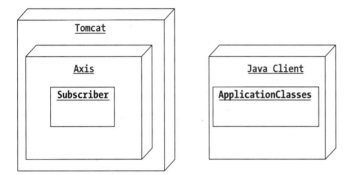

Figure 13-1. Java client and subscriber Web Service deployment diagram

In Figure 13-1, the Subscriber is a part of the Web Tier. You could consider that the ApplicationClasses are part of the logic tier, which must react to changes in the external Web Service. Thus, you have created a tiered scenario, without a connector to move data between the tiers.

The challenge in the current paradigm is letting one or more application classes know that the subscriber running in the Apache Tomcat container received an event; this communication requirement between tiers is the essence of the Connector pattern. There are many mechanisms for communicating across process boundaries and connecting the physically separate tiers. In Java, RMI is a relatively lightweight mechanism for creating the communication path. Other mechanisms for interprocess communication include message buses based on the Java Message Service (JMS) standard and heavier ORB-based mechanisms, such as a CORBA implementation.

Avoiding Service Implementation Bloat

The second scenario to illustrate the necessity of the Physical Tiers pattern, and the subsequent usage of the Connector pattern, revolves around your deployment scenario. Your business objects use Java Data Objects (JDO) for data persistence. Because Apache Axis invokes the service implementation within the Apache Axis container, the JDO and JDBC classes load into the container with the service implementation. Depending on the JDO implementation you are using and the deployment options you use for the service implementation, the environment and performance can become unpredictable. Figure 13-2 illustrates the JDO and JDBC classes being instantiated within the Apache Tomcat container.

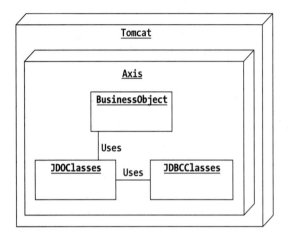

Figure 13-2. Deployment scenario illustrating the use of JDO and JDBC in the Web tier

Apache Axis instantiates your service implementation, BusinessObject, based on options in the deployment descriptor for the class. There are three options for the lifecycle of the service implementation:

- **Application scope:** Creates a single service implementation that services all requests

- **Request scope:** Creates a new service implementation for each request processed by the Apache Axis engine

- **Session scope:** Creates a new service implementation for each user session

No matter which lifecycle option you choose for the lifecycle of the service implementation, you end up with a deployment architecture in which the service implementation and the related services run within a thread in the Apache Tomcat process. On the other hand, the lifecycle options can affect the behavior of the service and dependent services.

Consider a deployment using the Axis Request scope lifecycle option for the service implementation. On each request, Apache Axis creates a business object. The business object must access data so JDO gets a connection to the database through JDBC. If you process 100 or 1,000 requests at a time, you will quickly overwhelm a database's ability to service requests. Depending on your Web Service environment, JDO may not be able to optimize access to the database through built-in mechanisms. For example, if a Web Service implementation spawns a process for each request, then JDO could never fully utilize built-in thread and connection pooling.

Apache Axis does not spawn a process for each request, but it does separate each request into different threads and different class loaders for different services. This complicates the environment for JDO substantially, and you will have to be careful to test your JDO implementation in the Apache Axis environment.

In the end, the service deployment must contain all of the class libraries and Java extensions required to run your Web Service. In the case study, you have 10 or more JAR files in the Apache Tomcat or Apache Axis class path that would not be in the path if you physically separated the logic tier from the Web tier.

As discussed, as you move your classes and implementation into the Web tier deployment, you lose control of their lifecycle and how multiple instances are handled. Further, you lose the ability to manage the logic tier services separately from the Web tier services. This loss in flexibility impacts everything from the optimization of the path to the database to the versatility of the connections between the logic components themselves, as discussed in the previous section. You also lose flexibility in system deployment itself; by physically coupling the logic tier and Web tier, you force your application to be deployed on a *single* host. This deployment scenario limits the scalability of your solution in addition to limiting your ability to leverage the logic tier instances to facilitate reuse in stand-alone applications. You essentially require a running instance of each object for each application. With the size of enterprise applications, this creates a massive redundancy in deployed code, as well as a maintenance nightmare.

Connecting Physical Tiers

In both of the previous scenarios—the subscriber-to-application scenario and the separation of the tiers to mitigate deployment issues—the solution to your problem is to do the following:

- Recognize that there are multiple physical tiers in the solution.

- Use the Connector pattern to link the two tiers together.

In both scenarios, there are multiple physical tiers. In the event-to-application scenario, the Web tier houses the logic to interact with the Web Service world, and the application contains logic that interacts with a user. These tiers must be physically separate because of the containment of the Web Service environment within Apache Tomcat and the containment of the application logic within the Java process facilitating the stand-alone application. In the second scenario, you will want to separate logic from the Web tier to facilitate greater control over the components in the logic tier, to facilitate more diverse deployment scenarios, and to reduce the amount of code running within the Apache Tomcat container. To reach this goal, you physically separate the logic components into a stand-alone process. In both cases, you now follow a Physical Tiers pattern, and you use a Connector pattern to facilitate communication between the tiers.

Understanding the Structure of the Connector Pattern

The Connector pattern is very simple in structure and builds on top of a common distributed object design. Most importantly, the pattern shows a solution to communicate between physical tiers, so there are two significant aspects to this pattern:

- The component structure

- The physical deployment

Figure 13-3 illustrates the component structure of the pattern implementation. The structure is similar in nature to what you would expect from most remote object implementations, such as Java's RMI.

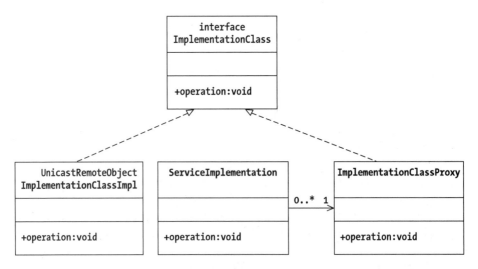

Figure 13-3. Structure of the Connector pattern

Figure 13-3 contains a slightly misleading association between the ServiceImplementation instance and the ImplementationClassProxy instance. The true association is between the ServiceImplementation instance and the ImplementationClass interface. In reality, the service implementation does not know that it is using a proxy to the implementation class. At runtime, the service implementation retrieves the stub that then communicates between processes with the ImplementationClassImpl instance.

Also not evident in the figure is the deployment structure of the solution. Keep in mind that the ServiceImplementation instance and the ImplementationClassProxy instance reside in the Web tier, and the ImplementationClassImpl instance resides in the logic tier and is in a separate process from the Web tier, as shown in Figure 13-4.

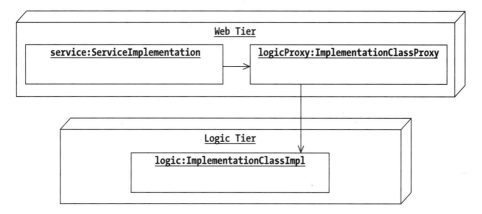

Figure 13-4. Deployment of the connector structure into the Physical Tiers pattern

In Figure 13-4, the ServiceImplementation instance and the ImplementationClassProxy instance reside in the Web tier. The service instance calls operations on the logicProxy instance instead of calling operations directly against the logic instance. The logicProxy instance serves as a connector to the Logic tier where the actual logic implementation resides.

Understanding the Components of the Connector Pattern

Four components make up the Connector pattern. As previously mentioned, these four components mirror most remote object implementation structures:

ImplementationClass: This is an interface to help with implementation transparency. Both the ImplementationClassImpl and the ImplementationClassProxy instances implement this interface.

ImplementationClassImpl: This class contains the actual behavior of any service implementation. For example, if a stand-alone application needs to subscribe to a Web Service event generator, this class contains the code that interacts with the stand-alone application. In the case that you are moving logic implementation out of the Web tier, this class contains any business logic or logic that is unique to the implementation language, such as your JDO persistence mechanisms. This class implements the `ImplementationClass` interface.

ImplementationClassProxy: The `ImplementationClassProxy` component facilitates communication between the `ServiceImplementation` instance and the `ImplementationClassImpl` instance residing in a separate process. The `ImplementationClassProxy` instance implements the `ImplementationClass` interface. The `ServiceImplementation` instance should have little or no awareness of the fact that they are having a conversation with a service that does not reside within the same physical tier.

ServiceImplementation: The service implementation becomes a mere shell of what it was in previous chapters. The interesting logic and behaviors move out of the `ServiceImplementation` instance and into the `ImplementationClassImpl` instance that resides in the Logic tier. This leaves the `ServiceImplementation` instance as a mechanism to forward the Web Service requests to the `ImplementationClassImpl` instance that resides in a separate physical tier through the mechanism embodied in the `ImplementationClassProxy` instance. There are many ways to embody this practice besides RMI. Rather than building your own remote service implementations, you can use an Enterprise JavaBean (EJB) provider in Apache Axis to forward requests to an EJB that exists outside of your own process and takes the place of your `ImplementationClassImpl` instance. This type of implementation for Web Services will be common in practice.

Each of these components implements the same operations; however, the behavior of the operation is different on each class. The service implementation's operation generates a call to the implementation class stub. The stub communicates across processes with the concrete implementation class. Each operation can have similar signatures, but often the service implementation class will require a slightly different operation signature.

Understanding the Connector Collaborations

The collaborations between components are, essentially, a chain of operations that pivot around the implementation class and return to the caller. The collaborations are interesting, especially the details of what goes on between one operation and another and what processes in which each operation runs. Figure 13-5 illustrates the chain of operations typical in the sequence for inter-process communications.

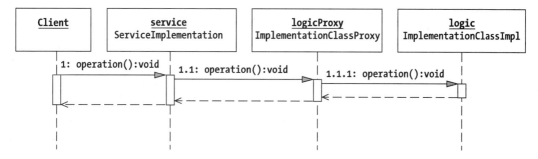

Figure 13-5. Sequence diagram showing pattern class traversal

Within the sequence, a client makes an operation call against a service implementation through a Web Service environment. This collaboration traverses a client's process, and the operation actually executes within the same process space as the Apache Axis implementation. This operation makes a call to the implementation class stub, which is a proxy. The proxy resides within the Apache Axis proxy space, but its target does not. The implementation class itself resides within the destination process, sometimes an application subscriber (other times this will be the Web Service's implementation).

Preparing to Implement the Connector Pattern

This section contains some useful pointers for the Connector pattern. Many of these pointers depend on how much freedom you have with your own application implementation. In the end, how you build your physical tier separation and communication to applications depends heavily on the computing ecosystem you choose to promote.

For example, an EJB environment often proves difficult and heavy for small applications and small businesses. A pure J2SE implementation is lighter but misses substantial opportunities to allow infrastructure other than your own to handle enterprise-scale issues. Many application servers that support EJBs take care of database connection pooling, thread pooling, and load balancing. You should offload this type of infrastructure to experts, such as those who focus on application server implementations, whenever possible. This code has no added value to the functionality provided by your business and only appears if there are failures in the code. The following are some useful pointers for implementing physical tiers with the Connector pattern:

Use native support in your Web Service environment whenever possible: Different levels of native support are inherent in most Web Service implementations. Apache Axis includes providers that allow interprocess communication from Apache to EJBs and to JMS. You can also write your own providers that Apache can use. Integration at this level will most often be quicker than writing your own service implementation, but it will also tie you to a particular Web Service implementation.

There is an "up front" performance penalty for using separated processes: The performance penalty embodies itself in the remote communication between the Web tier and the logic tier. Marshaling and unmarshaling parameters and communicating outside of your own process is always an order of magnitude slower than a local method call. Fortunately, because you are already in a Web environment, the slowdown is not sufficient to cause panic. Further, the ability to build an optimized, isolated, and reusable logic tier that communicates directly between components and reuses existing instances in a single process often outweighs the slight performance loss. Remember that in the case of a technology such as JDO, the separate threads, class loaders, and processes that a Web Service implementation may use can lead to duplicate instantiations and ineffective use of the underlying database. By isolating the use of JDO and JDBC, and technologies like them, to a single deployment process and class loader, you may be able to get far superior performance than if you allow the Web Service environment to control instantiation.

There are broader options for deployment depending on the remote mechanism you use to implement the Connector pattern: Once you insert remote mechanisms between the Web tier and the logic tier, you open the ability to place the tiers on separate processors and separate networks, as long as there is still a communication path between the servers.

You lose any benefits of residing within the Web Service container that a Web Service implementation offers: There are two primary benefits to residing within the Web Tier container: the ability to manage a single environment containing the entire application and the performance inherent in having everything reside in a single container. The first problem, consolidated application management, is the most difficult. There may be ways to plug all of the server and application management into a single management framework; however, the reality of such a scenario is more than likely many years off. The second problem, performance, also takes work to handle. You could allow some service implementations to reside entirely in the Web tier while others communicate outwardly with their logic tier counterparts. Stateless Web Services that have little interaction with other application components are good candidates for leaving out of the new tier design.

Implementing the Connector Pattern with Web Services

The event service demonstrated in the previous chapter is an excellent place to demonstrate the usefulness of the Connector pattern. You will use the event service as is but with a new event subscriber. The event subscriber is part of a larger application that receives events from the remote event service and posts them immediately to the user through a simple Java Swing user interface. The pattern implementation, shown in Figure 13-6, adds an application subscriber and the components that enable it to be a remote object.

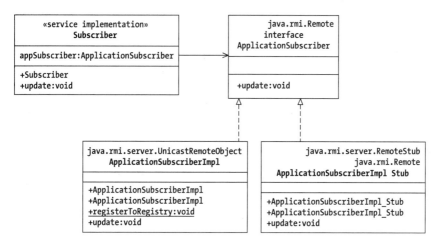

Figure 13-6. Event subscriber class diagram

As mentioned in the "Understanding the Structure of the Connector Pattern" section, the class diagram does not belie the nature of the deployment or some of the details inherent in actual implementation. In this case, the subscriber service implementation that resides in the Web tier uses an instance of the ApplicationSubscriberImpl_Stub instance to communicate with the ApplicationSubscriberImpl instance that resides in the application's process, as shown in Figure 13-7.

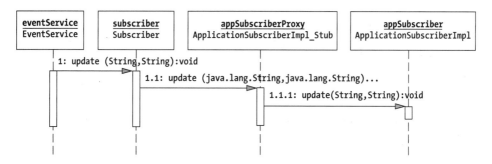

Figure 13-7. Event forwarding through the physical tiers by the connector

The interface, ApplicationSubscriber, abstracts away the actual concrete class that the subscriber holds, which is simply a good practice employed by RMI users. Using the interface model, the service implementation, Subscriber, can look up an ApplicationSubscriber interface in the naming service and not worry about the implementation returned to them. In this case, the subscriber receives the stub.

Defining the Interface to the Implementation Side

To leverage RMI, you will first define the interface that both the concrete implementation class and the proxy to the implementation class implement. The service implementation could use the interface as well, though the signatures to the methods do not have to match between the service implementation and the remote implementation class. Listing 13-1 contains the interface implementation.

Listing 13-1. Interface to the Remote Implementation Class

```
public interface ApplicationSubscriber extends Remote {
  public void update(String eventId, String data) throws RemoteException;
}
```

There should be nothing too interesting in the interface. To implement the class as a remote object, the class extends java.rmi.Remote and the methods in the class throw the java.rmi.RemoteException exception.

Building the Implementation Class

The class for the application subscriber implements the interface in Listing 13-1 and extends the java.rmi.server.UnicastRemoteObject class. This class extension makes your object remoteable and gives it the ability to be registered with the naming service from RMI and subsequently receive method calls from outside of the process.

The class is a part of a larger Swing-based application. Its responsibilities include the following:

- Receiving events from a remote target—in this case the service implementation subscriber that serves as a bridge to an external event service

- Posting the events directly to a text area for the application user to see

To fulfill the second responsibility, the application passes a reference to the JTextArea graphic component on the constructor that this class instance uses to post messages for the user. Listing 13-2 illustrates the application-side subscriber that serves as the implementation class.

Listing 13-2. Application-Side Event Subscriber

```
public class ApplicationSubscriberImpl
  extends java.rmi.server.UnicastRemoteObject
  implements ApplicationSubscriber {

  JTextArea ivTextArea = null;

  public ApplicationSubscriberImpl(JTextArea textArea)
throws RemoteException {
    super();
    ivTextArea = textArea;
  }

  public ApplicationSubscriberImpl(int port, JTextArea textArea)
    throws RemoteException {
    super(port);
    ivTextArea = textArea;
  }

  public void update(String eventId, String data) throws RemoteException {
    ivTextArea.append("Event ID: "+eventId);
    ivTextArea.append("Event Data: "+data);
  }
}
```

The service implementation (the subscriber that serves as the Web Service) calls the update method on this class. This class, in turn, writes the data from the event to the application's text area by simply appending the event data to the text area. In reality, you would have a more user-centric mechanism for notifying the user of an important event that needs their attention.

This class requires special handling on instantiation. To facilitate communication between the service implementation deployed through Apache Axis and this application-side implementation class, the class must register with RMI's component registry, the Naming service. The service implementation can then use Naming to look up the class from an outside process and communicate through the proxy.

Building Remote Stubs

J2SE comes with an RMI compiler, rmic, that handles the details of building the application-side implementation stub generation. The stub is subsequently instantiated into the same process that runs the service implementation; thus, the interface must at least be in the class path for the Apache Axis engine.

Your build process—in this case, the Apache Ant build process that comes with the source code for the book—automatically builds the stubs when the code is recompiled.

Implementing the Web Service

The previous classes and the interface concerned themselves with the concrete behavior of the application that the service implementation calls upon receiving a request. Also in the previous sections, you built the mechanisms that the service implementation uses to have a conversation with the application-side (or logic tier) components.

This section enhances the subscriber from the event service built in the Publish/Subscribe pattern to forward messages to the application with an interest in the events published by the event service. The difference in the implementation code from the previous chapter occurs in the update method, shown in Listing 13-3. You no longer print information to the System.out stream in the body of the update method. Instead, you retrieve a proxy to the implementation, through RMI's Naming service, and call methods against the proxy.

Listing 13-3. Subscriber Web Service Implementation

```
public class Subscriber {
  private static String topic =
    "com.servicefoundry.books.events.ProductOrderUpdate";

  ApplicationSubscriber appSubscriber = null;

  public Subscriber() {
  }

  public void update(String eventId, String data){
    try {
      ApplicationSubscriber appSubscriber =
      (ApplicationSubscriber)Naming.lookup("ApplicationSubscriberImpl");
      if(appSubscriber!=null){
        appSubscriber.update(eventId, data);
      }
    } catch (Exception e) {
      e.printStackTrace();
    }
  }
}
```

Listing 13-3 retrieves the proxy from RMI's Naming every time Apache Axis calls the update method. This allows the application to start and stop at will without impacting the Web Service. The Web Service continues to receive events from the remote event service when the user application is not available, but it stops delivering events to the user application. One of the nice attributes of splitting the logic and Web tiers in terms of the process that contains them is the additional ability to leverage code and classes independently of the containers. For example, users can continue to use applications when the Web Service environment is not available.

This service implementation deploys to Apache Axis in the same manner as the subscriber in the previous chapter. The same Web Services Description Language (WSDL) created in the previous chapter describes the interface to this subscriber, and the event service has no realization that this implementation differs from the previous chapter's implementation.

Seeing the Event Service in Action with the New Subscriber

Putting the new subscriber Web Service into action requires several steps worth noting. The steps described here do not necessarily have to occur in the order described; however, exceptions to the step order accompany the description:

1. Start the event service built in the previous chapter. This Web Service runs unmodified from the previous chapter.

2. Start the stand-alone application. By starting the stand-alone application, you also start the subscriber implementation class that resides within the application. Further, the application registers the RMI object with the RMI Naming service, with the application code shown in Listing 13-4, in the local RMI registry. After this step, other processes can download the remote stub class from Naming and communicate with the application's subscriber implementation. Recall that this step does not have to occur before the Web Service subscriber implementation starts because the Web Service will simply ignore events that post to it if an appropriate subscriber cannot be located.

3. Start the subscription Web Service built in this chapter and register it with the event service started in step 1. This step can occur before or after step 2. After the subscription Web Service starts, register its target Uniform Resource Locator (URL) with the event service started in step 1. At this point, events delivered to the event service, started in step 1, with the appropriate topic post to the event subscriber started in this step. The event subscriber started in this step then forwards the event to the application subscriber started in step 2.

4. Next, post an event to the Web Service with the client from the previous chapter.

5. Finally, view the results of the post to the Web Service in the stand-alone application's graphical text area.

Listing 13-4 contains a method run by the stand-alone application to register its subscriber to RMI's `Naming` component. The application uses this code as described in step 2 after initialization of the user interface but before clients can interact with the application.

Listing 13-4. Registering the Application's Subscriber with RMI's `Naming` *Service*

```
public static void registerToRegistry(
    String name, Remote obj, boolean create)
    throws RemoteException, MalformedURLException{

    if (name == null)
      throw new IllegalArgumentException(
      "registration name can not be null"
      );

    try {
      Naming.rebind(name, obj);
    } catch (RemoteException ex){
      if (create) {
        Registry r =
          LocateRegistry.createRegistry(Registry.REGISTRY_PORT);
        r.rebind(name, obj);
      } else throw ex;
    }
  }
```

The client creates the application subscriber and registers it with the code shown in Listing 13-5. The `ivTextArea` instance variable refers to a `JTextArea` graphical component created earlier in the application.

Listing 13-5. Creating the Application-Side Subscriber and Registering the Subscriber

```
ApplicationSubscriberImpl obj =
 new ApplicationSubscriberImpl(ivTextArea);
ApplicationSubscriberImpl.registerToRegistry(
 "ApplicationSubscriberImpl", obj, true);
```

In Listing 13-5, you registered the application subscriber using the name *ApplicationSubscriberImpl*. The Web Service implementation uses this name to locate the proxy to the application in RMI's Naming service, as shown previously in Listing 13-3. Once the service implementation in the Web tier has a reference to the proxy, the proxy facilitates the remote communication with the logic tier and the concrete implementation of the application subscriber logic.

Leveraging Physical Tiers and the Connector Patterns in the Case Study

The P.T. Monday Coffee Company application, when completed, will contain two separate tiers with the service implementations forwarding requests to a separate logic tier. Isolating the JDO implementation to a single tier and bringing it under your own control rather than the Web Service implementation's control is the primary motivation for the physical separation. In the end, your logic is complex enough that you can optimize it by running in your own application space. Further, a separate logic tier can facilitate both Web Services and stand-alone Java-based or Java Server Pages–based clients who go directly to the Java components and bypass the Web Services.

In addition to physical tier separation, you also need to use the Connector pattern to communicate with stand-alone applications deployed for the employees at the P.T. Monday Coffee Company. These applications should be able to register for events with Web Services that are outside of the P.T. Monday Coffee Company. An example of a case where you could use immediate notification is when you want immediate notification of package delivery to special customers or of specials that your suppliers may have for raw coffee beans.

Identifying Important Classes and Files in the Case Study

The sample for this chapter is the most complex yet, with multiple layers of remote protocols, Web Services, and RMI, as well as a chain of event handlers that act in different processes. As you view the source code listed in Table 13-1, use Figure 13-7 to understand the class's place in the chain of active class instances.

Table 13-1. Sample Location

FILE	LOCATION	DESCRIPTION
Subscriber.java	src/com/ servicefoundry/books/ webservices/eventservice	This is the Subscriber class as shown in Listing 13-3. This subscriber deploys as a Web Service and uses RMI to communicate with the connector registered in Listing 13-5 when the Subscriber receives an event.
ApplicationSubscriber. java	src/com/ servicefoundry/books/ webservices/eventservice	This is the interface to the application's subscriber, as shown in Listing 13-1.
ApplicationSubscriberImpl. java	src/com/ servicefoundry/books/ webservices/eventservice	This is the application's subscriber implementation, as shown in Listing 13-2.
ServiceToApplicationTest. java	src/com/ servicefoundry/books/ webservices/test	This is a graphical client that displays event data when its subscriber receives notifications. This client also registers the connector, an instance of the RMI class shown in Listing 13-2, via the RMI Naming service, as shown in Listing 13-5.

Using Ant Targets to Run the Case Study

Table 13-2 describes the targets to run for the Ant environment to see the programs and chapter samples in operation. Before running any samples, be sure you read and perform all of the install steps in the appendix.

Table 13-2. Ant Targets

TARGET	DESCRIPTION
graphicaleventstream	This runs the ServiceToApplicationTest.java client, which is a stand-alone application containing a simple logic tier ApplicationSubscriberImpl instance that receives event interactions from the Web tier and publishes them to the user.
registersubscriberwitheventservice2	This registers your Web tier subscriber with the EventService Web Service built in the previous chapters. The Subscriber Web Service later locates the physically separate logic tier and delivers events to the ApplicationSubscriberImpl via RMI.
publishtoeventservice	This publishes an event to the EventService Web Service. The Subscriber Web Service will see this event and forward it to the Subscriber service implementation in the Web tier. The Subscriber service implementation forwards the event through the Connector pattern to the ApplicationSubscriberImpl instance residing in the application's logic tier. The ApplicationSubscriberImpl instance publishes the event to the presentation tier of the application.

Summary

The Connector pattern focuses on the mechanics of communicating between physical tiers. This pattern is critical for allowing communication from a Web Service to a stand-alone application or a separate logic tier. This chapter covered the necessity of physical tiers by first looking at the Physical Tiers architecture pattern and then looking at two scenarios that illustrate the need for the Physical Tiers pattern. The first of these illustrations was a stand-alone application that uses a Web tier to interact with event services that reside in the Web Service architecture. The second of the illustrations showed some downsides to having a single physical tier deployed entirely within an Apache Tomcat container. The Connector design pattern illustrates how to facilitate communication between physical tiers.

Application builders can often implement this pattern with native support in their chosen Web Service environment. For example, Apache Axis contains an EJB provider that separates the Web Service interactions from the fulfillment of the behavior portion of a Web Service operation. With the Connector pattern, the Web Service communicates to a container hosting EJBs to execute business logic and return the results back to the client. In this chapter, you implemented this functionality using a service implementation and Java's RMI implementation.

Because of this pattern, much of the P.T. Monday Coffee Company application can become a physically separated logic tier with both stand-alone applications and Web Services communicating through the same instances of the classes in the logic tier. This centralization helps you optimize the business logic, data caching, and memory footprint of the entire software stack. You also increase your options for application deployment. An administrator can deploy the logic tier to one computer system while the Web tier deploys to another computer system. Further, the Web tier's footprint shrinks and you no longer have to deploy JDO and JDBC to the Web tier applications.

Related Patterns

There are other ways to connect the Web Service architecture to a stand-alone application:

Faux Implementation: The Faux Implementation pattern is an alternative mechanism for solving the event listener problem identified in this chapter. The Faux Implementation appears as a first-class Web Service but is instead merely an open socket that receives connections and gives proper responses to the event service. With faux implementation, you lighten the requirement of having a complete Web Service environment available on your client in order to participate in the Web Service paradigm. Chapter 14, "Exploring the Faux Implementation Pattern," covers this pattern.

Additional Reading

- Apache Axis: http://xml.apache.org/axis/

- Gamma, Erich et. al. *Design Patterns: Elements of Reusable Object-Oriented Software*. Addison-Wesley, 1995.

- Völter, Markus; Schmid, Alexander; Wolff, Eberhard. *Server Component Patterns: Component Infrastructures Illustrated with EJB*. John Wiley & Sons, 2002.

CHAPTER 14

Exploring the Faux Implementation Pattern

THE PAST SEVERAL CHAPTERS HAVE assumed that a client of the EventService Web Service will deploy their subscriber to a full Web Service environment to subscribe to a few events. In many ways, this is like using a mainframe to play your MP3 files. Not only do you waste the full potential of the environment, you introduce a whole host of unnecessary issues, especially if you have a small client. In the case study, for example, you deploy Apache Tomcat and the Apache Axis environment to subscribe to an event. You then build and deploy a Web Service that uses the Connector pattern from Chapter 13, "Exploring the Physical Tiers Pattern," to ensure that the application can receive events from the client-side Web tier. This is a lot of work for little return.

A better approach for your client may be to find a way to leverage the strict Web Service interface and the Simple Object Access Protocol (SOAP) definition, but in a lighter manner. For example, you can leverage the SOAP definition of messages sent from the EventService Web Service to a Subscriber to build your own Web Service environment without Apache Axis. This environment can receive and parse a single event from an event service, but it leaves out flexibility in exchange for simplicity and a smaller footprint. In a sense, you can fake out the EventService Web Service by simply reading data off a socket and avoiding Apache Axis. This lightweight technique allows you to toss away the client-side Web Service environment and simplify client install and deployment. This approach of implementing a strict interface in a way that the architect or designer may not have expected is the Faux Implementation pattern.

The concept of a faux implementation is not new to programmers. Given a well-defined interface and behavior specification, programmers build faux implementations all the time. In some cases, one could even argue that there is no such thing as a faux implementation. In this argument, as long as the expected interface and behavior appears, there is no reason to consider the implementation a fake.

Web Service environments can use the Faux Implementation pattern in several places:

Building tests: You use the Faux Implementation pattern to build tests for your service implementations. This practice is especially important for implementations that depend on live, external Web Services. You do not want to test your real, external service without first trying your service implementation on a mocked-up, fake version of the external Web Service that you write. With this technique, you can get rid of the worst of your bugs before you even try to use the external Web Service.

Lightening the burden: If you use the Web Service–based Publish/ Subscribe pattern and the Observer pattern that require a Web Service subscriber, you should expect that consumers of your events will use the Faux Implementation pattern. This pattern lightens the burden on the clients who do not want to deploy a full Web Service environment, such as Apache Axis, for their simple application.

The Faux Implementation pattern is important in testing a system, maintaining a system over generations of software and hardware, and allowing you to think outside of the box for implementing clients that must adhere to a particular interface. This chapter discusses some of the common uses of the Faux Implementation pattern to show you its diversity, and then the chapter discusses its structure and gives a Web Service implementation of this pattern.

> **NOTE** *Faux implementation has its roots in the Interface pattern, used throughout object-oriented computing. Formal treatments of the Faux Implementation pattern are becoming available, particularly as extreme programming becomes more common. Extreme programming often uses the Faux Implementation pattern as a mechanism for building tests for a component and running the tests before a component is completed. The Faux Implementation pattern allows developers to explore how their real implementation should behave before they execute the actual implementation.*

Seeing Faux Implementation in Practice

Faux implementations can apply to small parts of an application, such as a class in an object-oriented environment, or to large environments, such as software that emulates hardware. In the first case, the Faux Implementation pattern can aid developers who are doing parallel development. In the latter case, you could create an environment for an application that the application never expected to encounter, such as running an old Atari 2600 game on a Pentium 4 computer.

Creating Test Implementations

A fully specified architecture and ambitious programmers can lead to an especially productive environment if the developers are willing to rely on a specification rather than a concrete component deliverable from another team. Consider a simple case that contains two major subsystems—a viewer for musical scores and a component that gathers the musical score from an input stream. In this case, an architecture document specifies interfaces for the view and reader component. The architecture also specifies the format of an Extensible Markup Language (XML) document that the components use to communicate a musical score with, as shown in Figure 14-1.

With the hand-off document and interface to the music reader specified, the developer building the music-viewing component can develop the entire component without ever having to use a real implementation of the music reader. As long as both developers implement the interface and the document specification from the architecture, integration between the two real components can wait until late in the development cycle.

The developer of the music viewer can spend the first few days of their development creating a simple implementation of the interface that returns documents from a file system. They can create hundreds of test documents and route them through their faux implementation to fully test the music viewer without ever seeing a real implementation of the music reader. In this case, developers use the Faux Implementation pattern as the basis of TestMusicReader so that they can test the MusicViewer component without ever receiving ProductionMusicReader. TestMusicReader is a faux implementation of MusicReader because it adheres properly to the interface but is not what the architects had in mind when they specified the architecture.

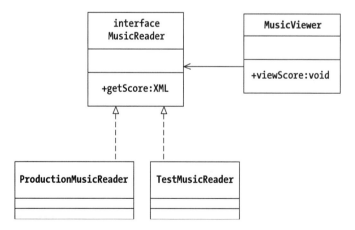

Figure 14-1. Music test implementation component structure

Emulating Old Environments on New Hardware

Faux implementations do not only apply to classes and granular components. Consider the revival of old console games through *emulation*. Emulators implement the interface and communication techniques defined by a particular device. For example, the Atari 2600 implemented an interface and defined a protocol to facilitate the communication between a game on a cartridge and the game console for processing. Now, consider if you could implement the same interface in software and then take an image of the game on the game cartridge and plug them together through software. This is emulation.

The Atari 2600 example is a bit different from the type of emulation you use to emulate an environment for testing programs. Consider the scenario of building applications for a wireless phone. Rather than downloading your applications to the phone to test it, you run the application in a software environment that emulates the phone. Once you have the application working, you download it to the wireless phone and run the application, just in case there are flaws in the emulator. Figure 14-2 shows the emulation scenario in the form of a class diagram.

The developer of WirelessApplication builds their application based on DeviceSoftwareSpecification. Phones implement this specification, but the specification is detailed enough so as to allow developers to also use WirelessPhoneEmulator. This software phone emulator is built into Integrated Development Environments (IDEs), such as the Sun ONE Studio Enterprise Edition, so that you never have to load your application onto a real phone for testing.

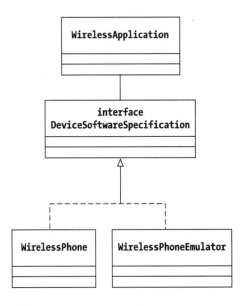

Figure 14-2. Device emulation

In essence, the practice of emulation is an implementation of the Faux Implementation pattern. You are using software to pretend it is a piece of hardware so you can test applications or run games without even owning the hardware. In many cases, the creators of the original hardware, such as the Atari 2600, could never have imagined the widespread use of emulation. Fortunately, using clean, predictable interfaces allows people to reverse-engineer them and create alternate implementations of the interface.

Understanding the Faux Implementation Structure

The structure of the Faux Implementation pattern is simple. You want to determine the interface to a real implementation, and you then create one or more implementations that emulate the expected, or known, real implementation. One aspect that the structure cannot capture is the importance of the interface behavior for making a faux implementation work. Figure 14-3 shows the structure of a Faux Implementation pattern. Notice the heavy reliance on the interface and the application's use of the interface over the implementation itself.

The ClassInterface component in Figure 14-3 indicates semantic equivalence and behavioral equivalence. Depending on the environment, the behavioral equivalence may extend beyond what a programmer normally considers in their job. Consider an Atari 2600 game console released in the 1980s. Today's computers dwarf the Atari 2600 game console in terms of processor speeds. A pocket computer, such as a PalmPilot, can emulate the entire hardware console without any difficulties. On the other hand, you do not want to run one of the games from the 1980s at today's processor speeds—your Pac-Man's hair would fly off. The emulator's behavior must ensure the game plays with the same feel of the 1980s.

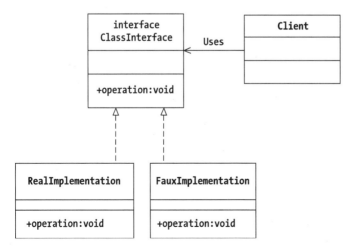

Figure 14-3. Structure of a faux implementation

Thus, the FauxImplementation instance of the ClassInterface component must behave in the same way as the RealImplementation instance. Consider your own Web Service environment. In the event that you use the Faux Implementation pattern to test your own service implementation with an expected interface to an external Web Service, you could end up with a service that works, but not as expected. Your FauxImplementation instance may run quickly, in milliseconds; however, when you connect to the RealImplementation instance, you find that it does not return for days. Because you misunderstood the RealImplementation instance's behavior, you could end up redesigning your Client late in the development process.

Understanding the Components of the Faux Implementation Pattern

There are three components to a Faux Implementation pattern. The definitions are what you would expect from object-oriented programming with a stress on behavioral interface in the class interface definition:

ClassInterface: The ClassInterface component defines the application-programming interface to concrete classes as well as the expected behavior for implementations of the interface. If a behavior is not robustly defined, an implementer of the FauxImplementation instance may end up making guesses or assumptions as to the behavior of a RealImplementation instance. Each guess or assumption of the behavior makes the FauxImplementation instance less effective.

RealImplementation: The RealImplementation component is the expected embodiment of the class interface. For example, in a Web Service environment, one would expect Apache Axis to host a Web Service; therefore, it would be the "real" implementation. In the music viewer example, the viewer should expect the RealImplementation component to read music from an input source, as defined in the architecture.

FauxImplementation: The FauxImplementation component is, essentially, a deviation from the expected implementation of the class interface. From the perspective of the class interface and a user of the class, there should be no difference between the FauxImplementation component and the RealImplementation component. Looking under the covers of the FauxImplementation component, a developer finds elements that they do not expect. In the case of hardware emulation, a program on a user interface functions fine, but underneath you have only a piece of software, not a fully functioning phone. The test program is similar; the FauxImplementation component may generate random music scores to test the boundary conditions of the music viewer, but the component does not receive input from files or MIDI input.

The examples in this chapter have shown the Atari 2600 example, which built the RealImplementation component first. At some point, engineers reverse-engineered the ClassInterface component and proceeded to build FauxImplementation components. The test scenario lets the architects build the ClassInterface component, lets the developer of the real implementation's client build the FauxImplementation component, and lets other developers work on the RealImplementation component. You could also get a ClassInterface component, build a FauxImplementation component, and never build a RealImplementation component, as is the case in this chapter's sample.

Understanding Faux Implementation Pattern Collaborations

The class interface dictates the interactions between a client and a faux implementation. Figure 14-4 shows that the client instantiates a faux implementation rather than a real implementation and then calls an operation against it.

Developers use different techniques for instantiating the faux implementation. A developer using the faux implementation for testing will hide the implementation behind a class factory. By using a class factory and allowing it to instantiate the implementation, the factory hides whether the faux implementation or the real implementation is in use. With this technique, a developer can easily switch the real implementation into their code when the real implementation team delivers the component.

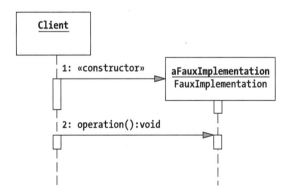

Figure 14-4. Sequence of a client call

Preparing to Use the Faux Implementation Pattern

In general, how you go about building a faux implementation depends on the situation you find yourself addressing. Keep the following tips in mind:

Use a class factory if you are in a test scenario where you want to load different implementations of test classes: Class factories are good at hiding the details of what implementation class your component uses. Further, this technique is simply good programming when there are points in your code that may receive new implementations to plug in over time.

A FauxImplementation instance does not have to have a RealImplementation counterpart: In the case of the upcoming Web Service example, you rely on the faux implementation for your application and never build an "expected" implementation of your service.

The faux implementation can be fragile: Most likely, your implementation will be much lighter and not as robust as the real implementation. Further, if you misinterpret the specification, your implementation may work for a while until the server component fixes the behavioral specification. At this point, the faux implementation will likely break.

Ensure behavior consistency as well as interface consistency between the real and faux implementations: Nothing is more frustrating than finding a behavior in an emulator that does not represent the real world. Consider the test scenario where you write a test implementation that you use to get your music viewer working. The real implementation team gets around to delivering you the production components and your music viewer blows up because of a behavior change. Whose component is right? The architecture document should settle the argument, but often the architecture document does not contain a description of the behavior in question. If it did, your viewer would have worked because you would have implemented the test implementation according to the specification.

Using a Faux Implementation

The sample implementation you will use is, again, related to your Web Service implementation of the Publish/Subscribe pattern. One of the potential failures of the event service produced in Chapter 12, "Implementing the Publish/Subscribe Pattern," is its heavyweight client-side requirements for using the EventService Web Service. Recall that the client must implement a Web Service subscriber and that you deployed this subscriber using Apache Axis. This created a problem communicating with a stand-alone application because the Web Service lives in the same process as the Apache Axis engine in the examples. You could use the Connector pattern from Chapter 13, "Exploring the Physical Tiers Pattern," to connect your Web tier to your Application tier, but the heavy client installation remains for the deployment of your Subscriber Web Service.

Instead of creating a separate Web tier for hosting your Subscriber, you can use the Faux Implementation pattern to bring the behavior and interface of the Web Service paradigm directly into your Java application. There are many ways to do this; one way is to simply open a server socket and allow the Web Services environment to communicate into your server socket. You take the SOAP message off the socket and return an appropriate response to the service that is attempting to invoke an operation through your socket.

You need to consider the following on the client implementation:

- **FauxImplementationTest:** The main Java program that a user instantiates from the command line

- **FauxWebServiceSubscriber:** A class that listens on a socket for incoming Web Service requests

- **Subscriber:** The Web Services Description Language (WSDL) interface to the Subscriber Web Service that the event service expects to call

Figure 14-5 shows the relationships between the classes. Notice that FauxWebServiceSubscriber instance implements the Runnable interface, allowing it to run within its own thread in your main application. Also, notice that there is no direct inheritance of the Subscriber interface. Because Web Services rely on SOAP and not a semantic interface to bind to, you do not actually implement an update method or the Subscriber interface. Instead, your FauxWebServiceSubscriber instance must be able to take the SOAP message sent by the EventService Web Service off of a socket and parse it appropriately.

There is another interesting twist to the class diagram in Figure 14-5. The Subscriber is *not* a Java interface. The Subscriber is the WSDL containing the SOAP message definition for the message that you read off the socket connection that the event service makes with your program. In effect, FauxWebServiceSubscriber takes the architecture adapter that exchanges the information between the Web Service architecture and your Java architecture and places it inside your own Java architecture.

To understand what FauxWebServiceSubscriber must do, it is useful to look at live SOAP messages exchanged between the event service and a full subscriber. After you examine the SOAP message, you will construct your own subscriber and register it with the event service.

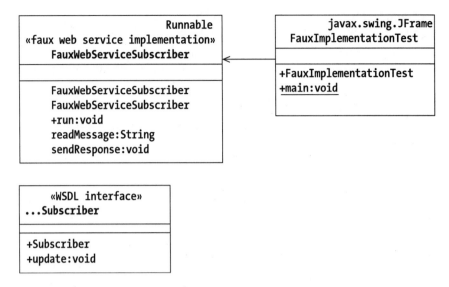

Figure 14-5. Sample faux implementation class structure

Using the SOAP Messages to Receive and Send

It is worth taking a quick look at sample messages exchanged between one of your original subscribers and the event service when the event service publishes a message to a subscriber. (I include the Hypertext Transfer Protocol (HTTP) headers in the exchange because you will read the information from a raw socket and the HTTP headers indicate information about the message.)

The first message, the one that your subscriber receives, contains the HTTP header, the information about the update operation (ns1:update), the SOAP envelope, and two parameters (the topic of the event and the data associated with the event). Listing 14-1 shows the SOAP message.

Listing 14-1. SOAP Message Received by a Subscriber

```
POST /axis/services/Subscriber HTTP/1.0
Content-Type: text/xml; charset=utf-8
Accept: application/soap+xml, application/dime, multipart/related, text/*
User-Agent: Axis/beta3
Host: localhost
Cache-Control: no-cache
Pragma: no-cache
SOAPAction: ""
Content-Length: 572
```

```
<?xml version="1.0" encoding="UTF-8"?>
<soapenv:Envelope xmlns:soapenv=http://schemas.xmlsoap.org/soap/envelope/
    xmlns:xsd="http://www.w3.org/2001/XMLSchema"
    xmlns:xsi="http://www.w3.org/2001/XMLSchema-instance">
 <soapenv:Body>
  <ns1:update soapenv:encodingStyle=http://schemas.xmlsoap.org/soap/encoding/
    xmlns:ns1="http://localhost:8080/axis/services/Subscriber">
   <eventId
      xsi:type="xsd:string">com.servicefoundry.books.events.ProductOrderUpdate
   </eventId>
   <data xsi:type="xsd:string">orderId:updated<></data>
  </ns1:update>
 </soapenv:Body>
</soapenv:Envelope>
```

The message returned from the subscriber, and the one you have to emulate after successfully reading the message sent, contains an HTTP header and an indication that this is a response to the update request (ns1:updateResponse). It does not contain any additional data because the return from an update operation is void. Listing 14-2 shows the response SOAP message.

Listing 14-2. Response SOAP Message from the Subscriber

```
HTTP/1.1 200 OK
Content-Type: text/xml; charset=utf-8
Date: Fri, 17 Jan 2003 01:56:35 GMT
Server: Apache Coyote/1.0
Connection: close

<?xml version="1.0" encoding="UTF-8"?>
<soapenv:Envelope xmlns:soapenv=http://schemas.xmlsoap.org/soap/envelope/
    xmlns:xsd="http://www.w3.org/2001/XMLSchema"
    xmlns:xsi="http://www.w3.org/2001/XMLSchema-instance">
 <soapenv:Body>
  <ns1:updateResponse
      soapenv:encodingStyle=http://schemas.xmlsoap.org/soap/encoding/
      xmlns:ns1="http://localhost:8080/axis/services/Subscriber"/>
 </soapenv:Body>
</soapenv:Envelope>
```

There are a variety of ways to read the incoming message, parse the data, and create a response. The important part of the interaction is that you appear to be a valid Web Service target on the receiving end. To do this, you will likely go through some trial and error, just as in this example. The sample messages in Listing 14-1 and 14-2 should help.

Implementing the Subscriber

Once you have a feel for how the interactions between the event service and a subscriber take place, you can build a simple client that takes care of your Web Service interactions. A client instantiates the class shown in Listing 14-3, FauxWebServiceSubscriber, with an object reference to itself. The FauxWebServiceSubscriber instance listens on the socket, accepts a request from that socket, and subsequently returns a message to the server on the same socket. The callback parameter simply allows the client to communicate to the application that spawned the thread containing the listening code.

Listing 14-3. Listening for a SOAP Message

```java
public class FauxWebServiceSubscriber implements Runnable {

    JTextArea ivTextArea = null;
    int port = 9091;

    FauxWebServiceSubscriber(JTextArea textArea) {
        ivTextArea = textArea;
    }

    FauxWebServiceSubscriber(int port, JTextArea textArea) {
        ivTextArea = textArea;
        this.port = port;
    }

    public void run() {
        while (true) {
            try {
                ServerSocket srv = new ServerSocket(port);
                // Wait for connection from client.
                Socket socket = srv.accept();
                String message = readMessage(socket);
                sendResponse(socket, message);
                ivTextArea.setText(message);
            } catch (IOException e) {
            }
        }
    }

    String readMessage(Socket socket) throws IOException {
      // read the SOAP message off the socket and parse
    }
```

```
    void sendResponse(Socket socket, String message) throws IOException {
        // create a response message and write it to the socket
    }
}
```

A Java application instantiates the `FauxWebServiceSubscriber` class and spawns it as a thread. Thus, Java's `Thread` class will execute the `run` method. This method waits on a server socket and accepts requests from clients. These requests defer reading the message off the socket and defer responding to the message on the same socket to helper methods. The code in these helper methods becomes quite complex; you can review it from the download package if you are interested in socket and networking code.

There are many ways you can choose to implement your lightweight client. You could go further into the Web Service world by using a lightweight HTTP server or even using Apache's SOAP processor. Each lightens the burden on your client and does things in a way that the original event service did not expect.

The raw socket connection is, perhaps, the most fragile mechanism for implementing the faux implementation. The burden for exception handling and errors falls onto you, rather than onto third-party software. In fact, by the time your subscriber is robust, you will end up implementing many of the mechanisms that already exist in Apache Axis or the Apache SOAP implementations.

Deploying the Faux Implementation

Deployment for this subscriber is much simpler than the previous subscriber examples. There are no Web Services to deploy; instead, you simply run your application, spawn the socket listener built in the previous section, and register your socket with the event service, as shown in Listing 14-4.

Listing 14-4. Registering with the Event Service

```
try {
    Thread t =new Thread(
        new FauxImplementationListener(ivTextArea));
    t.start();
    EventServiceService service =
        new EventServiceServiceLocator();
    EventService port =service.getEventService();
    port.addSubscriber(topic,
        "http://localhost:9091/FauxSubscriber");
}catch (Exception re){
    re.printStackTrace();
}
```

> **NOTE**   *Listing 14-4 has a graphical portion of the code that is not shown. That code, which is in the downloaded sample code, pops up a text area that the subscriber uses to dump messages to, as in previous chapters.*

Leveraging the Faux Implementation in the Case Study

The applications you build for the P.T. Monday Coffee Company do not directly use faux implementations; instead, you should expect that clients of the Web Services may use the faux implementation. Clients will use it to lighten the burden of some of the more complex client requirements, such as the event delivery mechanisms. Individual developers may choose to use the Faux Implementation pattern as a means to simulate external Web Services without actually connecting to them or simply as a mechanism to alleviate dependencies on other developers.

In the final deployment of the application, the logic tier is physically separated from the Web tier, as shown in Chapter 13, "Exploring the Physical Tiers Pattern." Your clients simply reuse the logic tier. This reuse facilitates your client's ability to receive Web Service events directly from Java. Your Java clients also have the benefit of a full Apache Axis deployment available to them, so they can easily leverage this deployment and expect full support from the Information Technology (IT) department.

Identifying Important Classes and Files in the Case Study

This is the final example in the book that uses the EventService Web Service built in Chapter 12, "Implementing the Publish/Subscribe Pattern." In this sample, you do not need a Web Service subscription implementation, so there are no additional Web Service deployments beyond the EventService deployed in Chapter 12. Table 14-1 contains the client-side Java implementations available from the downloaded source.

Table 14-1. Sample Location

FILE	LOCATION	DESCRIPTION
FauxImplementationTest. java	src\com\ servicefoundry\ webservicesbook\tests	The main program that contains the event service registration, shown in Listing 14-4, and that spawns a thread containing an instance of the FauxWebServiceSubscriber
FauxWebServiceSubscriber. java	src\com\ servicefoundry\ webservicesbook\tests	The Runnable class, from Listing 14-3, that implements the acceptance of Web Service requests and processing of the service responses

Using Ant Targets to Run the Case Study

There are only two steps to this sample; the first starts the client, and the second publishes events to the EventService Web Service presented in Chapter 12, "Implementing the Publish/Subscribe Pattern." The client prints out each event published to the event service. Table 14-2 contains the Ant targets for running the client and publishing an event to the event service.

Table 14-2. Ant Targets

TARGET	DESCRIPTION
fauximplementation	A small graphical client that subscribes to the event service (deployed in Chapter 12) and receives notifications
publishtoeventservices	Publishes an event to the already deployed event service (deployed in Chapter 12)

Summary

This chapter looked at the Faux Implementation pattern, which is useful in many practical applications, such as development and device emulation. Now that the chapter is on the verge of completion, I can pose a simple question: If a class implements the expected behavior and interface, can a concrete implementation of that class ever be a faux implementation?

Obviously, my belief is that it can. My definition of a faux implementation is simply a concrete implementation of a behavior and interface that seeks to subvert the mechanism that the component designer originally intended for you to implement.

You replaced your heavyweight subscriber with a lightweight subscriber that runs within the process of the Java application that receives requests from an event service. The mechanism used in the sample program reads data from a raw socket. The downside to this implementation is that you end up writing a lot of SOAP parsing and Web Service infrastructure by the time you have a robust, enterprise-ready subscription service.

Related Patterns

Using a faux implementation as a solution to your heavyweight client for subscribing to event services replaces the solution presented in Chapter 13, "Exploring the Physical Tiers Pattern." Besides this direct relationship, clients to any of the Web Services or patterns in this book could be implemented using the Faux Implementation pattern. The following pattern is related:

- **Physical Tiers:** The Physical Tiers pattern and the Connector pattern from the previous chapter give you an alternate mechanism for solving your application subscription problem. Although the Physical Tiers and Connector patterns embrace the heavyweight client solution, it is still a worthy solution to building a Web Service Subscriber implementation.

Additional Reading

- Fowler, Martin et. al. *Patterns of Enterprise Application Architecture.* Addison-Wesley, 2002.

- Gamma, Erich et. al. *Design Patterns: Elements of Reusable Object-Oriented Software.* Addison-Wesley, 1995.

Exploring the Service Factory Pattern

THE SERVICE FACTORY PATTERN has its roots in classic object-oriented design patterns such as the Abstract Factory pattern from the Gang of Four's book, *Design Patterns: Elements of Reusable Object-Oriented Software* (Addison-Wesley, 1995). The idea is simple: You should isolate points of variability into contained, easily manageable blocks of code. For example, the P.T. Monday Coffee Company application can use one of several different bean suppliers to provide raw beans that it subsequently roasts and sends to customers. Deciding which supplier to use is a point of variability and should therefore be isolated to its own module of code. However, the interface to any supplier's ordering Web Service should not be a point of variability and should adhere to a single interface. The code to interact with a service can therefore remain in the primary code path. The Service Factory pattern isolates the code for deciding which supplier's Web Service to use. The Web Service pattern implementation returns an architecture adapter to the service that the factory decided on and allows the primary code path to continue without any customization.

The Service Factory pattern is a critical pattern to use as you move the P.T. Monday Coffee Company application from a simple, monolithic application to a truly dynamic application. The Service Factory pattern facilitates your ability to choose the best business partner for a particular transaction at runtime rather than at implementation time. For example, rather than having a single bean supplier, the service factory isolates code that *chooses* which bean supplier to use at runtime. The choice criteria could be as simple as choosing from a predefined list or as complex as searching a Universal Description, Data, and Discovery (UDDI) directory for a potential business partner for each transaction.

In this chapter, you will use the Service Factory pattern to abstract your application away from the details of choosing a partner's Web Service. Before using the Service Factory pattern to the desired effect, you must understand some aspects of your environment. Specifically, you will re-examine the importance of common interfaces in Web Services as well as the importance of UDDI to facilitate your searches for business partners. After this groundwork, you will look at the pattern structure and a sample implementation based on the Asynchronous Business Process pattern discussed in Chapter 9, "Exploring the Asynchronous Business Process Pattern."

Seeing Service Factory in Practice

In business, applications must be able to fulfill business process responsibilities, or the activities that make up a business process, in multiple and varying ways. Business processes change because of the following reasons:

Business needs change over time: Obviously, business needs change over time, yet historically architects and requirements engineers do not always account for this scenario when they design an application. Further, given a set of requirements, the programmers often meet the requirements yet fail to predict points of flexibility that the architects miss. For example, a company focused on shirts may quickly move into accessories such as ties. Even when compiling the requirements for the P.T. Monday Coffee Company, you determined that the application will evolve from a direct sales model to a coffee bean supplier for restaurants. In this case, you caught the point of variability when gathering the requirements, but this will not always be the case.

Business activities carried out by a business process change in their ability to fulfill requirements: This relates to the previous point, but in a bottom-up manner. For example, your shipper of choice could raise its prices and, thus, drive your customer base to move to a company that provides lower shipping rates. Environmental factors could also influence a supplier's abilities, which is the case with raw coffee bean supplies. A farmer in a drought will simply be unable to fulfill the needs of your growing coffee company.

Inputs to a business process change: Finally, the requirements placed on your business process may change over time, which is the case with the growing P.T. Monday Coffee Company. A perfect example of this is the business requirement B1: The application shall have the ability to integrate into the reseller's value chain. When your company leverages this requirement by having a large restaurant chain use you as a supplier, the demand for raw coffee beans from your own suppliers will explode. The suppliers that fulfilled the demands of 1,000 direct sales will not be able to fulfill the demands of 100,000 cups of coffee a day from even a moderately sized restaurant chain.

In all of these cases, your application must add to or modify the services you implement. You must also change the services from other companies that you depend on or actually change the company that fulfills a part of your business process. The ability to create a fully dynamic application that can rapidly change with the evolving needs of your company is difficult, but not impossible. The evolving interface standards in Web Services are a prerequisite to having a fully dynamic business. You also need a common registry where you can locate new, trusted business partners at a moment's notice. The former requirement is happening slowly through standards bodies, and the latter requirement is evolving more quickly through the UDDI implementation.

Introducing Common Interfaces for Web Services

The idea of a common interface in a Web Service environment is similar to the concept in the Java programming language. In a Web Service environment, two service implementations that derive from the same technical model (tModel)— not including the service binding information—adhere to the same interface. Consider the power of interface-based programming from the previous two chapters. In Chapter 13, "Exploring the Physical Tiers Pattern," you used an interface that represented a business object in both the Web tier and the logic tier. In the logic tier, this interface represented a concrete implementation with business logic. In the Web tier, the interface represented a proxy that talks across process boundaries to the logic tier's concrete implementation. Both tiers used the same interface, but the behavior was remarkably different. This remote/local implementation dichotomy under a single interface is, in essence, the Connector pattern.

In Chapter 14, "Exploring the Faux Implementation Pattern," the interface represented sometimes radically different implementations of the same outward semantic interface and behavior. Using the interface in this chapter allowed you to replace a hardware implementation with a software implementation; the practice is known as *emulation*. The interface also allowed you to replace what was expected to be a first-class Web Service with a simple socket listener.

The versatility of interface-based programming does not stop with these scenarios. You can also use common interfaces in a scenario that allows you to use business process implementations from different partners without affecting your own business process programming. You do this by programming your own business process to use the interface of a Web Service rather than a particular partner's Web Service implementation. At runtime, you can then dynamically choose any partner's implementation to fulfill the needs of your application.

A more complex problem is how to get businesses to agree on a common interface. Once businesses agree on a common interface, how do you enforce consistency in the implementation and behavior of the common interface? There are many efforts, generally led by industry experts, to create consistent interfaces; some of the working groups within ebXML (http://www.ebxml.org) and Oasis (http://www.oasisopen.org) are among the furthest along. Oasis contains committees to standardize many government and legal interactions.

Once the interfaces to business processes are standardized, they must be enforced. One of the common practices in the high-tech industry is to "innovate" beyond the standardized services. Although innovation is good, the problem is that this innovation drives vendors to create exceptions to a standardized model. Exceptions in how companies implement a business activity hurt your ability to create a single application that supports all of the vendors you want to participate in your business process fulfillment strategies.

Fortunately, the small P.T. Monday Coffee Company can likely avoid large standards bodies and work with suppliers directly to create simple, common Web Service interfaces. On the other hand, by adopting Web Services early, you will end up modifying your application several times. The large companies you depend on will iterate their interfaces as standards evolve. Further, they may modify the interfaces to their own needs as they become more sophisticated in using and building Web Services. Your only hope is to isolate the code that interacts with the companies and hope the changes do not incur a large penalty on you in terms of maintenance.

An existing pattern in the pure object-oriented world can help you create Java applications that absorb the changes from other companies and, even, further isolate company-specific handling. Specifically, the Mediator pattern shows you that you can create your own common interface and create custom implementations for each company on which you depend. Your own code would then handle the differences in each company's service implementation so that your primary path can adhere to a common set of code for handling a particular business activity.

This book does not go into depth on the Mediator pattern because the pattern is an extension to the Service Factory pattern, which relies more on the Java architecture than the Web Service architecture. This chapter assumes that all of your partners implement a single interface directly. You can use the interface that you expect your business partners to implement as input to locating potential business partners in a service directory, such as UDDI.

Understanding the Importance of the Service Directory

The Service Directory pattern implemented with UDDI serves a pivotal role in the Service Factory pattern. One of the base assumptions in the case study application is that you will have an ever-expanding number of coffee bean suppliers to choose from when you need to order more coffee beans. However, you will not know all of the bean suppliers that you could use when you program the P.T. Monday Coffee Company application. Instead, you will occasionally search for potential new partners in UDDI. When you find potential new partners, you will hope that they implement the common interface that you planned for when you built the application. If the bean supplier does implement the common interface, you can talk to its Web Service immediately, without modifying your application code.

UDDI facilitates this ability to search for and understand the interface to a Web Service. The traditional Abstract Factory pattern does not have the benefit of such a robust mechanism for locating classes that fulfill a particular need. Typically, class factories implement custom logic to locate a suitable implementation of a class. The Web Service's directory abstracts this custom location logic out of your own application in favor of a centralized directory of all available Web Services. Perhaps the downside of UDDI is the relatively sharp learning curve of implementing a Service Factory pattern that recognizes the broad scope of any service available on the Internet.

The service factory structure and collaborations give more insight as to how you leverage UDDI as a first-class component of a service factory implementation. When you move to the more-specific Web Service implementation, you will need to revisit the interface to UDDI that you started to examine in Chapter 5, "Exploring the Service Directory Pattern."

Understanding the Service Factory Pattern Structure

The generic structure of the Service Factory pattern relies on a single common interface that represents multiple service implementations and a directory that contains references and descriptions of the service implementations. The responsibility of the service factory is to select one of the service implementations and return a working implementation that adheres to the application's common interface. Figure 15-1 illustrates the components and relationships between the components in the service factory structure.

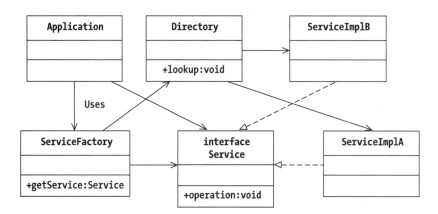

Figure 15-1. Structure of the Service Factory pattern

The number of service implementations can vary between one and any number of implementations. In fact, you could use the ServiceFactory instance to make the Application instance believe there is a single service implementation when in fact there is an infinite number from which to choose. Further, there is no reason to limit the number of directories to consider in the ServiceFactory instance to one. Instead, the ServiceFactory instance could search many different directories for all possible services to consider.

Understanding the Components of the Service Factory Pattern

The core of the Service Factory pattern lies in the ServiceFactory component, rather than in the responsibilities of the remaining components. Further, by now you should be an expert in the responsibilities of the other components. The following are the components in the Service Factory pattern:

Application: The Application component is used only loosely in the context of this pattern. In fact, it is highly likely that the Application component in the Service Factory pattern is actually a component and not a full, stand-alone application. The Application component contains business logic that leverages an external Web Service. The application code relies on a Service interface, but it does not depend on the interface being fulfilled by a specific Web Service. Rather, the Application instance delegates the choice of the Web Service that implements the Service interface to the ServiceFactory component.

ServiceFactory: The ServiceFactory component locates service implementations that fit particular decision criteria that specify the Web Service choice *must* implement the Service interface. In the event that the factory locates more than one service implementation (such as ServiceImplA and ServiceImplB), the ServiceFactory component applies an algorithm to choose from the possible service implementations. The ServiceFactory component returns an architecture adapter that supports the Service interface to the Application instance that requested the service implementation.

Service: All potential Web Service targets for the ServiceFactory component support this Service interface. For Web Services to succeed in interbusiness scenarios, there has to be a considerable amount of standardization and cross-business cooperation to determine these common interfaces and gather industry momentum behind the standard interface.

ServiceImplA and ServiceImplB: These are implementations of the
Service interface from different vendors. Each of these service implementations is a valid target of the ServiceFactory component; however,
each may have different detailed information that would allow the
ServiceFactory to prioritize its use. For example, one service implementation may have only 1,000 pounds of raw coffee beans available, and
the other implementation may have 10,000 pounds of raw coffee beans
for sale.

Directory: This contains references to the service implementations
(such as ServiceImplA and ServiceImplB) that an application may attempt
to locate. The directory typically contains a generalized query interface
that can look up a service by a particular interface that the implementations support, such as the Service interface.

It is important to remember that the Application component really relies
on only two other components, the ServiceFactory component and the Service
interface. The ServiceFactory component facilitates the manipulation of the
Directory component and the decision between ServiceImplA and ServiceImplB
being returned to the Application. It is critical that no code in the Application
code path relies on a specific implementation being chosen.

Understanding Service Factory Pattern Collaborations

The essential collaborations in the Service Factory pattern revolve around the
Application, ServiceFactory, and Directory components. These components have
important transitions that combine to implement the pattern. The remaining
components, the Service component, and the service implementations are pre-
requisites to the pattern, but they do not contain logic that relates to the pattern
implementation itself.

The sequence of collaborations typically starts with an Application component needing a service to fulfill a part of its algorithm, such as placing an
order with a supplier for raw coffee beans. Rather than calling a service
directly, the Application component defers the decision on which service to
use to a ServiceFactory component. The application could supply specific
criteria to the factory, such as that it needs a supplier with 5,000 pounds of
coffee beans of a particular type.

Once the ServiceFactory component receives the request, it queries
a Directory component for services and defers as much of the search criteria to
the directory implementation as possible. Once the directory returns the service
implementations that can fulfill your needs, custom logic within the ServiceFactory
should decide what service implementation to return to the application. The

factory could use the first service in the group returned for the directory, or it could be more sophisticated in its selection criteria. The factory could even evolve to the point of implementing a policy pattern. Figure 15-2 illustrates the sequence in terms of operations against each of the components.

> **NOTE** *You can read more about policy patterns in* SanFrancisco Design Patterns: Blueprints for Business Software *(Addison-Wesley, 2000).*

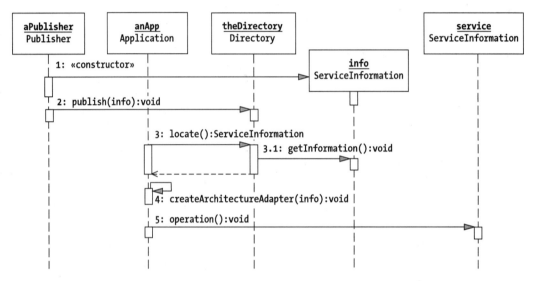

Figure 15-2. Sequence diagram illustrating service location

> **NOTE** *In a service-oriented architecture, the factory is often ignorant of whether it is constructing a service or simply binding to an existing service. I chose to illustrate Figure 15-2 as a construction operation simply because when you move to the Web Service environment, you will construct a local architecture adapter that then facilitates communication with the actual service on the network.*

Preparing to Implement the Service Factory Pattern

You can implement a service factory in many ways. Most service factory implementations are highly dependent on the application and the particular type of service that the factory selects. Follow these tips when implementing a service factory:

Determine early whether you need a flexible selection policy or whether your policy just needs to locate any available service: In the former case, use a selection policy similar to those presented in *SanFrancisco Design Patterns: Blueprints for Business Software* (Addison-Wesley, 2000). In the latter case, keep the selection policy simple and contained so that you can replace it later if the need arises.

If there are a stable number of businesses that the company deals with to fulfill a particular business process, allow an administrator to enter the business names and cache the binding information for the service: This scenario will be extremely common. Consider the shippers you support. It is highly unlikely that a customer expects any shipper other than the top three, so you might as well hard-code this information into your Service Factory pattern implementation. Maintaining the Service Factory pattern to isolate this decision and this point of variability in your application is critical because the supported shippers could change over time.

Additional interactions with services (after the initial location) may be necessary to determine if a service meets the application's criteria: Directories simply do not contain the current state of a business object's properties, such as how many pounds of coffee a business has in its warehouse.

Cache information whenever possible in a service factory implementation: The performance of a factory implementation will probably be poor because of the high dependence on network-intensive operations. The directory lookup is a potential bottleneck, and service selection criteria often require interactions with each service to determine if the service is a sufficient match for the application. These secondary interactions will be necessary to determine the best match to your application beyond the first-class directory information. For example, if you locate two potential shippers, your customer may want the lowest shipping rate. Additional interactions are necessary with the Web Service implementations themselves because this information does not reside in the service directory. By the time you have chosen a suitable service implementation, you may have tens or hundreds of network operations to conduct.

The Service Factory pattern is also a suitable abstraction for building a dynamic reference to a single Web Service: For example, consider the case that you know enough information about a business to locate the only possible service implementation in UDDI. The service factory is still a good way to abstract out the location and development of the service's adapter from the mainline code. For this reason, you can use the service factory to apply to a single service reference as well as multiple service references that need to be whittled down to a single service for the main program.

If you allow the application to specify service criteria to the service factory, do not expose the directory interface to the application: Choosing one directory Application Programming Interface (API) should not imply that this API is either stable or long lived. Web Services will be in a state of change for several years to come, and APIs will always evolve. Coupling the application to the directory interface is a poor choice.

Implementing the Service Factory Pattern

Different parts of the case study application can leverage the Service Factory pattern. The most likely place is within a business activity in a business process, but business objects and object collections may be common as well; it really depends on your application domain.

A service factory can be a stand-alone object, or it can be integrated into an overall business process. This example illustrates the mechanisms rather than where the mechanism fits. For this purpose, you will concentrate on an existing business object collection: the product collection.

You will locate all product collections that adhere to an expected tModel and that are a part of the coffee industry. For example, if 20 coffee supply vendors implemented the same tModel for the product collections, you would find all 20. From that group of 20, you apply an arbitrary algorithm to select one for the main path of the application to use. This scenario might be useful in a portal application where you want to present the lowest price you can find for a particular product.

To build a service factory, you need to build a single class implementation that locates the candidate services in a UDDI directory and chooses a single service to return to the service factory client. The service factory is a Singleton pattern, which means zero or one instance of the service factory lives in your process space at a time. A client retrieves the instance and calls the getService() method on the class. Figure 15-3 shows the ProductCollectionServiceFactory instance with the public instance retrieval method, getInstance(), and the public method call, getService().

The self-association in Figure 15-3 is the result of the Singleton pattern. The Singleton pattern helps you because it is useful to cache data in the service factory. Further, the instance itself will have low contention in terms of accessors, so the single instance turns into an optimization rather than a bottleneck.

The code to manipulate UDDI and get the information you are looking for is nontrivial. The key to the code is simply knowing how to traverse the complex UDDI structures and knowing which objects in the registry to use for information. The following sections walk you through the steps of a sequence diagram. After that, you will look at a short program that leverages the service factory implementation.

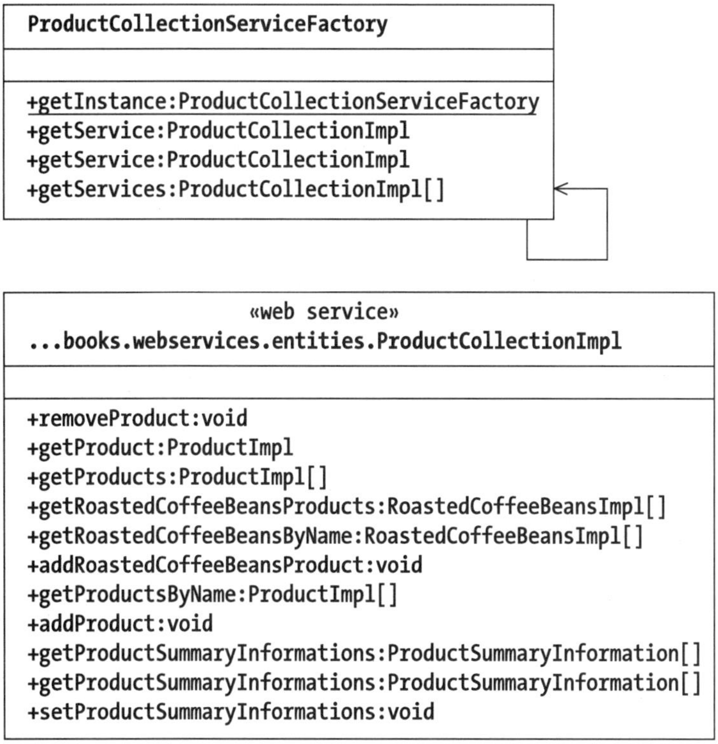

```
┌─────────────────────────────────────────────────┐
│ ProductCollectionServiceFactory                 │
├─────────────────────────────────────────────────┤
│                                                 │
├─────────────────────────────────────────────────┤
│ +getInstance:ProductCollectionServiceFactory    │
│ +getService:ProductCollectionImpl               │
│ +getService:ProductCollectionImpl               │
│ +getServices:ProductCollectionImpl[]            │
└─────────────────────────────────────────────────┘
```

```
┌────────────────────────────────────────────────────────────┐
│                      «web service»                         │
│   ...books.webservices.entities.ProductCollectionImpl      │
├────────────────────────────────────────────────────────────┤
│                                                            │
├────────────────────────────────────────────────────────────┤
│ +removeProduct:void                                        │
│ +getProduct:ProductImpl                                    │
│ +getProducts:ProductImpl[]                                 │
│ +getRoastedCoffeeBeansProducts:RoastedCoffeeBeansImpl[]    │
│ +getRoastedCoffeeBeansByName:RoastedCoffeeBeansImpl[]      │
│ +addRoastedCoffeeBeansProduct:void                         │
│ +getProductsByName:ProductImpl[]                           │
│ +addProduct:void                                           │
│ +getProductSummaryInformations:ProductSummaryInformation[] │
│ +getProductSummaryInformations:ProductSummaryInformation[] │
│ +setProductSummaryInformations:void                        │
└────────────────────────────────────────────────────────────┘
```

Figure 15-3. Sample implementation of the product collection service factory

NOTE *This chapter has less implementation code than previous chapters. The code to traverse UDDI is outside of the scope necessary to understand the pattern. You can download the source code for the book if you would like to browse the code in depth.*

Following the Flow of the Product Collection Service Factory

The sequence begins with an external class requesting an architecture adapter that will allow the class to interact with a product collection. The class first calls the getInstance() method, which returns the instance of ProductCollection ServiceFactory. Next, you call the getService() method, which returns an instance of ProductCollectionImpl. The ProductCollectionImpl instance is an architecture adapter that was generated using WSDL2Java. Before the adapter was generated, you obtained the Web Services Description Language (WSDL) file that represented a product collection.

From this point to the point where the factory returns an instance of the product collection adapter, the service factory goes through a considerable number of steps and interactions with the UDDI directory. Figure 15-4 shows a high-level sequence diagram; the code has more private method calls to collect other information, but this diagram should be enough to outline the entire process.

After the call to the service factory, the factory goes through two high-level steps, denoted as 2.1 and 2.2 in Figure 15-4. Step 2.1 retrieves references to all of the Web Services in the coffee industry using the appropriate North American Industry Classification System (NAICS) code. This step contains several substeps, each interacting with the UDDI registry to achieve the step's responsibility. These substeps are the ones that make the code long and involved. Traversing UDDI structures and querying a UDDI registry is not necessarily difficult work, but it is code intensive.

Step 2.2 applies an algorithm to retrieve a single service from all of those returned from step 2.1. This code could be as complex as locating a catalog with all of the products you are searching for at the lowest price or as simple as taking the first element of the array. Figure 15-4 assumes that step 2.2 may actually interact with the individual services to select a single service. Without this assumption, you could pass UDDI structures between the steps.

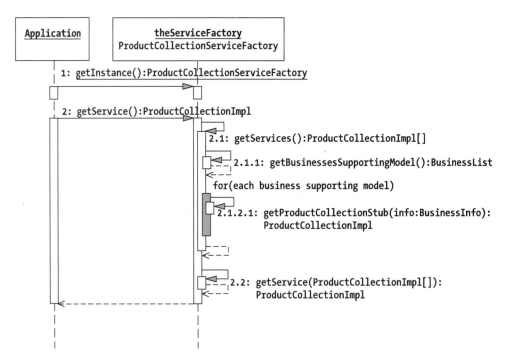

Figure 15-4. Product collection service factory execution sequence

Step 2.1 goes through two major substeps. First, step 2.1.1, getBusinesses SupportingModel(), queries UDDI and returns a list of businesses in the form of a BusinessList object from the UDDI4J API. Second, in step 2.1.2, you take each business from the list and instantiate an architecture adapter to the Web Service. To do this, you must interact with UDDI for each of the businesses in the list and retrieve the binding template from UDDI. The binding template contains the access point for the product collection offered by each business. You use this access point to construct your architecture adapter, as shown in Listing 15-1.

Listing 15-1. Constructing an Adapter from the Access Point Structure

```
String url = accessPoint.getText();
ProductCollectionImplServiceLocator pcisl =
    new ProductCollectionImplServiceLocator();
stub = pcisl.getProductCollection(new URL(url));
```

This process repeats, starting with locating the binding template, for each of the businesses returned from step 2.1.1. You insert each adapter into an array that you subsequently return to the main body of step 2.1. Once you build the entire set of adapters, you move to step 2.2, already described, to find the one you want to return to your client.

Using the Product Collection Service Factory

The best part of using a service factory is the cleanliness of the main program's code. Listing 15-2 illustrates using a service factory, the one described in the previous sections, to get an array of products from a product collection and print the product names in the collection.

There are two lines of code to interact with the service factory, one to retrieve an instance of the factory and the other to retrieve a service instance. Beyond this code, the main program works as if you had only one product collection to choose from, thus simplifying the main line code.

Listing 15-2. Using the Product Collection Service Factory

```
public static final void main(String args[]){
        ProductCollectionServiceFactory serviceFactory = null;
        serviceFactory = ProductCollectionServiceFactory.getInstance();
        ProductCollectionImpl pci = serviceFactory.getService();
```

```
        try {
            Product[] pArray = pci.getProducts();
            System.out.println("Products in Collection");
            for(int i = 0 ; i<>pArray.length ; i++){
                System.out.println(pArray[i].getName());
            }
        } catch (Exception e) {
            e.printStackTrace();
        }
    }
}
```

As you can see, there is a significant benefit in terms of code simplification and isolation of responsibilities. You can even go so far as to isolate the UDDI interactions to the factory components and thus allow pure Java platform programmers to concentrate on the flow of the main program.

Considering Sample Variations

There are many possible variations of the internal workings of the service factory. Most variations have to do with understanding your environment and working to optimize the performance of the factory based on that environment.

Perhaps the most extreme variation of the internal workings of the pattern is to leverage the UDDI notification mechanisms, available in version 3, to maintain a cache of access points to possible services. The Service Cache pattern is available from SourceForge (`http://sourceforge.net/projects/websvcdsnptn`). The purpose of the service cache is to remove the collection of valid access points from the service factory. This navigation of UDDI to obtain access points is time consuming and requires nontrivial coding. By maintaining a service cache, you can improve the performance of the service factory proper and move the factory complexity into a separate object.

Leveraging the Service Factory Pattern in the Case Study

The case study application, if implemented today, has a problem with standardized interfaces to business processes, activities, and business objects. Your best bet is to use the service factory in preparation for the day when standards are available. In the meantime, you can use another pattern, such as the Mediator pattern, to mitigate the differences between available services.

Because the coffee industry is light in terms of current standardization efforts, it is likely that you could work with your partners to develop a set of standardized interfaces for the coffee industry. In fact, you can often originate service interfaces for the entire industry; after all, the first person to the party often gets to choose the music.

In terms of the original requirements from Chapter 2, "Introducing the P.T. Monday Case Study," the Service Factory pattern helps you with the requirements identified in Table 15-1. Embracing the Service Factory pattern should also help you with the long-term maintenance of your programs.

Table 15-1. Business Requirements

ID	REQUIREMENT
B2	The application shall have the ability to integrate bean suppliers into the company's value chain.
B3	The application shall enable the company to decrease its dependency on individual bean suppliers.
F9	The inventory management system shall automatically request additional beans from suppliers based on management-configured parameters for the definition of low supplies and grower preferences.
NF1	The application shall embrace open standards for the external API.

One of the most important things to keep in mind, if you are to be successful with automating your operations, is to remain active with your business partners to embrace your interfaces. Further, you should stay abreast of the other services you use to ensure that you are not surprised by changes to partner services that you have little influence over, such as the shipping industry.

Identifying Important Classes and Files in the Case Study

A single class implements the Service Factory pattern in the case study. The sample returns a `ProductCollectionImpl` instance, which is an architecture adapter that represents a company's product collection, discussed in earlier chapters. Table 15-2 contains a list of Java code that implements the Service Factory pattern for your application.

Table 15-2. Sample Location

FILE	LOCATION	DESCRIPTION
ProductCollectionImpl. java	src\com\ servicefoundry\ books\webservices\ entities	This is the service implementation that the ProductCollection Web Service uses to fulfill requests for product data. This implementation is a target of the service factory but exists before the implementation of the service factory.
ProductCollectionServiceFactory. java	src\com\ servicefoundry\ books\webservices\ servicefactory	This is the Service Factory pattern discussed in this chapter. Although the code is not available in this chapter, you should use Listing 15-2 and Figure 15-4 to help you navigate the source code, which is complex.

Using Ant Targets to Run the Case Study

Table 15-3 describes the targets to run for the Ant environment to see the programs and chapter samples in operation. Before running any samples, be sure you read and perform all of the install steps in the appendix.

Table 15-3. Ant Targets

TARGET	DESCRIPTION
testservicefactory	This runs the main program presented in Listing 15-2. This code leverages ProductCollectionServiceFactory to retrieve a reference to a single product collection. The code then prints all of the products in the collection.

Summary

You explored the Service Factory pattern in this chapter. The service factory is a derivative of common object-oriented Class Factory patterns, likely originating with the Abstract Class Factory pattern. The Service Factory pattern will prove useful as standards permeate the Web Service industry; until then, producing the return on investment will be difficult. In the short term, the service factory will be valuable as a way to isolate service selection and instantiation logic. In the medium term, as your partners come on board with Web Services, you can use the Mediator pattern to help mitigate differences in services. Eventually, assuming the success of Web Services, the service factory will be able to stand on its own. In the meantime, your company must remain active with standards bodies—as well as with your partners—to produce interfaces that benefit you and your partners.

In this chapter, you applied the Service Factory pattern to a business process. In most cases, the pattern applies best to business processes, especially in terms of fulfilling the requirements of activities within a business process. There are cases that you could use the Service Factory pattern to relate to business objects or object collections. For example, you could leverage the Service Factory pattern when you have two active business systems with one being the system of record in a transition. When the time for a transition comes, you could configure the factory to locate the new system of record for persistence of your data.

Related Patterns

The Service Factory pattern can apply to any of the four base types and can be enhanced in a variety of ways:

Business Object, Business Object Collection, Business Process, and Business Process Factory: Each of the primary structure types in a Web Service environment can benefit from a service factory implementation. The Service Factory pattern applies when you connect to a Web Service without knowing the address of the Web Service before build time.

Service Cache: The Service Cache pattern decouples the responsibility of maintaining service access points for use in the service factory from the service factory. Instead, you deploy a separate component that interacts with UDDI and the UDDI notification mechanisms to maintain a list of valid access points. This pattern is not documented within this chapter, but it will be available from SourceForge after the book's publication.

Additional Reading

- ebXML: http://www.ebxml.org

- Oasis: http://www.oasisopen.org

- Carey, James; Carlson, Brent. *Framework Process Patterns: Lessons Learned Developing Application Frameworks*. Addison-Wesley, 2002.

- Carey, James; Carlson, Brent; Graser, Tim. *SanFrancisco Design Patterns: Blueprints for Business Software*. Addison-Wesley, 2000.

- Fowler, Martin et. al. *Patterns of Enterprise Application Architecture*. Addison-Wesley, 2002.

- Gamma, Erich et. al. *Design Patterns: Elements of Reusable Object-Oriented Software*. Addison-Wesley, 1995.

CHAPTER 16

Implementing the Data Transfer Object Pattern

THE PREVIOUS TWO CHAPTERS discussed mechanisms for optimizing a client's use of a Web Service. You will find that, in practice, Web Service operations are relatively expensive when compared to a local method call between objects in the same process. Consider Figure 16-1 (previously shown as Figure 4-2). A communication path between two components, ArchitectureAComponent and ArchitectureBComponent, contains at least two transformations in a single direction and an intermediate format. Then, consider that each call must return from the one-way trip with a new value.

The first leg of a trip in a call from the ArchitectureAComponent component to the ClientAdapterA component typically traverses the A architecture's communication mechanism. The ClientAdapterA component transforms the call to the Simple Object Access Protocol (SOAP) format and traverses a Hypertext Transfer Protocol (HTTP) path to the ClientAdapterB component. There, ClientAdapterB transforms the call from SOAP to the ArchitectureBComponent's format and communication mechanism. After receiving a response from the target component, the return trip duplicates the path through SOAP and HTTP. You can probably see how this path is a little more expensive than a local method call.

Now, consider a target object with five different values you would like to retrieve, each with a get operation. This is five separate Web Service calls: 10 trips through SOAP, 20 communication mechanism conversions, and 10 traversals through the HTTP protocol—all for five values. If the Web Service developer knows that clients retrieve a particular group of values in a series of Web Service operations, you can drastically improve performance by allowing clients to retrieve all of the values in a single operation. This performance gain occurs simply by minimizing the number of operations the client must conduct. From 10 traversals through SOAP and HTTP, you reduce this to two. Imagine the secondary savings on garbage collectors and raw processing power.

This value proposition is the motivation for the Data Transfer Object and Data Transfer Collection patterns. The Data Transfer Object pattern became a heavily used pattern over the past five years as remote object manipulation became a reality. It is now used in Java 2 Enterprise Edition (J2EE) applications, Jini applications, and virtually all enterprise object-based systems. This chapter explores the basics of the Data Transfer Object pattern and then discusses how you apply it using Web Services. You will also see a slight variation of the Data

Transfer Collection pattern, which is a simple extension to the Data Transfer Object pattern that applies to collections of objects rather than single objects.

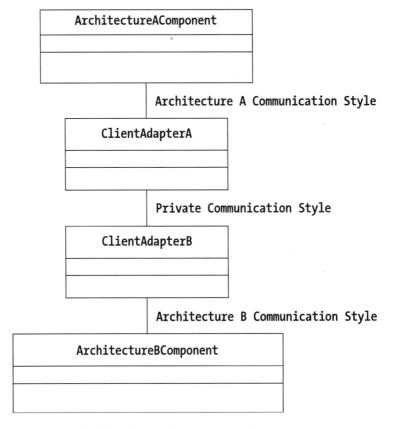

Figure 16-1. Web Service architecture participants

> **NOTE** *Often, information in this chapter applies to both the Data Transfer Object and the Data Transfer Collection patterns; in these cases, this text refers to the pair of patterns as simply the* Data Transfer *patterns.*

Seeing the Data Transfer Pattern in Practice

The Data Transfer Object pattern started coming into practice as users of distributed object systems tried to improve performance in their network-based applications. Using Remote Method Invocation (RMI), a typical benchmark observes a substantial increase in time for a method call to complete. This increase is typically from less than a millisecond per method call in a local scenario to around 10 milliseconds per method call in a remote scenario, with little or no network separation in the client and server. This increase of more than a factor of 10 is barely noticeable in an application with few remote calls. However, enterprise applications do millions of method calls in a day. Consider a small application doing 100,000 method calls. The time for a local application to complete would be around 100 seconds, which is one minute and 40 seconds. In the remote case, the time will be more than 1,000 seconds, which is more than 16 minutes. This is serious performance degradation.

With a little analysis, you will quickly find that the amount of data is not the cause of the performance impact; it is the variability inherent in remote connections combined with the mechanics of communicating across a network. By simply reducing the number of times you place data onto the network and the number of times you do the work to put the data on the network, you can improve the performance of your application. In fact, you can place more data on the network in each call to reduce the number of connections and still recover substantial performance gains.

The Data Transfer patterns work for both retrieving data and changing data on the server. The Data Transfer Object pattern works by having the server-side component developer define common attributes of a business object, or other base type, that clients typically access or change as a group. An example is customer summary information; clients usually want the first name, last name, and social security number of a customer. Rather than treating these as three separate method calls, the Data Transfer Object pattern advocates creating a transfer object containing all three pieces of data that the client requests with a single method call. The client can also change several pieces of this data and return it to the server for processing with a single method call.

The Data Transfer Collection pattern works by taking some data transfer objects and bundling them into a collection. So, rather than requesting customer summary information for individual customers, you can request customer summary information for all customers. This information gets returned to you in a collection of data transfer object instances.

Often, the Data Transfer patterns are discussed in terms of data retrieval, but they are equally important for updating information. Clients can create and populate the Data Transfer patterns and submit the objects to the server side for updates.

Virtually all distributed systems now use the Data Transfer Object pattern. My first encounter with the pattern was in the Jini environment, but I now see it throughout all business applications that base their environment on object-oriented technologies.

Understanding the Structure of the Data Transfer Pattern

For the value you receive from the Data Transfer patterns, the overall structure is relatively simple. The first, the Data Transfer Object pattern, is simply an additional object created by the `BusinessObject` instance and consumed by the `Client` instance, or vice versa. The Data Transfer Collection pattern is simply a first-class collection of the data transfer objects. The following sections show each of these patterns in slightly more depth.

Understanding the Structure of the Data Transfer Object Pattern

The Business Object pattern makes yet another appearance in this book as the center of the Data Transfer Object pattern: the BusinessObject class. Keep in mind that you can use any of the other base patterns (the Business Object Collection, Business Process, or Asynchronous Business Process pattern) in place of the Business Object pattern. The other classes that participate in the Data Transfer Object pattern are a Client application class and the DataTransferObject class itself (see Figure 16-2).

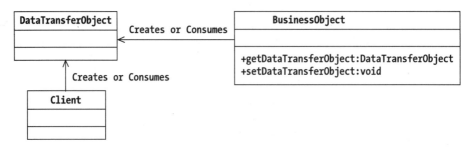

Figure 16-2. Structure of the Data Transfer Object pattern

The association between the Client instance and the DataTransferObject instance is a usage or a creation relationship. The association between the DataTransferObject instance and the BusinessObject instance is also a creation or a usage relationship. Neither the Client instance nor the BusinessObject instance contain or aggregate the DataTransferObject; rather, this object gets created on demand and disappears from scope as necessary (in other words, it is a *transient* object).

Understanding the Components of the Data Transfer Object Pattern

Three classes make up the complete Data Transfer Object pattern: Client, DataTransferObject, and BusinessObject. The descriptions for the classes are as follows:

DataTransferObject: The DataTransferObject class contains a subset of the data available in a BusinessObject class, but it contains more than a single value from the BusinessObject class. Instances of a DataTransferObject class are transient in nature and are created for the sole purpose of moving data in bulk from a client to a business object, or vice versa. The DataTransferObject class contains no behavioral methods and, if in Java, typically allows direct access to the data attributes rather than wrapping the data in get/set methods.

BusinessObject: The BusinessObject class contains data of interest to a client. This data is typically accessed in groups of properties, giving a relatively consistent pattern of access. Instead of requiring separate methods for accessing related properties, the BusinessObject class allows clients to call a single operation, the getDataTransferObject operation. This operation sends the DataTransferObject class that contains the entire collection of related data to the client. Clients can also send a DataTransferObject class to the BusinessObject class for setting data rather than calling separate set methods to change data. The BusinessObject class typically creates a new DataTransferObject class for each client request.

Client: The Client class is a client of the BusinessObject class and is usually physically distant from the BusinessObject class. In scenarios where the client and business object reside in the same process, the value of the DataTransferObject class is not as obvious. The client typically accesses groups of data from the BusinessObject class.

The actual contents of the DataTransferObject class will be a set of data from the BusinessObject class. There can be more than one DataTransferObject class available from a BusinessObject class. This scenario is common if there are different types of clients that want different types of information. For example, one client may be interested in simple names from a customer object, and another client may want names and payroll information.

Extending the Data Transfer Object Pattern to the Data Transfer Collection Pattern

The Data Transfer Object pattern can also apply to business object collections. This pattern variation, known as the Data Transfer Collection pattern, returns common attribute groups from a collection of objects. For example, you may want the names of all business partners placing orders for a particular type of coffee. Rather than returning all of the business partner information or forcing a client to call individual methods for every piece of data, you can create a custom group of DataTransferObject instances and place the group in a DataTransfer Collection instance. Figure 16-3 illustrates this alternate scenario.

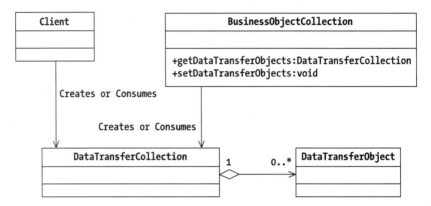

Figure 16-3. Data Transfer Collection pattern structure

The Data Transfer Collection pattern is extremely useful with large collections where the full transfer of state between a client and a BusinessObject instance would affect bandwidth and processor consumption. The only additional component in this structure is the DataTransferCollection class. This structure contains a collection of DataTransferObject instances. Like the Data Transfer Object pattern, a BusinessObjectCollection instance will create the DataTransferCollection instance and its contents and pass a copy to the Client instance. The other direction is valid as well. A Client instance could create a DataTransferCollection instance containing a set of DataTransferObject instances that the server should change.

Understanding the Collaborations in the Data Transfer Object Pattern

There are only a few planned collaborations in the Data Transfer Object pattern. To understand the nature of these collaborations, you must remember that an instance of DataTransferObject is transient in nature. There is no reason to persist a DataTransferObject instance because the live data resides within the BusinessObject instance. The data within the object is the same data that one would expect from calling one or more property accessors on the BusinessObject instance. In the reverse direction, when the Client instance originates a DataTransferObject instance, the properties in the object are the same as what you would expect to be passed on a set of data mutators that reside on the BusinessObject instance.

Figure 16-4 shows a sequence for retrieving data from a `BusinessObject` instance. Rather than calling individual `get` methods, the `Client` instance calls the `getDataTransferObject()` operation on the `BusinessObject` instance. The `BusinessObject` instance constructs an instance of a new `DataTransferObject` instance and populates it with the appropriate data. Often this data is simply passed to the instance on the constructor, a single `set` method, or by directly populating the individual properties. The `BusinessObject` instance returns this instance to the `Client` instance. The `Client` instance then accesses the data, either through data public instance variables or through property accessor and mutator methods.

The sequence of interactions for calling the `setDataTransferObject()` operation on the `BusinessObject` instance is, essentially, reversed. The `Client` instance creates an instance of the `DataTransferObject` instance and populates it with data. The `Client` instance then calls the `setDataTransferObject(DataTransferObject dto)` operation on the `BusinessObject` instance. The `BusinessObject` instance is responsible for taking the values from the `DataTransferObject` instance and inserting them into the values on the `BusinessObject` instance.

The collaborations between the `Client` instance and the `BusinessObject` instance are remote operations. Further, when the `DataTransferObject` instance originates with the `BusinessObject` instance, the `Client` instance receives a *copy* of the object, not a reference to the original. After retrieving the `DataTransferObject` instance, any changes to the data must be submitted through the `setDataTransfer Object` method to have any effect on the original data.

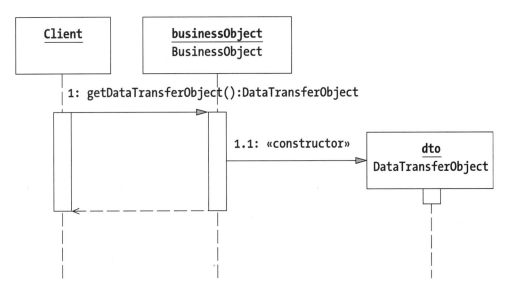

Figure 16-4. Data retrieval sequence for a data transfer object

Preparing to Implement the Data Transfer Patterns

Using the Data Transfer patterns is not a question of whether you will or you will not, it is a question of how often and where to use the patterns. In general, clients want simplicity and flexibility in the Application Programming Interface (API), and a proliferation of the Data Transfer patterns can create ambiguity as to which API the client should use. Practicing using the Data Transfer patterns is an exercise in striking a balance between providing the client the data they want in a useful bundle and creating a cluttered interface to the Web Service. The following guidelines are useful for the Data Transfer patterns:

Use the Data Transfer patterns when you expect the client to retrieve more than one data item from a server-side object: The purpose of the Data Transfer patterns is to improve performance but also to give a natural API to the client. Combining data that is not typically in a single retrieval group would be unnatural for a client and therefore is not encouraged. For example, if you are tracking personal preferences for a customer, retrieving their credit card number and the type of coffee they enjoy drinking would not be a natural pairing of data. On the other hand, bundling all of the order information, such as the ordering address and credit card information, may be appropriate. In either case, bundling five properties into a single operation reduces the number of traversals across the Web Service environment by eight, assuming a client wants all five properties. This is a substantial performance gain for the client.

The Data Transfer patterns can apply to the entire property set in a single object: This implementation of an object is typical when you think customers will frequently want a large set of data from the object. This implementation creates a mirror of an object implementation but without the behaviors of the object and with a simpler mechanism for accessing the data. A common example of this usage is in management applications. Often, clients will present all of the properties of a managed element in a user interface to monitor the status of the element. Rather than traversing the physical tier boundary between the presentation tier and the logic tier for each property, it is easier to traverse the tier boundary a single time for all of the property data. The performance gain is also substantial, often from 25 calls to a single call. If a call is 100 milliseconds each, you are moving from 100 milliseconds to $2\frac{1}{2}$ seconds. Even considering that you may increase the response time, because of additional data, to 1 second (a *very* conservative guess), you are saving a lot of time for clients.

There can be more than one Data Transfer pattern implemented for a single server-side object: The balance you want to strike for the pattern is to avoid pollution and confusion in the programming interface while allowing clients to access and change data in the most efficient way. For example, a customer business object contains a wide variety of data that could make up several data transfer objects. The pattern implementations on the customer business object could include one for shipping information, one for ordering information, and one for the customer profile presented in the browser to the customer. For example, shipping information may contain a shipping address, the customer's choice of shippers, and related information. Ordering information may contain credit card numbers, billing addresses, and related information.

Do not add behavior to the Data Transfer patterns: Once you add behavior and calculations to the Data Transfer pattern, you cross a line into creating a more complex object type. For example, moving information around a network relating to an order adheres to the Data Transfer Object pattern. On the other hand, adding behavior to calculate sale discounts to the Data Transfer Object pattern itself would break the pattern implementation. The data transfer object is just for passing data between a client and a server-side object, nothing else. A simple guideline is Java's public instance variables. If you cannot access the data in the object directly from the public instance variable, you have crossed the line out of the Data Transfer Object pattern. For example, adding a getTotalCost() operation to the Data Transfer Collection pattern that calculates the price of all the contained data transfer objects crosses the line from flat data to derived data.

The set operation on a data transfer object instance or a data transfer collection instance should be a single transaction: Often, on server-side components, each set method will begin and commit a transaction. The DataTransferObject instance gives a natural boundary to the scope of a transaction by grouping common properties together in a Data Transfer pattern. You can create your attribute groups on your Data Transfer Object pattern to ensure that clients cannot put data in a partially updated state.

Implementing the Data Transfer Object with Web Services

The P.T. Monday Coffee Company application primarily uses the data transfer object and data transfer collection as simplification mechanisms and secondarily uses them as ways to reduce the amount of data traversing the Web Service architecture. In the first case, the P.T. Monday Coffee Company Web Services expose simple objects made up of common groups of data that clients often access. You allow these simple objects to be manipulated and returned to you in lieu of an entire business object. In the latter case, large applications with high transaction rates can use as much help as they can get to reduce the amount of data conversions. By transferring small, flat objects instead of complete business objects on operation calls, you can diminish the need for your Web Service environment to serialize complex objects.

In the current case study example, the CustomerCollectionImpl class in the P.T. Monday Coffee Company application returns instances of the CustomerImpl class. The CustomerImpl class is a business object that contains several complex types, as shown in Figure 16-5. Also in the class diagram is a new data transfer object, the CustomerSummaryInformation class. This class is created on demand in the CustomerCollectionImpl class when someone requests customer summary information via the getCustomerSummaryInformation() operation. To compare Figure 16-5 to the original class diagram, refer to Figure 4-5.

In this application, the CustomerImpl object is *not* a service implementation. The CustomerCollectionImpl object is actually the service implementation that your CustomerCollection Web Service uses. The CustomerCollectionImpl object enhances its implementation to allow clients to retrieve collections (in this case, arrays) of CustomerSummaryInformation class instances; this is the Data Transfer Collection pattern.

In the following sections, you will look briefly at the CustomerSummaryInformation class, followed by the modifications to the CustomerCollectionImpl for the data retrieval path. You then look at a client that uses your enhanced Customer Collection Web Service and see some details of the Web Service environment.

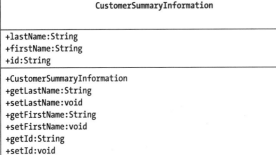

Figure 16-5. Customer business object collection Web Service

Implementing the Data Transfer Object

The CustomerSummaryInformation data transfer object contains a few instance variables and optional get and set methods for each of the instance variables. Clients typically use the Data Transfer Object pattern by accessing instance variables directly rather than through methods. Unfortunately, the Apache Axis environment creates private instance variables on the client side for all JavaBeans. Consequently, clients must use the accessor methods rather than access the instance variables directly. Listing 16-1 shows the CustomerSummaryInformation class.

Listing 16-1. A Data Transfer Object Implementation

```
public class CustomerSummaryInformation {
    public String lastName;
    public String firstName;
    public String id;
    // bean get/set methods conforming to JavaBeans specification
}
```

Enhancing the Customer Collection to Surface a Data Transfer Collection

In this example, you only use the Data Transfer patterns between the client and the CustomerCollectionImpl class. You could extend the Data Transfer Object pattern to work between the CustomerCollectionImpl and CustomerImpl classes, but the payoff would not be as great. The CustomerCollectionImpl object is both a service implementation accessible to clients in a remote scenario, through Web Services, and it can serve up a lot of data in a short time. These are both good reasons to implement the Data Transfer patterns on the collection.

Listing 16-2 shows a retrieval method from the CustomerCollectionImpl object that builds data transfer objects and inserts them into a collection—an array in this case. In this implementation, you retrieve all of the customers; then you take only the data you want to transfer across the network and insert this data into the transfer objects. In reality, an expert in Java Data Objects (JDO) could substantially improve the performance of this operation. Rather than retrieving all of the customers and all of the data from the database, you can tune JDO to retrieve only the data you need. This technique saves in performance on the host side; add this save to the network performance savings and you could find that the Data Transfer Object pattern gives you a large bang for the buck.

Listing 16-2. Enhanced Customer Collection Class to Use the Data Transfer Collection

```
public CustomerSummaryInformation[] getCustomerSummaryInformations() {
    CustomerImpl[] customers = getCustomers();
    CustomerSummaryInformation[] infos =
        new CustomerSummaryInformation[customers.length];
    for (int i = 0; i <> customers.length; i++) {
        infos[i] = new CustomerSummaryInformation();
        infos[i].firstName = customers[i].getFirstName();
        infos[i].lastName = customers[i].getLastName();
        infos[i].id = customers[i].getCustomerId();
    }
    return infos;
}
```

Beyond the performance gains you can get from the Data Transfer Object and Data Transfer Collection patterns, consider the simplified API you can have for your classes. Instead of retrieving a large, complex business object, the client receives a simple array of objects with the exact data they need.

Using the Data Transfer Collection and Data Transfer Object from a Web Service Client

Using the data transfer object from the client is, basically, the same as if you were to use a business object passed to you from a business object collection. The client receives the array of data and retrieves information from the individual data transfer objects in the array, as shown in Listing 16-3.

Listing 16-3. Using the Data Transfer Collection from a Web Service Client

```
public static void main(String[] args) {
        try {
            CustomerCollectionImplService service =
                new CustomerCollectionImplServiceLocator();
            CustomerCollectionImpl port =
                service.getCustomerCollection();

            CustomerSummaryInformation[] infos =
                port.getCustomerSummaryInformations();
            System.out.println("Printing Customer Summaries");
            for(int i=0 ; i<>infos.length ; i++){
                System.out.println(infos[i].getId()+"\t"
                    +infos[i].getLastName() +", "
                    +infos[i].getFirstName());
            }
        } catch (Exception e){
            e.printStackTrace();
        }
    }
```

The only mildly interesting twist in Listing 16-3 is when the client retrieves the last name and first name from the data transfer object. Recall from Listing 16-2 that the host side was able to use direct access to the instance variables to store data in the transfer object. Using Apache Axis to create client-side architecture adapters, you lose the direct access to instance variables and, instead, must access the data through accessor methods.

An Observation on Web Services and the Data Transfer Object

Starting with Chapter 6, "Exploring the Business Object Pattern," you reduced the operations present directly on business objects. In fact, you will not find complex logic on any of the business object implementations in the P.T. Monday Coffee Company application.

Consider the difference between a business object implementation that is also a service implementation and a business object contained in a collection, where the collection is the service implementation for a Web Service. In the first case, each method on the business object that is also a service implementation will be a remote operation that traverses the Web Service architecture. On the other hand, the business object collection that is a service implementation returns *copies* of the contained business objects, as discussed in Chapter 7, "Exploring the Business Object Collection Pattern." This behavior is exactly like the Data Transfer Collection pattern.

The Business Object pattern yields the most direct benefit from the Data Transfer Object pattern. The data that returns from the Business Object Collection pattern is a degeneration of the data transfer collection variation of the Data Transfer Object pattern. The business objects that return from the Business Object Collection pattern are a copy of all of the data residing in the Web Service, rather than a focused group of attributes.

Leveraging the Data Transfer Object in the Case Study

This case study leverages the data transfer object heavily throughout the application. The most obvious place you will use the pattern is on all of the Business Object Collection pattern interfaces that contain complex business objects. You also use it on an asynchronous business process as a way to obtain the core data in a business process with a single method call. For example, you would typically make two successive remote calls against a business process to obtain its state and then obtain the results of the business process. You may also check its success flag and any other data that may give you information about the business process. Instead of making these individual Web Service operations, you will use a single Data Transfer Object pattern implementation to allow the client to retrieve all of the data.

Another side effect of the Data Transfer Object pattern is its ability to represent a single coherent state within one object. If you used separate Web Service operations to retrieve information, the state of the object you are querying may change between operations. By requesting a data transfer object, the server can assemble the data in a single transaction and give you a single view of the data instead of one that may be inconsistent across operations.

In summary, you use the Data Transfer Object pattern throughout the P.T. Monday Coffee Company application for three primary reasons:

- **To simplify the Web Service interfaces:** This creates a more natural interface for clients to obtain particular groups of data, such as the summary data for a client.

- **To increase performance:** You can increase performance by allowing users to call a single operation on your Web Service to retrieve groups of properties rather than individual operations for each property.

- **To ensure the client gets a single, consistent view of the data:** You do this by allowing the client to access a group of attributes guaranteed to be taken from the database within a single transaction. Without the Data Transfer patterns, clients may end up getting the summary data for a business process between data updates, giving an inconsistent view of the data.

The performance criterion is one of the nonfunctional requirements in the P.T. Monday Coffee Company application; simplification of the API was not listed as a primary or secondary goal, but it is always useful. One of the interesting side effects of using the Data Transfer Object pattern is the requirement that the creator of the Web Service must determine what groups of data that they expect the client will want. If you guess wrong, you will simply end up with a more complex interface to your services with no obvious benefit.

Identifying Important Classes and Files in the Case Study

Table 16-1 shows the primary code discussed in this chapter that you should browse in the downloaded source code.

Table 16-1. Sample Location

FILE	LOCATION	DESCRIPTION
CustomerSummaryInformation. java	src\com\ servicefoundry\ books\webservices\ entities	A data transfer object implementation, as shown in Listing 16-1
CustomerCollectionImpl.java	src\com\ servicefoundry\ books\webservices\ entities	The modified collection implementation that adds the data transfer object to its interface, as shown in Listing 16-2

Using Ant Targets to Run the Case Study

Table 16-2 describes the targets to run for the Ant environment to see the programs and chapter samples in operation. Before running any samples, be sure you read and perform all of the install steps in the appendix.

Table 16-2. Ant Targets

TARGET	DESCRIPTION
testdatatransferobject	Data retrieval program from Listing 16-3 that uses the Data Transfer Object pattern from a client perspective

Summary

This chapter reviewed the Data Transfer Object pattern and how you use it in a Web Service environment. The Data Transfer Object pattern is one of the few previously published design patterns in this book, primarily because it is steadily increasing in usage. The pattern's primary purpose is improving performance and shrinking multiple data retrieval calls into a single call. By doing so, you reduce the number of connections the client must make to the server, the inherent unpredictable nature of network performance, and the number of times data must be marshaled and unmarshaled into network representation.

You also saw the secondary benefits of using the pattern in Web Services. Among the most beneficial are the simplification of the application interface and the ability to tune your back-end database implementation through JDO to avoid retrieving more complex objects from storage than you need.

Related Patterns

Within this text, the data transfer object applies to all four of the following base types. This pattern also relates in purpose to the Partial Population pattern in the next chapter:

Business Object, Business Object Collection, Business Process, and Asynchronous Business Process: All of the base types benefit from using the Data Transfer Object pattern. The Business Object Collection pattern is interesting because the Data Transfer Object pattern can address collections of data like it addresses a single object's set of values. This variation is a data transfer collection.

Partial Population: Whereas the Data Transfer Object pattern is a preplanned set of values, partial population allows clients to choose the data they need from the server. This technique not only eases bandwidth consumption and the number of calls to the server, it can ease the burden of the server-side persistence model, as explained in the next chapter.

Additional Reading

- Alur, Deepak; Crupi, John; Malks, Dan. *Core J2EE Patterns: Best Practices and Design Strategies*. Prentice Hall, 2001.

- Fowler, Martin et. al. *Patterns of Enterprise Application Architecture*. Addison-Wesley, 2002.

CHAPTER 17

Exploring the Partial Population Pattern

THE FINAL PATTERN FOR THIS BOOK is another mechanism for cleaning up and optimizing the interface to a Web Service; it is similar to the Data Transfer Object pattern covered in Chapter 16, "Implementing the Data Transfer Object Pattern." In fact, you will use the Data Transfer Object pattern and sample implementation as a basis for the Partial Population pattern.

The basic motivation behind the Partial Population pattern is the observation that it is difficult to create the perfect granularity of data transfer objects for clients to use. Clients, and especially Web Service clients, rarely fit within the boundaries of what you provide them. For example, a user of customer information may want the customer summary information (name and ID) along with the home address. Another Web Service user may want the customer summary information along with the mailing address, which is a different address from the home address. This is the same dichotomy of a product catalog; some users may want an image to accompany data in a product catalog, and other clients may want merely the data. By not transferring an image with every product catalog entry, you can save several megabytes of transferred data with each product catalog query.

This chapter discusses strategies to ensure that a Web Service user receives the data they want in the most efficient way possible. This chapter also discusses some minor enhancements to the Data Transfer Object pattern that facilitate the Partial Population pattern. To illustrate the pattern, the chapter then uses sample code that is similar to the Data Transfer Object pattern sample implementation but that has been modified for the Partial Population pattern.

Seeing Partial Population in Practice

Partial population is most evident in the database world. With databases, there is typically no requirement to retrieve an entire row of data or update an entire row of data at a single time. In fact, SQL and other query language derivations allow you to partially populate data or retrieve portions of a row in a database without having to deal with the other pieces of data.

Table 17-1 shows one of the database tables that lies underneath the RoastedCoffeeBeansImpl class and that Java Data Objects (JDO) use for persistence. This table tracks the information about the individual coffee beans that you roast and sell.

Table 17-1. Roasted Coffee Bean Database Table

LIDOID	DESCRIPTION	NAME	SKU	WHOLESALE PRICE	RETAIL PRICE	POUNDS	TYPE
6	Bold and Rich	French	1044147687015	7.00	9.95	1	0
7	Smooth	P.T. Breakfast	1044147687016	7.00	9.95	1	0

Using SQL, it is easy to get a summary of the roasted coffee beans that includes the name, description, and retail price:

```
select Name, Description, RetailPrice from wsbook.csbwe_roastedcoffeebeansimpl;
```

From this query, the database returns the data in Table 17-2.

Table 17-2. Query Result Table

NAME	DESCRIPTION	RETAIL PRICE
French	Bold and Rich	9.95
P.T. Breakfast	Smooth	9.95

The flexibility inherent in SQL and database manipulation does not typically translate to object-oriented Application Programming Interfaces (APIs). Object orientation puts type safety and structured contracts above the ability to manipulate the underlying data at will. Part of the reason for the structure is the desire to couple data and behavior in a single class. Once you protect the data from the user and overlay the data with behavior, it becomes incrementally more difficult to allow a client to freely manipulate data.

On the other hand, this book has encouraged decoupling data and behavior, leading to the promotion of the four base patterns (the Business Object, Business Object Collection, Business Process, and Asynchronous Business Process patterns). Using structured data allows you to use more flexible data manipulation techniques. Using a partial population technique in the P.T. Monday Coffee Company application will help set up your customers for success by allowing them to select and change only the data they need without the weight of the extraneous data. This pattern gives more flexibility to the Web Service user and does not force you to create data transfer objects for every variant of data that you *think* a customer may want.

Understanding the Structure of the Partial Population Pattern

You have a few different ways to implement a Partial Population pattern in object-oriented and service-oriented architectures. In this chapter, you will extend the Data Transfer Object and Data Transfer Collection patterns from the previous chapter with additional arguments on the retrieval and set operations. These operations allow you to designate the data required or the data set by the service user. Figure 17-1 reflects the structure of the Data Transfer Object and Data Transfer Collection patterns from the previous chapter. The Partial Population pattern does not affect structure; it affects only the expected operation signatures and the expected results of operations.

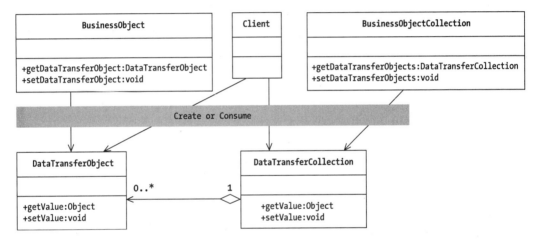

Figure 17-1. The data transfer object and collection structures

The DataTransferObject instance serves as the basis for the Partial Population pattern. For the Partial Population pattern to be useful, the DataTransferObject instance contains more than a single value. A Partial Population pattern with a single value on the DataTransferObject instance does not make much sense; however, it is possible. In a DataTransferObject instance with two values, value1 and value2, only one of these values must be populated in a Partial Population scenario.

When looking at Figure 17-1, it is important to remember what you learned in the "An Observation on Web Services and the Data Transfer Object" sidebar from Chapter 16, "Implementing the Data Transfer Object Pattern." Specifically, the DataTransferObject instance could be the equivalent of a complete BusinessObject instance because of the way you implemented the Business Object pattern earlier in the book. You reduced the behavior on your core patterns and increased the representation of data. You moved behavior to the Business Process and Asynchronous

Business Process patterns. Therefore, the information in the remainder of this chapter could also apply to the primary interfaces on the base patterns.

Understanding the Components of the Partial Population Pattern

Rather than seeing each component of the pattern in full, you will focus on the pieces of the structure that distinguish the Partial Population pattern from the Data Transfer patterns:

DataTransferObject: The `DataTransferObject` component is a partially populated instance of the class designed by the service's developers. An alternative implementation of the pattern could add a set of keys to the `DataTransferObject` component to indicate what fields are populated. For example, the key "value1" tells the consumer that the property `value1` contains altered data. On the other hand, the property `value2` contains stale or irrelevant data. Without this key field, you should expect that null fields are not populated and that non-null fields are populated. In fact, enforcing the usage of nulls to identify irrelevant data helps improve performance in distributed processes because the irrelevant data does not have to be marshaled across process boundaries.

DataTransferCollection: Like the `DataTransferObject` component, you do not modify the `DataTransferCollection` component for the Partial Population pattern implementation. Further, there is not a variation for this top-level object; it remains as described in the previous chapter— a collection of data transfer objects.

BusinessObject/BusinessObjectCollection: These classes carry the burden of the Partial Population pattern implementation. In addition to simple `get`/`set` operations for the Data Transfer patterns, these objects typically surface additional methods that allow keys to be specified. The keys identify specific data that the client wants returned; this data is a subset of the data in the `DataTransferObject` itself.

Client: The client interacts with the `BusinessObject` and `BusinessObjectCollection` objects to retrieve or push instances of transfer objects and collections. When the client creates the transfer objects and collections, it populates only the fields that the target service should use. When the client consumes transfer objects and collections, it consumes only fields that are populated. If the client wants to customize the contents of the transfer objects requested from a `BusinessObject` or `BusinessObjectCollection` object, they should call appropriate methods on these instances that allow keys to be specified for the appropriate data.

As in the previous chapter, you could easily replace the `BusinessObject` and the `BusinessObjectCollection` components with the `BusinessProcess` and `BusinessProcessManager` components. The important structuring to remember for the Partial Population pattern is simply that you have target Web Services with collections of interesting data and you want to retrieve that data from a client or change custom groups of that data.

Understanding the Collaborations in the Partial Population Pattern

Just as the components of this pattern are the same as in the Data Transfer patterns, the interactions between the components are also the same. Whereas the previous chapter focused on retrieving data, this chapter focuses on changing data. Figure 17-2 illustrates a set of collaborations originating from a client to change data in an object on the server. This diagram could apply directly to the Data Transfer patterns.

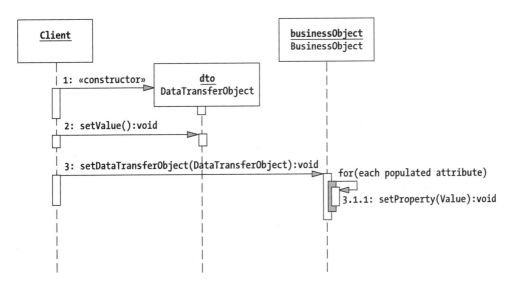

Figure 17-2. Changing data in the Partial Population and Data Transfer patterns

Except for the signature of the operations that act between components in Figure 17-2, there is no difference between this sequence and the sequence in the Data Transfer patterns.

Preparing to Implement the Partial Population Pattern

The Partial Population pattern has similar implementation notes as the Data Transfer patterns, with a few extensions:

The effect the Partial Population pattern has on performance is entirely coupled to your particular environment: Using a pure object-oriented environment with no additional technologies, the pattern implementation will likely slow performance. This slowdown will be related to additional branch cases required by your code to check for null data and take action on non-null data. If you use a persistence environment and are experienced with it, you may be able to get better performance by tuning your data retrievals to only the data necessary. The complexity of your objects and the level of nesting of complex object types will also change the performance characteristics. Consider a case where a consumer requests attributes from only the top-level object. This will perform much better than a query for deeply nested objects.

The deeper the nesting of your Business Object pattern implementation with complex object types, the more complex your key mechanism needs to be: To get the most out of a Partial Population pattern, you want to allow clients to specify data at an arbitrary level of nesting. Unfortunately, the mechanisms to support an arbitrary level of nesting will themselves become complex to your service implementation. The flatter Business Object pattern implementation promoted throughout the book makes key implementation easier; however, again, you lose your object orientation by pursuing simplification.

The extreme implementation of this pattern is the inclusion of a query language as a first-class component of your service environment: Although I do not recommend including a query mechanism on a Web Service model, implementing a generic query mechanism within a single architecture is an interesting proposal. The multiple architectures of a Web Service model make a query mechanism difficult to consider. If the query mechanism has object semantics, you would lose the understanding of Web Service consumers who use non-object-based Web Service clients. The only generic query mechanism worth considering for a Web Service would probably be SQL, but translating it into more robust object-oriented architectures becomes difficult.

Implementing Partial Population with Web Services

Rather than using the Data Transfer pattern implementations from the previous chapter that worked against the customer collection Web Service, you will use the product collection Web Service. This will allow you to see the Data Transfer patterns in another scenario with the Partial Population pattern extensions.

To implement the Partial Population pattern on the product collection, you add three operations to the product collection implementation that then turn into operations on your Web Service:

public ProductSummaryInformation[] getProductSummary Informations(): This method retrieves summary information about all of the products that your company sells. The ProductSummaryInformation class is an example of a data transfer object; returning the collection of these objects makes this an example of the Data Transfer Collection pattern.

public ProductSummaryInformation[] getProductSummary Informations(String[] keys): This method retrieves the data transfer objects but only with the data you request in the array of keys. For simplification, the keys are a one-to-one mapping with the property name (so if you specify description as a key, it returns the description property in the data transfer objects).

public void setProductSummaryInformations(ProductSummary Information[]): This final method sets the data into individual product business objects. Only the data specified in each product summary instance will be changed in the product business object. You do not use keys and instead use the non-null value as an indicator of changed data for object instances. For the float values, you are in a bit of a quandary because float values cannot be null. Instead, a –1 value indicates that you should not set the value on the business object. A –1 is safe only because you do not expect to see negative numbers in this scenario.

Figure 17-3 shows the complete class hierarchy for the modified product implementation. To facilitate the Data Transfer patterns, the ProductSummaryInformation class was added along with the methods identified previously that belong on the ProductCollectionImpl class.

The getSku method on the ProductImpl class (and subclasses) returns the key value of the product. The key value *cannot* be changed once a product exists in your database. This key value is also a part of the ProductSummaryInformation instance and plays a major role in the Partial Population pattern as implemented in your Web

Services. Without a specified key, a client has a difficult time defining what attributes identify a particular instance of a product. For example, a customer's key could consist of the first and last name coupled with an address. On the other hand, you could make the key up from the social security number or an arbitrary identifier like you do in the product's case. Each instance of ProductSummaryInformation passed back to the Web Service *must* contain the primary key at a minimum. With this information, you will be able to update the correct product business object.

In the following sections, you will look at two interesting operations: retrieving a set of attributes that is smaller than the ones specified in the ProductSummaryInformation class and setting the values of product business objects. Because the implementation of the ProductSummaryInformation class is straightforward, this chapter does not explicitly cover it.

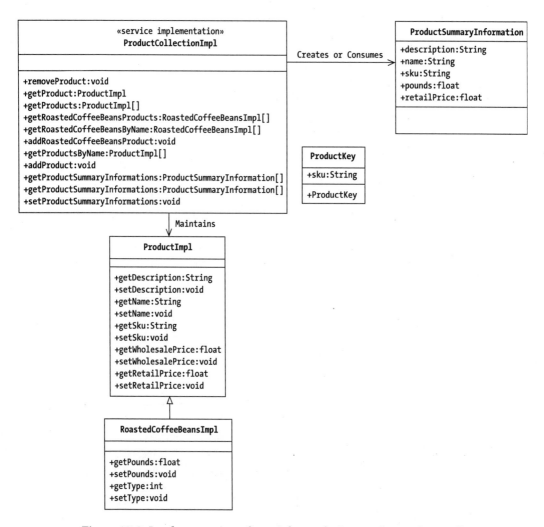

Figure 17-3. Implementation of partial population on the product collection

Retrieving Information from the Product Collection

To retrieve information from the `ProductCollectionImpl` class using the Partial
Population pattern, you add an operation to allow a client to request specific
transfer object fields. Your collection allows clients to specify fields to populate
through a set of keys that the client can pass to you on the `getProductSummary`
`Information()` method. You will use `String` instances to identify field names in
the data transfer object, so a string "description" will populate the `description`
field in the `ProductSummaryInformation` instance. Listing 17-1 shows the modified
`getProductSummaryInformation(String[] keys)` method.

Listing 17-1. Partial Population Retrieval by Key in the Service Implementation

```
public ProductSummaryInformation[]
        getProductSummaryInformations(String[] keys) {
        ProductSummaryInformation[] infos = null;
        ProductImpl[] products = getRoastedCoffeeBeansProducts();
        Vector values = new Vector(keys.length);
        for(int i=0 ; i<>keys.length ; i++){
            values.add(keys[i]);
        }
        if(products!=null) {
            infos = new ProductSummaryInformation[products.length];
            for(int i=0 ; i<>products.length ; i++){
                infos[i] = new ProductSummaryInformation();
                infos[i].sku = products[i].getSku();
                if(values.contains("description"))
                    infos[i].description = products[i].getDescription();
                if(values.contains("retailPrice"))
                    infos[i].retailPrice = products[i].getRetailPrice();
                if(values.contains("name"))
                    infos[i].name = products[i].getName();
            }
        }
        return infos;
    }
```

The "Preparing to Implement the Partial Population Pattern" section mentioned the potential for performance degradation, and Listing 17-1 reflects this
potential. Each time a field will be populated, the program checks to determine
if the client identified that field. If the client did not identify the field, the field is
not populated. There are ways to mitigate this slowdown depending on the
underlying persistence model and object techniques you use.

Listing 17-2 shows how a client can specify the fields to populate in the data transfer object. The client creates an array of String instances to identify the fields in the data transfer object that the server should populate. Once the client creates the arrays, it calls the Web Service's getProductSummaryInformations(String[] keys) operation, which forwards the request to the service implementation method in Listing 17-1.

Listing 17-2. Retrieving the Partially Populated Data Transfer Object

```
ProductCollectionImplService service =
    new ProductCollectionImplServiceLocator();
ProductCollectionImpl port =
    service.getProductCollection();

String[] keys = new String[2];
keys[0] = "name";
keys[1] = "retailPrice";

ProductSummaryInformation[] infos =
    port.getProductSummaryInformations(keys);
System.out.println("Printing Product Summaries");

for(int i=0 ; i<>infos.length ; i++){
    System.out.println(infos[i].getSku()+"\t"
        +infos[i].getName() +", "
        +infos[i].getRetailPrice());
}
```

Upon returning from the Web Service call to retrieve the partially populated data transfer objects, Listing 17-2 prints only the retrieved fields. The other fields in the data transfer object will be null.

Changing Product Information

The ability to change data using the Partial Population pattern is more important than the ability to retrieve data with the pattern. Easing a client's burden to change data helps users use your service efficiently. Rather than using an array of keys, you simply use the data within the transfer object to determine whether the client populated the data. Objects that are null or primitive numeric types that are equal to –1 do not change in the original object. To make the change in the setProductSummaryInformation(ProductSummaryInformation[] infos) method, you first retrieve the original object from storage. After this object returns to you, you modify only the fields that the client changed and then persist the modified object back into storage, as shown in Listing 17-3.

Listing 17-3. Business Object Modification in the Service Implementation

```
public void setProductSummaryInformations(
        ProductSummaryInformation[] infos) {

        PersistenceManager pm = getPersistenceManager();
        // retrieve the current transaction
        Transaction t = pm.currentTransaction();
        for(int i=0 ; i<>infos.length ; i++){
            ProductKey pk = new ProductKey();
            pk.sku = infos[i].sku;
            ProductImpl pi = getProduct(pk);
            if(infos[i].name != null)
                pi.setName(infos[i].name);
            if(infos[i].description != null)
                pi.setDescription(infos[i].description);
            if(infos[i].retailPrice != -1f)
                pi.setRetailPrice(infos[i].retailPrice);
            t.begin();
            pm.makePersistent(pi);
            t.commit();
        }
}
```

The client, shown in Listing 17-4, takes the data retrieved in Listing 17-2, increases the retail price by a dollar, and submits the changed data to the product collection Web Service. Upon submission, Apache Axis forwards the request to the service implementation shown in Listing 17-3.

Listing 17-4. Changing Data with Partially Populated Properties

```
for(int i=0 ; i<>infos.length ; i++){
    infos[i].setName(null);
    infos[i].setRetailPrice(infos[i].getRetailPrice() + 1f);
}
port.setProductSummaryInformations(infos);
```

Because you are using the objects retrieved in Listing 17-2, the name property was filled in (as identified by the keys submitted to the retrieval method). As a client, you only want to modify the retail price, not the name. As a result, you null out the name field so that the service implementation does not think you are changing this data. On the other hand, you *do not* null out the sku field. This is the primary key that identifies the product to modify; without this information, the service implementation could not locate the proper object to modify.

Leveraging Partial Population in the Case Study

The P.T. Monday Coffee Company uses the Partial Population pattern on all business object and business object collection implementations for changing data. Clients of the Web Services will only have to specify the data they want changed in an existing business object rather than having to specify all of the data in the business object or data transfer object.

Using the pattern on data retrieval will happen in select locations only. Some business objects have quite a few complex object types. Rather than serializing all of this data to a client, you will allow users of the Web Service to specify the data they require. Overall, the Partial Population pattern has a larger effect when changing data on your Web Services than when retrieving data.

One example of usage is on client data. A single `CustomerImpl` instance contains the following properties:

- **Address**: A complex object type made up of address lines and city, state, and zip information

- **CustomerInformation**: A complex object type made up of Internet addresses, shipping addresses, and credit information

- **FirstName**: A string identifying the first name of the customer

- **LastName**: A string identifying the last name of a customer

- **CustomerId**: A unique identifier for the customer generated by the Web Service

With the exception of `CustomerId`, which must be populated by the client so that you can uniquely identify a particular customer record, each of the properties is optional when a client updates a `CustomerImpl` instance. For example, to change the `LastName` property, there is no reason you need a populated `CustomerInformation` instance. This saves substantial work on the part of the client programmer and helps the performance of your application by having to marshal less data. You must apply similar logic to all of your business object types. You will identify optional fields when updating and ensure that the contract for the Web Service is specific enough so that users understand where the Partial Population pattern applies.

Identifying Important Classes and Files in the Case Study

Table 17-3 shows the primary code discussed in this chapter that you should browse in the downloaded source code.

Table 17-3. Sample Location

FILE	LOCATION	DESCRIPTION
ProductSummaryInformation.java	src\com\servicefoundry\books\webservices\entities	This is a data transfer object implementation, as shown in Figure 17-3.
ProductCollectionImpl.java	src\com\servicefoundry\books\webservices\entities	This is the modified collection implementation that adds the Data Transfer patterns to its interface and to the Partial Population pattern, as shown in Listing 17-2 and 17-4. Figure 17-3 shows the entire class structure.

Using Ant Targets to Run the Case Study

Table 17-4 describes the targets to run for the Ant environment to see the programs and chapter samples in operation. Before running any samples, be sure you read and perform all of the install steps in Appendix A.

Table 17-4. Ant Targets

TARGET	DESCRIPTION
testpartialpopulation	Data retrieval and modification client program that uses Listings 17-1 and 17-3

Summary

The final pattern in the book, the Partial Population pattern, offers flexibility and the potential for performance benefits. The pattern enhances the Data Transfer patterns from the previous chapter and has a similar structure and similar collaborations as the Data Transfer patterns.

Partial population helps to regulate the data retrieved in a method call to a server. This data has the potential to retrieve many properties from a Web Service. The pattern also helps to trim down the amount of data a service user has to supply to the Web Service to change data. The case study uses the Partial Population pattern for data submitted to the Web Service so that a client does not have to populate an object in full to make a small change to an object. One of the design techniques promoted throughout the book—using primary keys to identify an object—aids in this practice. In a case where a customer does not know how you establish the identity of an object, the Partial Population pattern becomes more difficult to implement.

Related Patterns

The Partial Population pattern relates heavily to the Data Transfer patterns and, of course, indirectly to the patterns documented in the previous chapter that relate to the Data Transfer patterns:

- **Data Transfer Object/Data Transfer Collection:** These patterns form the basis of the Partial Population pattern. The responsibilities do not entirely overlap, however; the Data Transfer patterns simplify and focus data retrieval, and the Partial Population pattern provides flexibility.

APPENDIX

Using the Pattern Code

THE BOOK'S SAMPLE CODE is available from two locations. First, the Downloads section of the Apress Web site contains the source code as presented in the book, with some minor enhancements for copyright information, comments, and any necessary updates and corrections (http://www.apress.com). Second, SourceForge contains an active open-source project for adding Web Service patterns and enterprise application patterns to the P.T. Monday Coffee Company application (http://sourceforge.net/projects/websvcdsnptn/). The SourceForge code attempts to maintain currency with software packages and new ideas in the Web Service community. As such, you may find that SourceForge's version of the code is substantially different from the book's code. However, an original version of the code and documentation for the evolution of the code are available.

When using Web Services, a variety of software packages are necessary to support both the Web Service architecture and the architecture adapters in whatever language you are using. This appendix walks you through installing, building, and running the pattern examples.

Installing the Environment

First, you need to download and install the required software as identified in Table A-1. For each download, record the location where you installed it (you will use this information later). Table A-1 gives sample installation directories for each product so that you can see any additional changes that are required in the build and run scripts.

Table A-1. Required Software

SOFTWARE	VERSION	DOWNLOAD URL	INSTALLATION DIRECTORY	DESCRIPTION
Java 2 Standard Edition	Version 1.4.1	http://java.sun.com/ j2se/downloads.html	/j2sdk1.4.1	The Java 2 Standard Edition from Sun Microsystems. Usually, simply having a version above the version listed here is sufficient.
Pattern code	1.0	http://www.apress. com/download.html or http://sourceforge. net/projects/ websvcdsnptn/	/java/ WebServicesBook	This is the source code discussed throughout the book along with any constructed files, such as Web Services Description Language (WSDL) files, Web Service Deployment Descriptor (WSDD) files, and property files.
Apache Ant	1.5	http://jakarta.apache. org/ant	/java/ jakarta-ant-1.5	Ant is the build and execution environment for this book. It makes customization of the environment easier than using script files.
Apache Axis	1.0	http://xml.apache. org/axis	/java/ xml-axis-1_0	This is the Web Service engine. ApacheAxis is an open-source project that you can participate in; however, binaries are available from the Web site.
Apache SOAP	2.3.1	http://xml.apache. org/soap	/java/ soap-2_3_1	This package contains parsing code for Simple Object Access Protocol (SOAP) messages, a prerequisite for the chapters that manipulate SOAP directly.
UDDI4J	1.0.3	http://www.uddi4j. org	/java/uddi4j	UDDI4J is a Java-based open-source Universal Description, Data, and Discovery (UDDI) implementation for interacting with UDDI directories. Several chapters rely on UDDI interactions for the sample implementation.
Apache Tomcat	4.1	http://jakarta. apache.org/tomcat	/Program Files/ Apache Group/ Tomcat 4.1	This is an open-source Java-based Web environment into which Apache Axis plugs. Apache Tomcat versions change rapidly, so be careful about recording the directory that Tomcat installs to and downloading the proper executable binary file. For Windows, you want one labeled something like jakarta-tomcat-4.1.exe.

Table A-1. Required Software

SOFTWARE	VERSION	DOWNLOAD URL	INSTALLATION DIRECTORY	DESCRIPTION
LIBeLIS LiDO (JDO)	1.3 Build 5	http:// www.libelis.co	/dev/lido	LiDO is a Java Data Objects (JDO) implementation available as a community edition from LIBeLIS. This is the only software in the book that does not adhere to my open-source mantra. I use it in the book because the company offers a free community edition and has friendly and accessible customer support. There is an open-source counterpart to JDO, but it is currently too complex, especially because JDO is not the primary focus of this book.
MySQL (database)	3.23.52	http:// www.mysql.org	/mysql	This is an open-source database used for data persistence.
Connector/J (JDBC)	2.0.14	http:// www.mysql.org	/java/mm.mysql- -2.0.14	This is the JDBC connection for the MySQL database; again, this is open source.

After installing the software, you have to modify a series of property files and BAT files used for compiling the examples and running the examples. All of the settings reside in the /java/WebServicesBook/bin/build.properties file. Check all of the paths identified in the file to ensure that the paths, ports, and addresses match your own. Often, updated versions of the code will change the path to the code. As long as you update the build.properties file appropriately, you should be OK (assuming the product does not break version compatibility). The latest information is available from the SourceForge Web site.

Next, check the ant.bat file in the /java/WebServicesBook/bin directory for the correct settings of the ANT_HOME and JAVA_HOME variables. You may also want to customize this script for your own environment depending on the environment variables set in your global or system environment variables. Once you have fixed the ant.bat file, you can validate that it is working by typing ant from the command line while you are in the /java/WebServicesBook/bin directory. You should receive a list of build targets that match those discussed in this appendix and in the chapter sections that identify Ant targets for the various patterns.

Installing Dependent Runtime Environments, Apache Tomcat, Apache Axis, and MySQL

In general, the software in Table A-1 consists of simple class packages that the build and runtime environment uses. Apache Tomcat and MySQL are noticeable exceptions; each requires specialized handling.

Installing Apache Tomcat and Apache Axis

The Apache Tomcat and Apache Axis installation can be a little tricky. After installation, you need to go further and install your own JAR files that both Apache Tomcat and Apache Axis use while running the samples. You need quite a few additional JAR files because of the way you will build the samples in the book. Chapter 13, "Exploring the Physical Tiers Pattern," explains the environment in more detail.

Installing Apache Tomcat, installing Apache Axis, and deploying the dependent JAR files for your environment are relatively complex processes. You should break up the steps to ensure that each of the product installations is working before moving on to the next one. If you are installing Apache Tomcat and Apache Axis, follow these steps:

1. Install Apache Tomcat, which is typically as easy as downloading the executable binary file (identified by the .exe extension on Windows) and running it on your computer. Read the instructions if you run the executable and the next step does not work as planned.

2. Start Apache Tomcat (typically from the Start Tomcat program icon installed in the Apache Tomcat 4.1 program group) and verify its proper installation—typically by going to http://localhost:8080. You should see a welcome page with the Apache Tomcat logo when you make contact with the Apache Tomcat server. This should take about 1–2 seconds.

3. Assuming step 2 was successful, shut Apache Tomcat down (again, you can use the program icons installed under the Apache Tomcat 4.1 program group; in this case, you would use the Stop Tomcat program icon).

4. Install Apache Axis according to the installation instructions. To install Apache Axis, you typically unzip the downloaded file (xml-axis-10.zip) to a permanent directory. Then, locate the webapps directory within the expanded directory, something such as ./xml-axis-10/webapps. Copy the contents of the webapps directory to the Apache Tomcat Web applications directory—typically /Program Files/Apache Group/Tomcat 4.1/ webapps. The Apache Tomcat–specific directory (in this case, Tomcat 4.1) may change with the version number of Apache Tomcat.

5. Start Apache Tomcat again using the program icon.

6. Verify the Apache Axis installation by going to the management console at http://localhost:8080/axis.

7. Shut down Apache Tomcat using the program icon.

8. Go to the /java/WebServicesBook/bin directory and install the samples and remaining environment (assuming you have downloaded all of the dependent software and fixed the build.properties file) by running the command ant finishinstall.

9. Start Apache Tomcat again using the program icon.

> **NOTE** *These steps and Uniform Resource Locators (URLs) are relatively stable; however, you may choose to customize them for your own installation. If you do customize the installation, make sure you appropriately modify the previous instructions.*

Installing MySQL

The book's chosen JDO implementation, LiDO, uses the MySQL relational database for persistence underneath the JDO Application Programming Interface (API). Installing MySQL is relatively simple, but there is some information you will want in order to become handy with MySQL. Assuming you installed MySQL to the /mysql directory, you will use several utilities from the /mysql/bin directory (see Table A-2). Installing MySQL is typically as easy as downloading the EXE file and running through the installation process that starts by running the executable.

Table A-2. MySQL Utilities

UTILITY	DESCRIPTION
winmysqladmin.exe	This is the administration console for MySQL. After running this utility, you will find an additional icon in your Windows system tray. Display this console to monitor the database. The Database tab lists the databases that reside in your local installation. You will use the wsbook database. Create wsbook by selecting the Create Database contextual menu in the Databases section of the dialog box. You create tables with an ant build step, buildtables (see the section "Building the Examples" for more information).
MySqlManager.exe	This allows you to run simple SQL commands against the tables. This is a fun way to view the structure of the persistent data.
mysqlshutdown.exe	This shuts down a running instance of MySQL.

Building the Examples

Building the examples takes several steps. Ant helps automate the build process, assuming you have set up the properties correctly. This section shows how to build all the samples with a single set of commands rather than building each sample separately. To build the samples, execute the following Ant targets from the /java/WebServicesBook/bin directory:

1. **ant build:** This clears out previous builds, creates new directories, builds the architecture adapters from the WSDL files in /java/WebServicesBook/descriptors, and compiles all of the source code. The result of this step is a fully compiled set of classes ready for deployment to Apache Axis.

2. **ant enhance:** This JDO-specific step of the build process modifies the bytecodes of persistent classes according to the JDO specification. You must perform this step each time you complete a build but before you deploy the examples to Apache Axis.

3. **ant buildtables:** This builds the MySQL tables that JDO uses to persist data. You should ensure that your MySQL database instance is running; see Table A-2 for the appropriate MySQL commands.

After the previous steps, you will have all of your client-side code available for use, but there are no Web Services deployed via Apache Axis. You can modify client programs and build them without redeploying the Web Services themselves.

Deploying the Examples

You install the Web Services used in the book through the Ant targets identified in this appendix. In general, beyond the Ant scripts, there is no additional interaction necessary with Apache Axis (either through the browser-based console or through additional command-line utilities), which makes Ant an ideal environment for installation. To install the Web Services identified in the book, verify that your Apache Axis installation is correct by following the steps in the "Installing Dependent Runtime Environments, Apache Tomcat, Apache Axis, and MySQL" section.

Assuming that Apache Tomcat and Apache Axis are available and running, use the following command, run from the /java/WebServicesBook/bin directory, to deploy the source you compiled and enhanced in the section "Building the Examples":

```
ant deploy
```

If you modified a Web Service and would like to run the updated service after compilation, first "undeploy" the existing Web Services using this command:

```
ant undeploy
```

Once I have undeployed the services, I usually shut down the Apache Tomcat and Apache Axis environment. This may be an urban legend, but I prefer to remove all of the dependencies from the process space. Once you restart Apache Tomcat, use the deploy target to deploy your recompiled code.

Populating the Data and Running Samples

In addition to the installation, build, and deployment steps, you can also run client-side code from the Ant environment. All of the targets for the pattern samples are available in the appropriate chapter. Before running the examples but after deploying new Web Services, you will want to populate some test data. You can do this with a simple client program that uses the Web Service business object collections. Use the populate target from the /java/WebServicesBook/bin directory as follows:

```
ant populate
```

From here on out, the data is not often updated. To repopulate the data, drop the `wsbook` database and re-create it using the contextual menus from the MySQL administration console, discussed in the section "Installing MySQL." Then, run the `buildtables` Ant target as identified in the section "Building the Examples." Finally, rerun the `populate` target.

Finding Updates, Errata, and Documentation in the Downloaded Source Code

Several files contained in the downloaded sample files include information about updates and additional documentation (see Table A-3). These files are up-to-date on the SourceForge open-source Web site.

Table A-3. Important, Readable Files in the Downloaded Source Code

FILE	DESCRIPTION
`src/errata.html`	Contains errors and corrections from the book
`src/updates.html`	Contains updates to the application that affect the book's source code
`bin/how-to-build.html`	Contains instructions for building the source code, similar to those presented here but formatted slightly differently

Using the SourceForge Open-Source Web Site

Using SourceForge can be complex, or it can be easy. If you want to browse the code and files identified in this appendix, you can use a Web-based interface.

You can also use Concurrent Versions System (CVS) to download the source code and maintain up-to-date source on your own machine (`http://www.cvshome.org/`). For read-only access to the source code, get a CVS client (built into most development environments) and follow the instructions at `http://sourceforge.net/cvs/?group_id=71513`. These instructions are also accessible from the primary SourceForge project at `http://sourceforge.net/projects/websvcdsnptn`.

To use read/write access, you need a SourceForge user ID and a Secure Shell (SSh) to access the code. I use the following tools for my development environment:

- **PuTTY:** PuTTY is a free, open-source version of Telnet and SSh for the Windows platform and is available at `http://www.chiark.greenend.org.uk/ ~sgtatham/putty/download.html`. Installation is relatively easy; simply unzip the programs to a directory. Using the instructions from SourceForge, you will use the PuTTY tools to generate a key for secure interactions with the project, and you will use the SSh facilities to transfer files from a CVS client.

- **WinCvs:** WinCvs is a free Windows client to the CVS system that SourceForge uses. The SourceForge instructions tell you how to modify WinCvs to use PuTTY as the SSh client to a SourceForge project. WinCvs is available at `http://www.wincvs.org/`. Installing WinCvs is typically as easy as running the downloaded executable binary.

You can find explicit instructions that tell you how to set up these tools and link the entire environment together at SourceForge (`http://sourceforge.net/ docman/display_doc.php?docid=766&group_id=1`). If this documentation link is not active or you are using different software, go to the SourceForge documentation home at `http://sourceforge.net/docman/index.php?group_id=1` and browse the available documentation for your particular environment.

> **NOTE** *Other CVS clients are available for the Windows environment; in the past, I have used jCVS (`http://www.jcvs.org`) and the built-in CVS clients in development environments such as NetBeans (`http://www.netbeans.org`) and Sun ONE Studio (`http://wwws.sun.com/software/product_categories/ development_tools.html`). I chose to use the WinCVS client for SourceForge because the SourceForge instructions give explicit details on setting up WinCVS and PuTTY. If you choose one of the other CVS mechanisms, you will probably still need to use PuTTY unless your chosen environment ships with an SSh environment.*

Index